GOOD

TROUBLE

Good Trouble

Building a Successful Life & Business with Asperger's

© Joe Biel, 2016
This edition © Microcosm Publishing, 2016

Cover by Meggyn Pomerleau

Interior photos:
Ken Blaze, kenblaze.com, pages 17, 47, 56-57, 134-135, 188-189
Dave Roche, page 13, 133, 146, 169
Autumn Sabin, page 38
Debbie Blotnick, page 43
Stefanie Manley, page 41, 44-45
Brandon Williams, page 46
Caroline Wallace, page 62
Tim DeWine, page 64
Eleanor Whitney, page 92, 99
Erik Diffendaffer, page 75, 104
Siue Moffat, page 112
Chris Boarts Larson, page 121
Robyn Bassani, page 125
Joel Davis, page 150
Rebecca Bolte, page 223

For a catalog, write or visit:
Microcosm Publishing
2752 N Williams Ave.
Portland, OR 97227
www.microcosmpublishing.com

ISBN 978-1-62106-009-3
First published March 15, 2016
First printing of 4,000 copies
This is Microcosm #200
This work is licensed under a Creative Commons
AttributionNonCommercial-ShareAlike 3.0 Unported License.

I'D RATHER BE READING BOOKS FROM
Microcosm Publishing .com
2752 N WILLIAMS AVE • PORTLAND, OR 97227

creative commons
CC BY NC SA

Distributed by Legato / Perseus Books Group and Turnaround, U.K.

Printed on post-consumer paper in the U.S.

The events detailed in this book are meant to tell the story and context of the author's life, experiences, and journey and should not be read as indicting or condemning the actions of others. Everyone behaved in the best way that they knew how at the time of reporting. Some names have been changed because it's not about them; it's about me. No real person, living or dead, committed any of the crimes or misdeeds depicted in this book. Because that would be wrong.

GOOD

TROUBLE

Building a Successful Life & Business with Asperger's

JOE BIEL

MICROCOSM
PORTLAND, OR

mr. narrator
this is bob dylan to me
my story could be his songs
I'm his soldier child
—The Minutemen, "History Lesson Part II"

"The ease with which a person can be ostracized generally has less to do with the severity of their offense than with their proximity to the margin to begin with."
—Red Durkin, comedian

Dedicated to the underdogs and those who support them, especially the ones who never stop working hard but can't seem to keep their heads above water.

And for Elly, who has dragged my corpse out of burning buildings more times than I probably realize.

FOREWORD
by Sander Hicks, founder of Soft Skull Press

Way back in 2003, I was running Vox Pop, Brooklyn's bookstore/café, when a guy named Joe Biel sent us a box of books from a company called Microcosm. These books were rugged, fresh, direct, and energetic. I was fired up. I displayed them all together as a unit. I went down to the basement of the café that week, and built a special rack. I put up a sign on the display that said, "Independent Press of the Week: Microcosm Publishing!" That sign and that rack stayed up there for a good while, as the books sold well, moved around the neighborhood, got read and talked about, and re-ordered. Microcosm was all about independent living, fierce direct action, passionate determination to change the world with small steps, big ideas, and daily practice. People connected to them.

Good Trouble is the manual on the man behind Microcosm. Joe doesn't give you all the answers but he does open up wide. He is honest about his own contradictions, and lays bare the big questions that have driven his unique and gutsy life thus far. Like, how can you be both a lefty punk rocker and a smart business person? How can an idealistic small business keep its nimble advantages even as it begins to quickly grow? And can a political activist publishing company survive the implosion of the messy romantic relationship of two of its key people?

Joe holds up his struggle, and his success with Microcosm, the same way he holds up the failure of his marriage. With punk intensity, just a hair shy of too much, he pushes us past our comfort level. He starts with an abusive childhood and how he rose above it. He learned a lot about himself, and he acted on that knowledge. His pattern is to take a beating, turn around, and work harder to improve. "Rise above." In a society that has failed us, he has figured out how to be a better person, not in the name of fear, or "God," or Law, or government, but because at his essence Joe is a kind of "bodhisattva" someone interested in liberating others more than liberating himself. I don't know another guy who would endure the torture of a spasmodically bad marriage, and then check himself in to years of psychoanalysis with a feminist therapist, because his ex-wife advised him to do so. But that's exactly what Joe did. While there, he was given the keys to understand a few secrets about his mysterious self.

Joe Biel had the idealism to turn Microcosm into a worker-run collective, and the leadership to take it back, when faux-left, non-committal politics failed, and political immaturity threatened to destroy the company. Joe's diagnosis of Asperger's Syndrome helps give one scientific name to an obsession with truth, to doing things right, and paying attention to details. He has found a bright side even to his medical liabilities. And if he's not sensitive to other people's feelings enough, well, he knows he has to work on this, and he's been practicing to improve.

When I went down to the basement and made that Microcosm book rack, it was out of a deep sense of connection. Microcosm's work and aesthetics reminded me of my own, starting Soft Skull Press in '92 as a college student working at Kinko's, taking advantage of all the access to technology, and the "five finger discount" offered by the place where I worked.

And that's not all that Joe and I have in common. He might kill me for saying this, but his future biographers should ask about the influence of his Catholic school education, or that of his Catholic grandma. Maybe Joe's drive, zeal, and vision are from some kind of "calling." It's a calling when you write post-cards to every single zine maker who sends you their zine, to send free books to every prisoner who writes asking for a little guidance. Joe's calling is prophetic—to publish books that radically change the way we think about social justice, and capitalism itself. I love it when the business professor later in this book says "you don't want to make $1 on ten books, you want to make $10 on one book," and Joe is like "heck no, that's totally wrong." He'd rather spread the message than make the money.

More important than Joe's success with Microcosm, with this book, he shows that it is possible that you yourself can do something as great or greater.

Good Trouble is living proof that paradigm-shifting projects, ventures, cooperatives, collectives, and corporations don't start thanks to privilege or luck, family or fate. We start rolling these small snowballs down a big hill out of a hunger to end the kind of suffering we know all too well. To liberate others from the abuse we felt at the hands of those closest to us.

Joe Biel is a part of a legacy—a lineage of independent publishers who scraped up just enough spare change to begin to put new voices into print. He's right up there with Lawrence Ferlinghetti of City Lights, Virginia Woolf and the Bloomsbury Group, Henry Rollins with 2.13.61, ...even Walt Whitman, making blissed out connections of universal love by personally type-setting and printing his visionary *Leaves of Grass*.

After I read *Good Trouble* my head was buzzing, my ears heard a silent ringing, I suddenly had new eyes to see my own life. It's 2015, 23 years since I was a Kinko's copier and publisher. At age 44, I'm not publishing that much any more. But that could change.

These days, I'm working as a carpenter, and I'm having a great time making loft beds in New York City. But there's more I could be contributing to political and spiritual liberation, through independent publishing. *Good Trouble* fires me up like a blowtorch. May it have this same effect on you: to do more, to publish, start a zine, to write, to speak out, to organize, to start shit, to make money, to plow all the money back into the project with absolutely no clinging to any of it, to lose all your money, or make a lot, to help others get sober, get conscious, expand, get liberated, learn new things, teach, make huge mistakes, and make something awesome, weird, and majestic.

Can we be true to who we are?

And make a living at the same time?

Can you see what I can see? How much we can change the world if we engaged in the *Good Trouble*, of doing what we love, spreading that love to others' lives, on a daily basis. That's what we call some serious *Good Trouble*.

INTRODUCTION
by Joyce Brabner, co-author of Our Cancer Year with Harvey Pekar

I should probably introduce myself, if for no other reason than what happened last week when I was standing next to a plaque indicating the site of my city's tiny corner Harvey Pekar Park.

A version of my life with Harvey, my late husband, was turned into a popular biopic that was called *American Splendor*. Together, we tried to, and I think did, raise the bar for comics as both literary and journalistic nonfiction for adults. We began by self-publishing out of a crowded apartment. We ended up para-celebrities, finally able to keep working without having to fill orders from home and each of us better known, living in a house that was paid for, carrying no debt, and owning a car that starts in the winter.

"Harvey Pekar?" said a young man in his early 20s to his friend, as they walked by me. "They're this really cool new punk band... "

Well, yes they are. (And I gave them my permission to use the name.) But, lately I've found myself asking, "Punk as defined by my times or yours?" or "What's the demographic?" This last has to do with idiot cultural assumptions that someone my venerable age has nothing in common with, no reason to listen to, and no need of information, education by or skills learned from... another demographic.

That useless attitude blows. Big wet ones.

Since I discovered Microcosm Publishing, I've been thrilled, inspired and at times confounded by its treasure chest of comics, zines, books, posters, and patches, most useful because I mend my own clothes. (That's one way of remaining debt-free, oh thou youth of America.)

I also wrote a book about my own crew up against the AIDS epidemic, circa 1981, explaining:

> Besides always wanting to write a "gang of misfits" caper, I really started this [book] in 2006 because I saw another generation of outcast artists and young punks growing up without affordable health care and trying to take care of each other. Nothing brings that home to me more than all kinds of little pamphlets, comix, and self-published zines you will have not seen by such folk, many of which I found through Portland's Joe Biel at Microcosm Publishing. Find, read, and support.[1]

And I mean that, with all my heart. I would like to think that I read some of Microcosm's catalog as part of a promise I demanded of myself in my diary, when I was thirteen: "I am going to always remember how smart kids are and how much we already do understand and can think for ourselves. I will listen to them."

---

1 *Second Avenue Caper: When Goodfellas, Divas, and Dealers Plotted Against the Plague* Pub. 2014 Hill and Wang

Younger me and young Joe Biel of *Good Trouble* might have traded little self-made books, drawings, and music and, hopefully, had each other's back against school bullies or principals who demanded we go home and change clothes for something more "appropriate." But that's the story of most outsider, reject, unpopular, weird, queer, or otherwise non-normative kids, even those of us who were all different in the same conforming black jeans, safety pins, and T-shirt way.

You just never know who, skulking along the margins of a school cafeteria or trying not to go home to abuse, will end up being *that* writer, *that* musician, *that* creative person who had time to figure out an escape route towards their passion, while everyone else was at the popular kids party. Some of us devour autobiographies growing up, or *bildungsroman*. (I can use that word. Mine is the last generation to get an adequate liberal arts education, which makes public libraries more important than ever.) Okay. I never became a photographer like Margaret Bourke-White, but she reassured young me I could keep my own name and showed me more of what women's work could be. Anne Frank let me know little girls could and should write books. *Good Trouble* fits in a bug-out bag (or a bookshelf in any bedroom that now feels too small).

Growing up unhappy, perhaps because of awful secrets, family violence, or other trouble puts you pretty much on your own when you finally break out. Few of us get handed a map when exiting, but most of the kids I knew left home with at least some clues (or even money) in hand, even those holding on to strictures or scriptures they would later reject. Unhappily, when growing up like Joe (and me), unable to trust what surrounds you, perhaps because it is *bad trouble* or because you, too, are a "smart kid" too aware too early that something is missing... finding your way out can be rough.

In *Good Trouble*, we watch Joe draw his own map, and, as did a lot of us from broken, unsettled or bound-by-secrets homes, relentlessly searching for an ethical world, an ethical and reasonable way to live, to relate. Does he take it too far; is he sometimes very hard to live with, until he finds his balance? Most of us trying to break away overreact until we figure out how to act. A few years after the above, my diary then dictated that I would *"never take a job tricking people into buying what they do not need or really want. If you have to, tattoo your mouth like the hairy Ainu [Japan] so you can never work at Braunstein's department store."*

I was out of sync with my time. Rebel girls wore only white frosted lipstick in my day, dear children. Such tattoos on American white girls, or lip/nose piercings, came along much later and, again, on kids all different but the same. But Chapstick or black kohl stick, youthful fervor is what powers us through the utter confusion and absolute certainty that comes with making ourselves into the people we'll want to be able to live with later.

So much happens in *Good Trouble*, this document of the also fervent first half[2] of a very creative, difficult person's life that it was hard to choose what I wanted to talk about. The book is punk autobiography, an indie small business manual, a reason to worry about what urban sprawl does to cut young people off from diversity and culture and a painful look at what hides in some homes, hurting too many of those kids. It's also about Gen X mating, Gen X marriage, Gen X mess. My crowd imagined they were inventing multilateral relationships. I don't know anyone who ever made that work after age 35. (If they are still at it, they probably write and sell books about polyamory.) Joe mucks conscientiously through his own *tsoris*, trying to untangle the ties that bind in a relationship that might have been kinder to everybody if there had been less theory and more empathy.

Empathy does not come naturally to some folk. What I think is most exceptional in *Good Trouble* is Joe's unflinching account of growing up not knowing "that people express emotions when they talk and you can tell when someone is about to talk by looking at their face."

The word "neurotypical" has not yet made it into my computer's spell checker, so you, too, might not catch on immediately that Joe there is beginning to find out about himself, that he is "on the Spectrum." He has Asperger's Syndrome, with all of its two-faced blessings and curses: Asperger's can be hell on relationships, and we get to see that—but we also see how a brain difference helps him create Microcosm Publishing. Numbers talk to him, even when co-workers won't.

In the interest of full disclosure, I must say I laughed, winced, and got a bit of a sore neck nodding vigorously as I read my way through *Good Trouble*. I got to read this book and write something for it because, a few months earlier, I told the elite New York "activist" publisher who expected to publish the book I am working on now to fuck off, perhaps because he told me that most of his authors are so eager to get their message out and "so grateful to be published, that they don't really care about royalty payments or consider them important."

Instead of shopping the manuscript around, again, I brought the book straight to Microcosm. I don't expect to be earning big royalties on it, because Joe agrees we'll send a lot of copies first to people in trouble, to people helping them, and to places where I think what I'm writing now is needed. Here I am, revisiting my indie roots after a straight up yes from Joe. I know to expect some bumps later. There always are. But as I expect such trouble will be *Good Trouble*.

---

2 Maybe first *third*. Joe bicycles almost everywhere and has been vegetarian for most of his life.

PROLOGUE
by Joe Biel

My favorite DIY punk records of yesteryear contained not only lyric sheets but were also stuffed with every imaginable booklet, piece of trash, insert, goofy scrap, advertisement, matchbook, letter, or photograph. Unloading someone else's trash from a record sleeve made the exchange feel like a relationship; disheveled scraps somehow extended an act of consumption into feeling like a conversation, suggesting that a letter in return might be appropriate. I was always attracted to overly long dialogues from bands that talked about their intentions during their performance—especially if it was unwanted or awkward. I related to those moments, warts and all. Thinking about this made me realize that the right thing to do is to offer more exposition, not less.

In September and October of 2006 I was sailing down the East Coast in the back seat of Mary Chamberlin's van with her at the helm. Chef and queer punk pioneer Joshua Ploeg sat upfront, navigating and offering commentary on each person that we passed. I sat with punk writer Dave Roche, author of *On Subbing,* and punk illustrator Cristy Road, whose queer-powered illustration work and stories of growing up Cuban had appeared in more places than anyone would care to count before she turned 30. I was surrounded by dozens of to-do lists with various items crossed off as I wrote out new ones and consolidated multiple lists onto a single piece of paper.

Mary, like me, was a pioneer in punk-literature publishing and distribution. As a teenager she took over the established Tree of Knowledge, a mail-order house filled with all kinds of literary and iconographic artifacts with punk roots or touchstones, moved it into her living room, and took it on tour with every band from her home state of Arkansas.

It had been nearly ten years since I'd last been involved in the musical aspects of punk rock, and I was achieving my latest dream: To establish that these young voices, illustrations, ethical concerns, and cultural trappings were just as much a part of punk as the rock-and-roll bands that had dominated the scene for the previous 30 years. It seemed that the best way to champion and demonstrate this idea was to take the leading voices on a punk tour where we could each perform our talents and showcase the same kind of ethical decision-making and amplification of ideas that bands did. So I organized one.

I felt that even the documentary short films that I'd made—about the board game Risk, the stray dog that my roommates and I had taken in after finding it on the street, the collapsing passenger rail system, and the iconic bike- lane markings painted by a rogue city employee—were representative of my views and interpretations of punk. I'd made them to screen on the tour to expand the audience's definition of punk, just as we'd ask the crowd to help load in our gear with us, having revolutionary slogans hanging over the venues' doorframes, or collecting only small donations of an unspecified amount to come in and see the show. When booking the tour, I fought hard for our performances to not be paired with bands. The promoters would always insist that it would get people to come out. One promoter suggested that we should play YouTube videos to "get people excited." But such logic de-legitimized our mission. If the point was to have a large audience, we'd be focusing on stadium rock instead of working on a framework within punk. It was more important to have six people who wanted to be there than 700 people who chatted and heckled while waiting around all night because they were only there to see their favorite band. We'd learned that the hard way on a previous tour.

Even though the van blew out the same tire twice in three days and broke down half a dozen times, causing us to miss eight shows, it only made the whole experience more authentic as a DIY punk tour. Dave liked to compare what we were doing conceptually to how stalwart punk pioneers The Minutemen reshaped the definition of punk's sound in the early 1980s to include jazz, funk, and classic-rock elements. Similarly to The Minutemen, we always made a point to grow the network and go to out-of-the-way small towns and places where a punk circuit wasn't yet built up or defined. As a result of this panache, we ended up performing in a farmhouse with a friendly chicken in the audience in North Carolina. When the chicken puked immediately after Dave's performance, we felt that punk had a new convert that day.

Four hours after we replaced the starter in Mary's van, it broke down for the final time, finding its resting place and stranding us for a week in Gainesville, Florida. Joshua and I pared down the merchandise, shipped my bike home to Portland, and finished the tour on Amtrak trains. We were demonstrating what was possible, even when our behavior was sometimes misguided and all systems were breaking down. If we could take our weird art, food, book, and film project on tour on a disappearing passenger-train system, we thought it might inspire others to take the same kinds of risks.

I was proud of what we had accomplished, but it was hard not to take it as an insult when audience members told me that their takeaway from our show was that the low production values of my documentaries made them feel like they could make films too. But, at the end of the day, that's my entire message in a nutshell. And by the end of the tour, we'd brought it to a couple thousand new friends, many of whom I'm still in touch with to this day.

Truckstop outside Greenville, NC, 2006. Photo by Dave Roche

Clockwise from top left: Fil, Joe, Cristy Road, Joshua Ploeg and Mary Chamberlin. Front lawn of a house named after some aspect of Star Wars in Washington, DC 2006. Photo by Dave Roche

PREFACE:
IT HAS TO GET WORSE BEFORE IT GETS BETTER

On a brisk fall day in 2008 I stepped off the Amtrak train in Portland. There was no one there to greet me. I've been a loner for most of my adult life, but, even so, it was grating to return to the city that I'd lived in for ten years with zero fanfare.

But, really, that was the least of my problems. I had no money to my name and had tens of thousands of dollars in credit-card bills. Because of extreme nearsightedness, I needed another eye surgery in a few months, despite having just finished healing from my third one. I was having mysterious medical problems that left my joints stiff and made walking difficult and painful. I gained and lost weight without explanation. Nonetheless, I carried my meager possessions on my back, waiting for my bicycle to appear in the baggage room.

The punk-rock operation that I'd founded twelve years prior, Microcosm Publishing, had fallen on rocky ground and was in real financial peril. I hadn't really ever planned for it to become a business—let alone employing twelve people—and most of my vision had been focused around the politics that it could hold dear and demonstrate in application rather than how to make it financially sustainable. After founding the company in 1996, it grew over the next ten years from fitting under a paperweight in a frigid, tiny room to sending out dozens of mail orders every day to all corners of the globe. Microcosm had sold over 1,000,000 paperback books that I'd gotten to publish and were written by my heroes.

In 2005, I made the decision that Microcosm would be managed collectively by its workers. I chose this path because of a combination of factors: feelings of moral obligation; my experiences growing up in the shadow of the dying steel industry; pressure from my then-wife, who was one of the workers; and because I had done too much reading about labor history. I figured that I had already far exceeded my expectations and dreams. Collective management seemed like a way to reduce my stress while allowing Microcosm to move into a new era and for others to find the kind of investment that I had once carried alone.

Unfortunately, things didn't shake out that way. We ended up with a dozen employee-managers, most of whom wanted to work part time but carry an equal say in decisions. Each year expenses would increase by 20 percent as we carried out each staff person's vision, even if these visions were in conflict with each other. This wasn't causing us to make more money, so every year the finances became more of a shell game. I was intent on trying to give people room to make the decisions that they felt were right and learn from that. Then the recession hit, slowing down sales as we had our busiest publishing season ever. The collective wasn't equipped to respond.

Because of the weird solutions to old industry problems that I had created, I was invited over the years to have my writing appear in academic textbooks and books from other respectable indie publishers and to speak at art museums, colleges, conferences, and sold-out events. I had done book, zine, documentary, and music tours through 48 states and most of Canada. I had been featured in popular Japanese magazines, and tourists from Tokyo would want to take my picture when they recognized me. I saw my design work used—and bootlegged—in places all over the world. I felt that I had seen and done all that there was to see and do. I had spent the last five years slowly resigning from various aspects of doing freelance design work and printing for respectable musicians and organizations, writing for magazines, and teaching at high schools and colleges. I felt like an esoteric and eccentric collection of skills. It seemed as if the highest levels of innovation, merit, success, and satisfaction that I would know in my lifetime had already come and gone before I turned 30.

For over six years I had lived with eleven roommates and felt more alone than at any other time in my short life. I would think up as many errands as I could each day and try to disappear for as long as possible. Then each night after eating a giant burrito on the way home I would ride the wrong way up the one-way street with my eyes closed and count how long I could keep them closed. Most nights I could add a second or two to my previous record. I'm still unclear what motivated this deranged behavior. I was deeply unhappy, but I wasn't suicidal—I had too much I wanted to accomplish still. I think it was just a challenge, a feat that couldn't be taken away from me. I couldn't see too much with my eyes open anyway.

I was returning to Portland to get some space to think and resolve some issues. At 30 years old I still had a hard time forming and building relationships. I wasn't close to even a few people. I had a bad problem with severely miscommunicating with people I cared deeply about, and I would often not notice when they made a request of me, especially if it related to emotional boundaries. This had gone south more than a few times, and I was at the point of feeling like the best course of action would be relocating to a desert island (at least for a while). For many years my life felt like Sisyphus', except I was carrying around a huge rock without directions or a goal.

My ex-wife Heather had gone so far as to call my behavior emotionally abusive, which stopped me cold. To borrow a phrase from author David Finch, ours had been a "neurologically mixed marriage" and was therefore quite painful for both of us. I still felt scarred from our relationship, which had ended four years prior. I was happy that it was over, but this new label that she'd attached to me was frightening and new territory. In a final letter, she itemized my meltdowns, control issues, and how I always put my needs before those of others. Like all challenges, I embraced this one. I responded by checking myself into intensive therapy with a feminist counselor and began extensive reading homework to get to the bottom of the matter.

I had lost my house in the divorce and couldn't afford to pay rent, so I asked a friend from my old board-games group whether I could stay on her couch for a few months, and she happily obliged. Eventually, I would be house-sitting for another friend whom I'd met during the lowest point of my divorce and who had been commanded by my ex to choose sides. What he'd seen in me, I still didn't know—but, like most people who stuck by me, I suspect that he'd say that he respected my ethics, saw that I rarely took the easy path in life, and it touched him that I'd given him a bicycle when the repo man came and took his car away. We'd only known each other for a few weeks at the time.

My bike box was handed to me by the Amtrak staff, and when the TSA agents[3] stopped hassling me I put it back together, wondering what the coming weeks would hold. I was nervous and scared about therapy but felt that I'd put it off too long already. I was embarrassed and ashamed and didn't even tell those who were closest to me. It didn't feel like the path of DIY self-empowerment that I had championed for my entire adult life. It felt like giving up, giving in, and giving control to someone else.

After months of therapy, the reality wasn't as scary as I'd imagined it would be. At the end of one 90-minute session, I casually mentioned that Heather had gotten upset with me when I told her about my discovery that people make facial expressions when they are about to talk and that these expressions sometimes reveal the tone or feelings that they are expressing. After six months, it was my therapist's turn to look perplexed.

"You didn't notice the expressions in people's faces before that?" my therapist asked.

"No. I had never noticed until I had edited about 70 hours of video interviews and then started to notice how people's faces moved when I advanced frame-by-frame."

She looked concerned and a little enlightened.

"Unless you had head trauma as an infant, that is very likely a sign that you have Asperger's Syndrome... newborn babies can see emotions in people's facial expressions—but we will have to talk about that next time. I have to see another patient now."

I was released onto the street to unlock my bike with this crazy newfound revelation. I had not, to my knowledge, had infant head trauma, but I had been joking that I had Asperger's since I learned that it existed.

I went home and took an online test. I scored 98% Aspie. I took longer and longer tests and each one placed me similarly. I started to research Asperger's and what it was, what it meant, and how it affected relationships.

Simon Baron-Cohen, one of the world's foremost experts on Asperger's and director of the Autism Research Centre at the University of Cambridge, defines Asperger's Syndrome (AS) as a "high-functioning" form of autism with four defining traits:

- Persistent and intense preoccupations
- Unusual or bizarre behaviors
- Impaired social-reasoning abilities and the inability to apply social rules properly
- Clinical-strength egocentricity.

In that split second my entire life made sense.

After this revelation, I got on my bike and rode to the east side of the river and then north. When I got to the one-way street near my old neighborhood, I closed my eyes and started counting but stopped myself. I was creating a new and conscious future.

---

3 The window when TSA agents had any jurisdiction in Amtrak stations was very brief because they had no authority to do much more than plead for you to show them the contents of your bag.

CLEVELAND
YOU'VE GOT TO BE TOUGH!

Section

I

Origin Story

OUT RAGE

The troubles started even before I was born. Both sides of my family immigrated to the East End of Pittsburgh, Pennsylvania between 1890 and 1910. My grandma, Helen Biel, was one of ten children, and her parents were seemingly seeking out some sort of better life by leaving Berlin. While I imagine that Pittsburgh would be preferable to living through World War I, moving to the United States just before the Great Depression was certainly bad timing. The gradual collapse of the steel industry being lost to Japan over the next 60 years was probably a bit rough on them as well, though it did little to prevent her nine siblings from having lots of children. Helen married a railroad worker, Theodore, who was accidentally electrocuted by a co-worker who turned on the power while my grandfather was working on the rails.

Helen only had one son, Donald, in 1929. They lived alone in Pittsburgh in a house near America's first co-operative grocery store. Beneath the house was what appeared to be an Underground Railroad apartment in their sub-basement. Donald, from all that I can tell, was always a big nerd. He worked on radios and TVs in the basement and, while he owned a deflated football, the idea of him tossing it around with his friends, with his lanky 6'6" frame, is hard to imagine.

Around the time of Woodstock, Donald met my mom, who was dating someone else but, as my mom tells the story, my dad won out by having a pronounceable last name. They got married around 1970 and moved to Mentor, Ohio—a new development in a new suburb of Cleveland. Cleveland was America's fifth largest city in 1949 but had been on the decline since about 1960. By the time my parents arrived, bankruptcies shook the steel industry and violent crime peaked, plummeting Cleveland down to the 29th largest city. The worst was yet to come—it's currently the 48th largest city in America. When my parents arrived, the City of Cleveland was on the verge of filing bankruptcy and electing the "boy mayor" Dennis Kucinich. The Cuyahoga River began catching on fire from being full of industrial pollution, and the federal government formed the Environmental Protection Agency as a result. Mayor Perk caught his own hair on fire during a televised ribbon cutting ceremony, and the next decade saw continued depopulation.

My parents were part of the problem. They were second-generation European immigrants who moved into a house that they had built in Lake County, in a scheme dreamed up and sold to them by the likes of the highway developer Robert Moses and the 1926 Euclidian zoning court case, where industrial, commercial, and various residential uses were zoned away from each other, creating massive urban sprawl.

The advent of cars and the city planning delusions of the 1950s convinced my parents that it was a good idea to live 21 miles from my dad's job and far from any entertainment or shopping opportunities. They believed that the family car would solve that problem. Lots of other people did too: The population of Lake County grew by 747 percent that year. My mom always insisted that the house cost a meager sum for something "quiet" and "nice." This facade and the availability of loans created the illusion of a middle-class lifestyle for many people.

When I mention Cleveland in conversation today, most people remember it as the city where three women were kidnapped and held captive for a decade by Ariel Castro. Some people remember Anthony Sowell, the loner serial killer, whose work had created such a terrible neighborhood odor that the sausage factory next door was blamed and dismantled. But the problems go back much further. Cleveland was nationally recognized in the '70s as a city in the midst of racial violence. The Hough (pronounced "Huff") Riots were the result of a white-owned bar's posting a sign reading "No Water For Niggers" in a neighborhood that was 87 percent Black. Over the next six days, the neighborhood was burned to the ground. A series of harsh responses and racially charged white "neighborhood patrols" all over the city ensued for years to come. The racial tension was exacerbated by the collapsing economy and resulted in firebombed cars and gangs of armed white men shooting solitary Black men who were minding their own business. Most were acquitted on the grounds of some proactive interpretations of "self-defense."

The stigma of the riots depreciates property values in "Rough Hough" to this day. So when laws, mobility limitations, and city charters making neighborhoods and suburbs white-only were found unlawful during the civil-rights era, middle-class Blacks began moving to the suburbs and white people continued their eastward exodus farther and farther away from the city. As Cleveland proper continued to suffer massive population loss, the eroded tax base couldn't pay the increasing costs of maintaining the city—let alone the suburbs.

While it's clear where this is headed, perhaps the greatest mistake of all was the creation of Lake County. Located on Lake Erie on Cleveland's East Side, many white people—including many of my neighbors and my friends' parents—saw Blacks as poor criminals. The wounds still haven't healed, and, as recently as 2015, when a Black family bought a house in neighboring Painesville, residents spray-painted "No Niggers" on the garage before they moved in.

Aside from the obvious racism and classism that created this eastward exodus, Lake County seemed to be built on the backs of the workers. Trade workers and union leaders who were willing to push their fellow co-workers off the proverbial ladder were the ones who could scrape together the money to move their families out of the city and grab a piece of that new suburban dream.

James A. Garfield's mansion is also in Lake County. A former Civil War commander, Garfield was elected U.S. President in 1880 before being assassinated three months later in a Baltimore train station by Charles J. Guiteau, who had run against Garfield and lost. Guiteau said that he was commanded by God to commit the murder and he sought protection from the mob for his misguided effort to "heal the Republican Party" from Garfield's moderate views. As Guiteau was arrested he shouted "I am a stalwart of the stalwarts!" Somehow he lived longer than any other Presidential assassin.

In 1996 I realized that the legacy of corruption and brazen entitlement in Lake County continued into the present. A local police officer was caught having sex in the back seat of his squad car with his son's high-school classmate. The day after the officer was caught, his poor son, who has the same name as his dad, went back to school to the jeers of his classmates. After the officer was fired he responded by prosecuting the city for violating the terms of his union contract, but the case was thrown out. Social dysfunction and abuse of power lurked behind almost every closed door in Lake County, and people in power were often so cocky as to leave them a little bit ajar.

In November of 2003 the public caught wind that the high school's treasurer since 1981, Jim Metz, had concealed the fact that the school district was on the verge of financial disaster. Metz, a father of three former students, would routinely backdate receipts and move income from the next calendar year into the previous one to make the finances appear stable. At the time, the fiscal district was shared with the Lake County Health Care Consortium, and Metz would move money back and forth to create the illusion of fiscal health in the district. Things came crashing down when he got caught taking out an unapproved loan without the school board's knowledge, and a deficit of around $20 million was discovered—while Metz was claiming there was a budget surplus. Some people I interviewed alleged that Metz was actually pocketing the money himself, but when I interviewed the current treasurer, Daniel Wilson, he vehemently dismissed this allegation. He said that Metz's professional misconduct was providing "false and materially misleading financial information," and no criminal charges were filed. Metz claimed that the deficit could be recovered by a property-tax increase of $8 million per year, but the taxpayers voted down a levy.

When Metz was eventually fired from his position while on sick leave (though one board member voted against firing him), he sued the school district for wrongful termination. The case was eventually settled out of court for an undisclosed amount. The school board hired a collection agency to track down everyone who had written bad checks to the school and laid off about 240 staff members. Taxpayers still had to pay for a $15 million deficit. Regardless of whether Metz stole the money or just misled the public, it remains a classic case of how one Lake-County person's selfishness hurt over ten million people when the state of Ohio had to bail the school out.

You can see the urban/suburban cultural divide in the voter's habits. While the city center always votes for pro-union Democrats, the suburbs are voting for the Republican who can best protect their money. Ohio has gone to the winner of every U.S. Presidential election, and the urban/suburban tension continues today.

On top of this dynamic of screwing each other over as a life practice, most people had to commute right back to the inner city for work, including most of my childhood neighbors. They were relatively poor, working-class people, but, thanks to their skin color (to this day Mentor is still 96 percent white as part of a city that is over 50 percent Black), credit lines, and living above their means, they generally were able to perceive themselves as middle class. In reality, income in Ohio was falling behind the national average and moving away from the core didn't make people any wealthier.

My sister Julie and I were born into this awkward situation in the late '70s just as the first wave of punk rock exploded across the U.S.

IT'S BETTER IN MENTOR

In 1983 my dad, while at his job in the steel mill, had a stroke. The blood flow to his brain was blocked and brain cells rapidly died, never to come back. I was five. I have very few memories of him before this, but I sure remember staying up late on this particular night, waiting for him to come home from work and wondering where my mom had gone. No one suggested that I go to bed as the sky fully pitched black, and no one would answer my most basic questions.

My mom finally appeared alone late that night, screaming about my dad for what felt like an eternity. After having a stroke on the job site, he had gone right back to working. Through casual conversation, his co-workers finally convinced him that he should go to the hospital. The amount of damage that a stroke causes depends on how long the brain is deprived of oxygen, how quickly medical care is received, and the amount of intensive therapy to rebuild afterwards. My dad had waited a long time.

I barely know anything about my parents. If they've told me, I have repressed those memories or wasn't paying attention. I know that my dad was fun and had a sense of humor before the stroke, but the brain damage gnawed at his personality. He lost control of his vocal cords and muscles. While he could develop thoughts, he had great difficulty expressing them. He couldn't walk and could barely crawl unassisted. He had always been smart, but, even when I could decipher his slurred speech, it didn't make any sense. He was demoralized and was unceremoniously placed in front of the TV for the duration of most days. He checked himself out of physical therapy after a few weeks. It's unclear whether he understood what he was doing or whether he was just frustrated, fed up, and feeling hopeless. In either event, leaving physical therapy became a major factor in his rapidly devolving condition and a major cause of screaming and blame in our household.

My dad was no longer able to work, and my mom had left her job as a high-school English teacher in the early '70s to raise two small kids. We received social-security and disability checks to pay our bills.

Everyone around me said that Cleveland was the center and source of all crime and violence, but 21 miles from downtown there was plenty of domestic violence behind closed doors in our home, in our neighborhood, and in my friends' houses.

The City's slogan, "It's Better in Mentor," posed more questions. Better than where? Better for whom?

I was still too young to even understand my feelings, but in 1984 I had an experience that gave me perspective. My mom was outside cutting the grass after some kind of intense fight with my sister. My sister had taken my mom's purse and wrapped her body around it like a tiger protecting a jewel. Not knowing or caring about the particulars of the situation, I felt that it was my duty to retrieve the purse. My sister and I had been raised to understand that my mom's purse and keys were her prized possessions, and I knew that this affront could not stand. I approached my sister, and she began lunging at me with her teeth and her nails. I managed to retrieve the purse but got pretty cut up and bloody in the process. Nonetheless, I marched outside, where I triumphantly handed the purse to my mom with a smile.

"That was a stupid thing to do!" was all that my mom said as she took the purse.

I was crushed. I wondered why she wasn't proud or even appreciative of my act of bravery. From that day forward, I began to put the pieces together and slowly understand the dynamic that was going on. Yelling, threats, and physical violence had been common in our house as long as I could remember, even before my dad's accident. Certain family members, especially my dad—who couldn't speak in his own defense—would be blamed and shamed for family or circumstantial problems. Accidentally breaking a glass of jam would result in a beating, which resulted in fear. While most neighbors were sympathetic to our situation and I had friends, I never felt that I could talk about what was *really* going on in my house. Most neighbors assumed that my sullen mood was a result of my dad's health and uncertain future. On the other hand, my mom didn't have close friends. She would demonize the neighbors and tell my sister and me about only the most horrifying neighborhood gossip, which made the violence in our own home seem normal or even mild. The fear and intimidation were expected, if not hopeless. The promises of Lake County had isolated our family, and my mom's behavior seemed almost normal there.

I once spilled my cereal bowl all over the floor in front of the front door and hurriedly tried to clean it up before my mom got home and saw the mess. She wandered in as I was still wiping up milk, and she seemed confused when I recoiled from her in fear and put my hands in front of my face. She helped me clean up and even offered sympathetic words. It confused me. There was so much pain in our household, but no one seemed able to do anything to make anyone feel any better. I felt nothing but fear at home, so I hung out at the neighbors' houses and wondered why I never detected any tension in the air. The neighbors understood that I needed to be away from home and tolerated my presence without ever talking about why.

My mom made my clothes, which I understand is no simple endeavor, but corners were always cut. For most of my childhood I remember this pair of faded grey sweatpants that were permanently stained with spaghetti sauce and had only a right pocket because she had run out of material. I never heard the end of the ridicule about these pants from other kids in the neighborhood.

My childhood was like a playground full of wasp's nests. Any time something fun would come along, my mom had to pick at it until I was not allowed to participate or it simply wasn't enjoyable. She would make fun of my few friends and criticize other people until they were in tears. Sometimes when she was anxious she would pick at her nails until it drew blood, and I was just happy that it wasn't my blood. She would scrape metal spoons against metal pots to get the last bits of burned food out of the bottom. For twenty years afterwards I couldn't be around people who picked their nails. When anyone scraped metal against metal, it felt painful in my head.

I learned to cope by developing a life inside my head. I was the kind of kid who couldn't walk past a luggage rack without rearranging it to make good use of the available space and then lecture the adults about how they should do things differently. I once corrected a stranger in the park about the difference between ducks and geese. After learning about the invention of the GMO square tomato in the 1980s as a solution to efficient packing, I spent much of my time in the far recesses of my head thinking about the most efficient ways to pack a truck with items of various shapes and volumes.

From about age four, I felt most emotionally proximate to a small torn piece of dirty blanket. I would hold it in my hands and rub my fingers back and forth on it. It was only about the size of the palm of my hand, but still it had various kinds of wear in different places that allowed for different sensations and textures when I ran my fingertips across it.

By 1985 I was sent to live with my grandma, now in her 80s, presumably to make things easier on my mom. My grandma didn't know what to do with me, but she was a good person with a good heart, at least as far as I could tell. She thought that teenage boys should work in coal mines and was perplexed when I wanted to play video games or read. But life with her was far preferable to living with my parents, even when she put me to work around the house. My grandma used strange catchphrases that confused me. If someone said their food was too hot to eat, she would smile and say, "It was cooked on fire!" But I had watched her cook it on the old electric stove in the kitchen. I would explain this to her in response each time. She always looked confused. If I was in the bathroom before we had to run errands or, worse yet, go to church, she would bang on the door and shout "Don't be taking longer in there than you have to!" The first few times I wondered what someone would possibly do in the bathroom that wasn't necessary. The room wasn't appealing enough to want to spend time in. Finally one day I asked, "What would I be doing?" She stuttered and stammered and eventually said, "You... know what I mean!" I had no idea what she meant, but years later I figured out that it related to her particular strain of Catholic guilt and getting into Heaven. My grandma was a sweet lady but we rarely saw eye to eye.

My dad and I in the late 70s, playing with a tire while he demonstrates that he dresses like the nerdiest member of The Ramones.

LONE BREW

When I was seven or eight my family visited a department store. I had enjoyed a recent fishing trip with my grandfather, so when we walked past the fishing aisle, I ducked in and stuffed some supplies into my pockets. We hadn't caught anything on the previous trip, which I assumed was because we didn't have the proper equipment. I'm not sure if I had a story concocted to explain where I had gotten the fishing supplies, but when my mom found them she made me return them to the store and apologize. She explained that this resolved the issue.

When I was growing up, my family was devoutly Catholic, meaning that everyone did whatever they wanted whenever they wanted and planned to confess away their sins before they died. My mom's brother was an officer in the military and was a selfish, threatening, and shaming person. Once he made me sit at the table for six hours after dinner because I had put something on my plate that he wanted to eat, a punishment that seemed completely pointless when I could have just handed him my plate if he wanted it so badly. I wondered how he could perceive himself as a Christian. But we were raised to hold onto this idea that blood relations, rather than mutual respect or appreciation for each other, kept us in the same room. The family would tease him at the table during Thanksgiving about how his subordinates would tip over his boat or otherwise work to dismantle his authority during the Vietnam War. I figured that they didn't like him either but later found out about the soldiers' organized resistance movement to the war in Vietnam.

My uncle's son, Billie, was largely raised by my mom's father. My grandfather brewed beer in the basement, did extensive woodworking, and built a house from scratch with his own hands after he retired. I feel like I got a lot of his genetics, but I barely got to know the guy before he died in the mid-'80s from food poisoning. He could be teasing or even mean at unpredictable times so I generally avoided him as a small child. For most of our overlapping lives, I thought his name was "Bird" because his wife, a German immigrant who had grown up in a Polish neighborhood, said his name, "Burt," with such a thick accent.

One thing I learned from Bird is that ours is a family of alcoholics. We never had alcohol in the house where I grew up. But, when he was alive, my grandfather had 30 gallons of homebrew going at a time. My cousin Billie had developed a daily habit of getting drunk by age twelve. He knew to turn the beer containers upside down and check for ones that no longer had any sediment. If nothing was settled on the bottom, you could drink it. Once I learned about this, it made sense why, even though my parents kept empty vodka bottles on display, I never saw either of them drink outside of church.

Billie taught me more about my bloodline than anyone in my immediate family. We had very little in common: he had a mullet; loved to collect and shoot guns; drove Ford trucks exclusively; had a closet containing only cowboy boots, blue jeans, and black T-shirts; and went to trade school to repair diesel engines. He didn't much care for politics but told me that he didn't vote for Obama because the man wanted to take his guns away.

I suspect that Billie had a harder time growing up than I did because he employed the same tactic that I did: He spent as much time as possible away from his immediate family. He moved in with our family, where he was respected and treated as an adult, something I suspect that he was not accustomed to. He was the only relative I thought I could trust, so I tried to tell him about how my mother treated me. He tried to brush off the violence and told me that I should "respect" my mom. I tried to explain that that wasn't the issue, but, in hindsight, I see that he was trying to teach me how to minimize the impact and severity.

He did get me out of the house though. We went to the arcade, to Chuck. E. Cheese's, and to the comic book store, and he'd even go pick up my friends and hang out with us. He didn't make fun of even my nerdiest hobbies (such as melting lead wheel weights that I collected from the street to pour into rubber molds to make my own Dungeons-&-Dragons figurines), and he was always supportive of my interests. He was the first person in my life who talked to me as an adult. His truck got rear-ended when I was thirteen, and he explained his plan to fix it with his buddies and submit fake receipts to the insurance company to get paid for his own work. He got married and inherited our grandfather's house but was having marital problems right off the bat and lost the house that he'd grown up in during the divorce.

When I started to have funny green haircuts and wanted to spent my time listening to punk music alone in the basement, he'd come down to "bother" me and then ask me to play each track that had an interesting name. He quickly concluded that none of them sounded like his beloved country songs, and he'd lose interest and leave me alone. I'm not sure if I would have preferred his company at those times or not.

My dad, my sister, my grandma, and I in 1982.
I can't stop focusing on my toy.

CHEESEBURGER IN PARADISE

Ten years after the fact, my family had still never talked about my dad's stroke, referring to it as "Dad's accident." That is, unless you count my mom's frequent violent outbursts as "talking about it." She blamed my dad for every one of our family's problems or failures or each time my sister or I acted out. My dad's inability to parent, let alone control his muscles well enough to walk or talk, was blamed on "selfishness." Given that this word was routinely screamed while my mom was bludgeoning him with her fists, I hesitated to request an explanation as to why she felt this way.

As a child, I had little trouble accepting my mom's version of events and I had few other viewpoints to even consider. But it didn't feel right to blame my dad for what I could understand had taken away almost all of his choices in life beyond what channel to watch on TV.

When I was about ten, a neighbor got lice and my mom washed my blanket scrap. It was completely destroyed in the washer. I cried for a few days afterwards and felt it as deeply as someone might feel the loss of a person who had understood and supported me.

As I grew up, somewhere in the back of my mind I knew that the violence my mom inflicted on our whole family would be more than just cause for us to be taken away from her. But that's the problem of dysfunction—its predictability is distressingly comforting. Part of me also somehow knew that getting put in a youth home would likely have even more negative consequences than staying where I was and enduring the beatings until I was big enough to defend myself.

I had a lot of anxiety at the dinner table. I would hurry through my meals to get away from my mom and her control. I would eat quickly, digest poorly, and had long gaps between meals. I stayed away from home as much as possible, mostly by riding my bike to the comic-book store after school every day. I went so frequently that I knew the schedule of every employee even though, honestly, there were things that I liked more than comics, but this routine accomplished what it needed to.

My grandma, who had grown up during the Great Depression, had spent years stashing $20 bills inside of and underneath every surface in her house, with the intention of saving up money to send my sister and me to "a good school." Perhaps the options were limited. The school that she chose, All Saints School, bore the initials A.S.S. and its classrooms were filled with asbestos that would flake and be vacuumed into the air for the students to breathe. After I graduated, the building was condemned. More vividly than anything, I remember the smell of the steel mills and how they reminded me of burnt ketchup on the 45-minute bus ride across town. For every seven teachers who ranged from boring me to tears to being downright insufferable, there was one exemplary teacher who made up for all of it. The school was the butt of the joke in the movie *Major League,* depicting a baseball team composed of losers and washouts set in Cleveland: two of the main characters eventually make reference to getting married at A.S.S. When we saw the movie and excitedly brought this up to our teachers, they told us that it was not an appropriate movie for us to watch. I had been thrilled because the movie felt like some of my first positive attention.

In third grade, my teacher selected me as the most promising artist in my class and sent me to join a special group, with one student from each grade, to learn origami, the Japanese art of paper folding. It was the first time in school when I actually felt engaged with the subject matter, and I picked up the folds, creases, and techniques faster than even the 8th-grade students. Our visiting Japanese mentor gave us a mission: The school was to make 1,000 paper cranes before the end of the school year. He explained that for every 1,000 paper cranes that you make, you get to make a wish. I gave myself a mission: I was going to make 1,000 paper cranes myself that year. I found thousands of sheets of paper in a closet at home left over from my dad's former job at the steel mill. I would bring a few dozen to school each day and, after getting in trouble a few times, I learned to fold cranes under my desk while maintaining eye contact with the teacher. Of course, when I was caught the next time by the same teacher, she was only more incensed and declared, "Joe Biel! It's great that you are so enthusiastic about the cranes project, but you are in math class right now!" I completed 2,000 cranes that year and stored them in garbage bags in the back of my closet but my wishes to escape my home life did not come true.

When I was ten years old, I ran into a kid getting beat up at school and I interrupted, shouting at the bigger kids to leave him alone. Surprisingly, they did. And the kid I stood up for spent the next three years making a pilgrimage across the entire church every week to shake my hand during the sign of peace, despite the *Roman Missal* explaining to only say "peace be with you" to the people seated nearest to you. Granted, few people ever read or followed these instructions; they just attended Mass and followed the lead of the person next to them. For whatever reason, I had read the rules and was always hyper-aware of them.

In the sixth grade, at the peak of everyone's sexual tension, we were shown an educational film from the '70s about conservation for Earth Day. The whole thing was boring and predictable without a hint of education until a segment about how to conserve water. The actor and on-screen text both declared that the most efficient way to save water was to "Shower with a friend!" This inspired laughter uproarious enough that the teacher had to stop the video. For the next three years, any time a question about how to conserve resources came up, someone would immediately shout out "Shower with a friend!" Punishments began to follow. Nonetheless, the students could not be stopped.

Overall I had a positive experience at A.S.S. Even though my brain is not programmed for empathetic ability and I had a hard time relating to others, I felt cared about even if I wasn't understood. Sometimes this could be awkward. At my sister's graduation ceremony, one of my classmates broke into tears for five minutes because she wouldn't see the graduating class at school the next year. Feeling nothing at all, I looked at the problem intellectually and tried to explain to her that she would see them around town still. Ironically, my mom appeared, asked what was wrong with me, and gave my classmate a hug. The situation made me look like an asshole but I didn't understand what had gone on. One problematic aspect of Asperger's is that I can't access the perspectives or feelings of others. I tended to have stronger emotional responses to TV commercials or what a dog might be going through than I did with my classmates' feelings.

Despite this, my A.S.S. classmates were patient and tolerant with me, sometimes intent on giving me helpful advice. One day a classmate approached me out of nowhere and said "You could be cool if you just wore your pants a little lower." It was a little hard to take well-intentioned advice like that after living under the delusion that I had been cool all along. I refused to lower my pants, out of pride and continued stubborn delusion.

The school was small, with about 40 kids in each grade. Most of the teachers were downright unqualified to educate anyone and incapable of focusing a discussion, but I never felt threatened or endangered there. Unfortunately, the school administration was forward-thinking enough to not allow us to get A.S.S. graduation rings, which I would proudly still wear to this day.

I was a compulsive shoplifter throughout my early teenage years and had quite the collection of stolen books to prove it. I would wear a bulky coat and load things into it. When I was fourteen I started to get sloppy and got caught at a WaldenBooks in the mall. Hilariously, the young, nerdy employee didn't have the chops to actually confront me about it and instead grabbed my friend's arm and said "Tell your friend with the coat never to come back here again." I didn't. For about two years.

Through the bulletin board at the comic shop and my friends, I started to understand that there was a history and an underground in Cleveland. My daily bike ride to the comic shop evolved into a daily bike ride to the record store, Wax Stax. I met a young Insane Clown Posse there, passing out free demo tapes and flyers for free shows to a disinterested populace. But it was much more exciting to dig through thousands of LPs by bands that I'd never even heard of but felt connected to, based on the artwork alone. My friends explained that, while it was not really hurting anyone to steal from WaldenBooks, I shouldn't steal from the indie comic shop or the tiny record store. I could understand those rules and it gave me some greater concepts to ponder.

After voting for Jimmy Buffett's "Cheeseburger in Paradise" to be our graduation song despite the protestations of our teachers, most of the graduating class of A.S.S. attended Lake Catholic, a private high school that happened to be within walking distance of my house. I figured that it wouldn't be much of a change at all. I planned to finally approach the people whom I had crushes on at the end of the year before but was too chickenshit to ask out. But Lake was ten times the size of A.S.S., and that changed many things in ways that I hadn't counted on.

Lake looked good on paper: there were progressive conflict-resolution policies, and the school tried to avoid punitive measures. But I was separated from most of my friends and was growing apart from the rest. My newfound interests in punk rock and trying to not come across as so much of a nerd were leading to conflicts left and right. I picked on friends who had never done anything to warrant being treated that way. I worked hard to make new friends but just wasn't meeting the right people—and the environment felt so vast. I started to get picked on quite a bit myself. One day while waiting for the bus home from the public pool, two friends and I got jumped by older classmates with gang affiliations after we refused to give them our money. I saw how easy it was for them to get away with this without consequence. Everyone looked the other way. We started asking some of our older friends to look out for us at the pool.

While there had always been a big shelf of zines at Wax Stax, it wasn't until I went to see The Smoking Popes at the Euclid Tavern in 1993 that I met a young Jake Kelly. Jake was working the room, asking each person to give him a buck for his zine, *Summer*. Closely following in Jake's footsteps was a young Beckett Warren, who accepted a mere quarter for his zine, *Beckett Tapes*. I sprung for both and spent most of that night in the corner, reading every word and feeling as if I had discovered my new religion.

I took these zines with me to school the next day. It was my first solace at Lake Catholic. I began bringing zines to school to read every day and picking up all of the ones I could from Wax Stax. Every month, I devoured *Maximum Rocknroll,* the Bible of punk rock news and reviews. It was *Maximum*, with its poor photographic reproductions of shock rocker GG Allin and interviews with bands like Whorehouse of Representatives, that really intensified my classmates' picking on me. Perplexed and alienated, they would condescendingly grab it out of my hands in the lunchroom and as one kid put it "try to find one eye-catching image anywhere in the whole thing." They could not decipher what about it excited my young imagination so. I couldn't explain what made the whole thing so interesting at the time, even as a kid cocked his fist back behind his head, demanding that I do so.

In hindsight it's clear that zines were the first meaningful and sincere pieces of writing that I'd stumbled across. They were made by my peers, fifteen-year-old kids from other schools. To me, they were a way to change the fabric of conversation around issues that were affecting our lives, as well as creating a pressure valve for our collective rage at a system that had left us behind to get beat up between inhaling asbestos and hiding from our terrible lives at home. Equally importantly, zines introduced me to political ideas and subject matter that my teachers didn't think I was mature enough to learn about. It was from zines that I learned about the massacre at El Mozote in El Salvador, the riots for gay rights at Stonewall, the Diggers finding food in San Francisco dumpsters and cooking for everyone in the Haight, and Kittie Knox standing up to racism in bicycle racing in the 1880s. They taught me that information didn't need to come from a clinical or journalistic distance but could be made personal.

During the summer after ninth grade, my first long-term relationship ended when my girlfriend cheated on me. We had been going out for a year and I was totally crushed. Thinking about our relationship was the only way that I could get through each day of high school. I had always believed that I would be a very loving and romantic suitor, but this was an outcome that I hadn't foreseen. I found that the only way that I could make the emotions go away for a few minutes at a time was turn up the abrasive hardcore of bands such as H-100s. Listening to Green Day or other lovestruck pop ballads just made the pain worse.

Some of the students at Lake had been kicked out of other schools. Our school had really strict policies on things such as hygiene (e.g., you would be sent home for not shaving), but in other regards it was weirdly lenient. On several occasions, kids would gang up on me, push me around, relentlessly kick me or my chair, or take my money—as a teacher watched—and punishments would not be doled out. These events were treated as if they were not notable. I'm not sure whether this was a convoluted way of trying to teach us students to stick up for ourselves or whether the administration just didn't want to deal with it. While these policies left me alone to have fun gambling during Scripture class, it also sent a clear message to the bullies: You are free to do as you please. And they did. I was called a fag so many thousands of times during those two years that the word ceased to have actual meaning, though the callous vitriol behind it was always evident.

Before the school day started, I spent most of my morning trying to avoid certain people so they wouldn't knock my books onto the floor—or worse. I tried to slip out of problem classes and go to the nurse's office as frequently as I could as a way of avoiding people. My locker was ransacked more times than I could count, and everything of value would be taken. I gave incredulous and helpless looks to my science teacher as he watched a kid kick my desk—with me in it—slowly across the floor. When skirmishes turned into fistfights, both sides would be put into mediation until the differences could be talked through. I believe our class was the first in the school's history that had so many repeat offenders fighting each other that the school gave up and started punishing them. Repeated requests for the administration to do something about my situation proved fruitless.

It wasn't the bullying that ended my time at Lake, though. Students had to attend a mandatory faith-healing service after school and bring a family member. When the State of Ohio said that this wasn't lawful, the school offered that a student could write a ten-page paper instead. This was the final straw. Maybe it would have gotten better, but I demanded to get out before I found out.

BROW BEATEN

By the time I was sixteen, after years of being bullied at home and at school, I was big enough to fight back and frequently demanded that my mom justify why she had moved us to Lake County, where I had to go into the city to have something to do. Helen, my grandmother who was paying for my schooling, had just passed away, and I refused to go back to Lake. My mom couldn't understand what that environment was doing to me. A.S.S. had been an escape valve from the environment of fear that she had created at home, but Lake was just heightening the tension.

I traded in my paper route for a job at Burger King when I turned fourteen to help me stay out of the house. I spent more and more of the time that was left with friends from my neighborhood. We never talked too deeply about it, but from what I saw and heard, my friends' home lives reflected relative shades of grim. From alcoholism to credit-card addiction to poverty to intimidation, violence, and fear, we could see what each other was going through and stuck together as social misfits.

During one afternoon of drifting aimlessly, we stumbled upon a wallet on the sidewalk in South Euclid. Bored and not thinking much of it, we snatched it up to find that the only contents were a handful of phone numbers and over $400 in small bills. Overjoyed, we went straight to the record store and spent it all. We justified it later by surmising that the owner *must* have been a drug dealer.

People with Asperger's Syndrome learn through a try-fail-try model. Each time we experience something, we refine our approach on the next attempt. When something goes wrong, we robotically use whatever feedback is available to approach the problem differently the next time. If things go well, we celebrate our success and repeat. While I never figured out how to behave in order to avoid bullying at Lake, my assimilation into this group of friends was relatively easy. I was naturally goofy, not afraid to do ridiculous things, and was always up for earning some laughs. At first I would just repeat quotes and other people's routines to see which ones got a laugh, like a talk show host in training. Gradually, I developed my own schtick. Such things naturally bonded me to my new group of friends as we each developed a deeper appreciation for the stylistic and humorous aspects of punk rock. I would sing along to the stereo at loud volumes from the back seat and was up for whatever mischief could be dreamt up.

During another boring afternoon, my friends and I found a plastic baseball bat in the trash at the park. We carried it around for hours and took posed photos with it as a feigned weapon or hanging out of the fly of someone's jeans. Hours later, we drove across town through a wealthy neighborhood to get ice cream, and I pretended to swing the plastic bat at various mailboxes that we passed. On the way home we were stopped by the police.

My friend Jason was sitting in the seat that I had been in an hour earlier. Two cops pulled him out of the car and threw him up against the curb. They kept demanding to know where "the weapon" was. Eventually he told them that I had done it and they pulled me out and threw me on the pavement. They demanded that I admit that I frequently smash mailboxes in that neighborhood. Completely confused, I asked them if they meant the plastic bat in the front seat of the car. When the cops saw the miniature plastic bat, they became more upset. They couldn't arrest me for a dumb joke and said that we could go.

Apparently one family whose mailbox gets a regular thrashing from passing bats tried to press charges against me. Since the bat we'd found couldn't damage much outside of the insect kingdom, the cops told them that they could only ask me to pay restitution but they could not require it. A few weeks later, the kid who was driving and I sheepishly went over there to apologize with our parents. My mom staged a big theatrical production out of transferring my dad out of the car into his wheelchair in front of their house.

The people who lived there tried to get stern with me and again asked if I had done it before. I tried to explain the joke of pretending to hit things with a plastic bat. They responded by explaining how expensive it was to constantly replace their mailbox. I wondered why they didn't just leave it be. They struck me as young, selfish yuppies who were making a big deal out of something small. And without a sense of humor!

It was one of the first times when I felt that my mom supported me in her own weird way. She had shown up and taken my side. It was also the first time that a cop was violent with me. I rationalized it in my mind that his behavior was justified. I hadn't broken the law, but he had every reason to think that I had.

Slowly, becoming part of a group of friends started to give me some confidence in myself instead of trying to rein in my oddities and tics. Rather than being ashamed of my quirks, punk celebrated them, and this helped us become more popular in a certain milieu. I came to accept that I was a weirdo at heart. I assumed it had to do with my dad's being disabled, my home life, and my eccentric sense of humor. My friends accepted me and even held up these as great qualities in me. But after this scuffle with the cops, some of my friends were told that I was bad news and that they weren't allowed to hang out with me. It was the first of many of my "jokes" that really blew up in my face.

Photos from 1994, clockwise from top left: Me, Jason, Me, Greg. My homemade shirt says "Eat Weiners" after I was told that I was not allowed to wear a shirt proclaming "I Hate Eddie Veddar" [sic] to school.

SOCIALISM

As I began to figure out and accept who I was, I had to take a good hard look at just how much trouble I had connecting socially with other people. When I was younger I got a free pass because everyone knew about my dad, but as I was becoming a teenager people expected me to overcome my upbringing. Once, when someone demanded my opinion about something related to some war or another in school, I refused to say anything. I hadn't been paying attention, and I became more upset when my teacher singled me out. I refused to talk and he eventually sent me to the principal's office. At the parent-teacher conference at the end of the year, he told me and my mom that I had talked more during those five nearly silent minutes than I had during the rest of my three years in his class. "What was the point?" I wondered. But as I was voted "shyest" in the yearbook polls, I realized that other kids related to each other in a way that I didn't.

It probably wasn't helping matters that by now I subsisted on a diet of cookies, beer, and coffee. That summer my mom figured out that I had taken on the family's genetic disposition to get drunk daily. First she found an empty 24-pack under my bed. Then she noticed that I had drunk a warm 6-pack of beer that she was going to use to clean the carpets. Then our dog began to sniff a bag full of 40-ounce bottles of malt liquor that I'd left on the floor of the living room. All of this culminated in her demanding that I stop listening to punk rock, take down all of the flyers adorning the walls of my bedroom, and stop wearing all of the ripped clothes that she hated so much. But after she hit me a few times, I realized my own stature and strength and hit back. She screamed "How dare you hit your mother?!?!" which really left me baffled, as it was apparent where I had learned this behavior. I'm not proud of this moment, but her violence was never directed at me again; it was now solely directed at my disabled father.

After much negotiation, my mom agreed that I could go to Mentor High School. With 2,500 students in my grade it was perhaps the largest high school in the state, and it was where all of my friends went to school. But it was overcrowded and was unattractive from most perspectives. Students got very little individual attention and the oft-repeated marketing of Lake was that at their school you had "a name," whereas at Mentor you were "a number." When my two worst bullies at Lake found out that I was transferring, I didn't need to tell them that they had played a part in this decision. They high fived each other and cheered. Years later, I wrote a letter to the school about the culture of bullying that I experienced there but didn't even get a formal letter in response.

But Lake isn't the school that is known for this or remembered this way. In fact, the documentary *Mentor,* was released in 2014 about that school's disproportionately high and nationally notable rate of bullying-related suicides and the administration's tendency to ignore this and sweep it under the rug. This culture certainly existed when I was at Mentor, but I was bullied twenty times worse at Lake.

Alix Lambert, director of *Mentor,* told the *Boston Globe* that she felt the residents of the city were more hostile to her than the guards were when she made a film about Russian prisons. She said that many students who were still being bullied contacted her and that one email sent to her during production unironically told her to kill herself.

City charters and laws from pre-civil-rights era Lake County continued having a huge influence in keeping the school system 96 percent white. Refugees from Croatia flooded the region in the early '90s during their struggle for independence, creating a large Croatian population with many of the parents' never learning English and living together in neighborhood communities. It was their kids who seemed to both have the worst home lives and suffer the worst bullying in school. Most of the deceased students profiled in the documentary *Mentor* are Croatian, as were many of my friends growing up. Next door to a city that was 51 percent Black, the bullies were beating up and discriminating against the Eastern-European white kids.

Mentor High had plenty of other problems. There were multiple incidents of a military recruiter or a teacher sleeping with various students, including some pregnancies. The year before I arrived, the principal was caught videotaping cheerleaders changing in the bathroom during pool parties at his home, but he later claimed to be healed by finding Jesus[4]. That same year, Robyn, one of my best friends, got kicked out for bringing a gun to school. But rest assured, she was not interested in hurting anyone. She brought it to school to sell it for drug money. Twenty years later, when I asked her what she had learned from this, she said that she discovered that she could pee and wipe successfully while handcuffed, so maybe the school system wasn't a total failure.

By the time I attended Mentor, I had undergone demonstrable changes. I was a punk rocker in a band with three kids from my neighborhood. During the year and a half that I attended Mentor, students, teachers, and bullies alike ignored me and let me do whatever I wanted. Discovering punk rock had changed me: I now walked around with confidence instead of fear. I wore sleeveless work shirts and patched jeans and while I was thin, I hid it in loose clothes. People assumed I was tough. My toughness was never challenged. It was the first time in my life that being a twitchy kid who talked to himself was an asset and helped complete my character instead of drawing taunts. My best friend Jason had gotten into a fistfight with a kid who claimed to be a high-ranking member of the Bloods on the last school day before I transferred in. So when the students returned on my first day at my new school, I was treated with equal parts respect, fear, and reverence as Jason's surlier, quieter, larger friend. It didn't hurt either that one of the other alleged Bloods was a kid that I had gone to grade school with and that he never seemed to think that our different paths in life were anything to be concerned about. He still treated me as a friend. I had

4 Here's the article: http://www.connectionmagazine.org/archives_old/principal.htm

met some of the other Bloods when I worked at Burger King, and some of them seemed to remember me fondly because of the free food that changed hands.

During my entire time at Mentor High, I didn't have one book assigned to me to read, though it didn't seem like I missed much. I slept through the school day, in between reading zines and daydreaming about the world that existed within their pages. I liked *Maximum Rocknroll*'s dogmatic view that punk *must* be independent and have integrity. It came with strident rules and iconic tropes, almost to the point of self-parody. But this appealed to me. I liked guidelines, and clear rules were very easy for me to adhere to. I would order 20 to 30 zines from the reviews in the back of each issue and soon discovered such joys as *Mylxine, Cometbus, Fun in a Bucket, Interbang, 7-11, Suburban Subway, Contrascience, HeartattaCk, 9 & A Half Left, Cooties, Punk Planet* (which I began to write for a few years later), *Slug & Lettuce, Fern, Sneer, Big Surprise,* and hundreds and hundreds more.

Each zine uniquely offered what was missing in my immediate environment: A production that was proudly amateur, usually handmade, and always independent, espousing views that my middle finger alone couldn't encapsulate and yet were rarely boring. More so, zines never tried to pull a fast one over on me by imposing fake bullshit or trying to convince me to do something that I wasn't interested in. Zines respected my experiences and my intelligence while engaging me where I was at. I felt that I had discovered a secret handshake that I needed to tell the world about. I worked with some friends to start publishing an underground school newspaper, *Fresh Fish,* where we talked about where we are at in our lives with a biting and dark humor. It became such an underground hit and scandalous publication that possessing one could result in a detention and that handing out copies resulted in an immediate suspension.

Weirdly, I discovered through zines that I *was* interested in education. The immediacy of reading a personal account was gripping and necessary, especially after years of watching desensitized newscasts and falling asleep while reading newspaper articles and textbooks that, because of efforts to project an unbiased view, came through as cold and unfeeling. Zines allowed me to relate to the emotions of others, something that I had always struggled with.

Through zines I discovered that I was interested in economics and world politics. I discovered literature that engaged my imagination and made the time pass without my noticing. I found out about random pieces of humorous history. So I kept devouring any zine that I could get my hands on.

Singing with my first band, Five Finger Discount, 1995. Left to right: Greg, Chris, me, and Jason.

XEROCRACY POWER

As a result of my newfound immersion in zines and punk, I again tried to relate to and invest in people. I still found it virtually impossible to form tangible emotional bonds. I didn't understand that asking a yes-or-no question would not result in a conversation, even if I thought the person was really cool. Oddly enough, wearing a shirt by a cool band that people liked or reading a zine that looked interesting were the best ways to attract people to talk to me. Sometimes the performance that I felt like I had to put on for conversation—especially for someone whom I respected—scared people away. But even when it didn't, I never felt like real bonds were formed. I wondered whether everyone felt this way.

When I learned that Speak in Tongues, a DIY punk club, had been operating on W 44th and Lorain in Ohio City since 1991, I felt that I had lost time to make up for and began spending several nights a week there. At first I just went as an attendee, but I quickly got involved working with a large group of other maladjusted people, who were even embracing the wacky and creative side of themselves, pain and all.

Most people in my life seemed unaware or actively in denial about their pain and how it affected them, and they went to great lengths to appear to be what they perceived as "normal." But the people at Speak in Tongues wore their hearts on their sleeves—sometimes literally as cut-up, sewn-on scraps of fabric—even if those hearts were bleeding and they had to drink to medicate. They were theatrical caricatures and overstated cartoons, running back and forth across the room, yelling at the top of their lungs, setting things on fire, literally picking up change on the dance floor to make fun of tough guys who did a dance called "picking up change," and bringing bicycles and hand trucks inside to use as dance partners on nights when the place was emptier. But, rather than overstated spikes, mohawks, and chains, they wore simple things: pants and shoes with holes in them, thrift-store T-shirts with funny slogans on them, and wildly tousled hairstyles, but nothing was ever intentional or overly posed. Everything was just thrown into the air to land as it did.

I met other kids my own age who were practically running the place. I became responsible and created a role for myself there as a way to form real bonds and take my own destiny and interests into my hands while creating a city that was more engaging to me. I started by passing out flyers for Speak in Tongues shows on the east side. I felt closer to the regulars at Speak in Tongues and the punk kids in my neighborhood than they often did to me. Nonetheless, it was a way to create the intentional family that I needed to move on from my upbringing and to let go of my anger.

The place was a proper celebration of emotion that carried the ever-important punk torch of empowerment—anyone could shape its future. There were cryptic messages scrawled in paint on the walls, posters for Ralph Nader's Presidential campaign in the front windows, an anything-goes spirit on the dance floor, an unbelievable mess in the bathrooms, and a gas station across the street that would happily sell beer to anyone who could see over the counter—if they hadn't been mugged on the way. While the place certainly had pretenses, they often had more to do with theatricality than standoffishness. Sometimes the theater could get wild, like the night that a car was set on fire.

Before long I was setting up and promoting shows there and singing and playing bass with my own bands on the stage. But before long, I felt like what was lacking in the place was zines. I was inspired by the concept of xerocracy—a word that I had learned about in zines, meaning influence achieved by copying and distributing thoughts onto paper. So I began hauling milk crates full of zines behind the bar to trade, give away, and sell at shows. There were some weeks that I spent four or five nights there.

One of my bands broke up and I started a new one. Before we'd even played a show, I asked the illustrator who had drawn the demo and T-shirt art for my previous band to draw a T-shirt for my new band. He produced an image of two half-naked women making out beneath the name of our band. Robotically, I didn't think about what it conveyed and began printing the shirts in my basement. The next day I brought them to school to sell but the image wasn't as well received as the previous one. Everyone declined to purchase one, even at a paltry six dollars, and one woman spelled it out clearly for me: "While I support your band even before I've heard it, I'm not going to pay for or wear a shirt like

In school I had to comb my mohawk over to one side of my head, 1995.

that for anyone." Disenchanted, I went home and was yelled at by my mom who had seen the image in our basement. It was a hard lesson, but an important one. And it got me to understand what I'd done. Even though the two cartoon characters on the T-shirt weren't real people, it came across as a statement about the value and role of women in the punk scene.

Shortly thereafter, I went to see Fugazi with my friend Liz. I didn't know her very well, but we had a class together and other friends assured me that she was "cool." I was slightly intimidated. Based on the patches on her sweatshirt, it was clear that she had strong feminist views, something that I knew I didn't yet fully understand. That night, several thousand people dancing made the club pretty hot, and people began taking off their sweat-soaked shirts. Liz, dancing right in front of the stage, removed her shirt too. The man standing next to her, whom she didn't know, offered to "protect" her. She punched him in the face and shouted "I can protect myself!" My education was coming together.

Through Speak in Tongues I discovered bands and zines that were directly connected to Riot Grrrl, a radical social movement within the punk scene. Partially in response to second-wave feminism focusing on creating women-only spaces during the 1960s, Riot Grrrl showed women in punk venues as equals while saying "we are creative and like to have fun too"—whether or not that meant choosing a feminine appearance. Riot Grrrl helped me to connect the dots and understand why feminism made me feel uncomfortable as a teenage boy—enabling me to see my misconceptions through to conclusions rather than stew on guilt or generalizations. Ranging the entire gamut of musical genres with very creative fashion, Riot Grrrl helped me understand how seeing a woman on stage was the one of the best ways for women in the audience to feel like they belonged there too. It also explained how I had likely alienated women in my past.

Cleveland had a long-standing tradition of punk festivals, and 1996 was no exception. I didn't realize how lucky I was to have 50 bands from all over the world perform within bike-riding distance from the house I grew up in. It was my first taste of controversy, boycotts, protests, a rented armory full of propaganda, cultural politicking, bumper-sticker sloganeering, and, most memorably, a riot. One Life Crew, a hardcore band that wasn't scheduled to perform, was given half of the set time allotted for Integrity, a world-famous band they shared members with. The previous two years had been full of debate about whether OLC's anti-immigration/anti-welfare message, delivered from the mouth of a Turkish immigrant, was, in fact, racism. So when singer "Mean" Steve Murad declared "Fuck the liberal fruits!" before tearing into "Pure Disgust," the song in question,

it escalated things until he was interrupted by a woman shouting at him. Not content to leave it there, Murad got in the face of the woman and shouted "Bitch, I'll fuck you up," which spiraled the thousand people in the room into violence. The

The cover of the demo tape by my second band, The Wimps. Left to right is me, Lawrence, and Mike, 1996.

band was soon dropped from their record label and responded by making strange prank phone calls to various other bands in the scene, with such tasteless nuggets as, "I love Black people. Everyone should own some." It was Scene Politics 101 for my young brain, demonstrating virtually every aspect of identity politics in five minutes.

While most of the style of hardcore punk at that fest was not musically interesting to me, the politics were fascinating. During this narrow window, hardcore punk was tightly wound around didactic radical politics, and I brought home dozens of new zines. Even issues like veganism, the condemnation of drugs and alcohol, rights to abortion access, and gender equality weren't seen as radical or even going far enough for many people who took to marching in the streets and gluing the locks of facilities that tested on animals. It was the kind of conviction I needed to find in my life and I swallowed the pill whole.

During a show at Speak in Tongues later in 1996, at eighteen years old, I figured out who I wanted to be. I have no recollection of this, but former Cleveland local and now L.A. show promoter Sean Carnage reports that I drunkenly babbled at him that I was going to build something but that I didn't know what it was yet.

I wouldn't have been so grandiose when sober, but build something I did. In 1996, I started using the name "Microcosm" in various ways as a name for what I was doing. Microcosm is a Greek word that roughly translates to "small world." It represented to me how the punk scene was a reflection of the real world, replete with many of the same flaws and problems. I felt that I could draw attention to issues through documentation and writing and to begin to right these wrongs and build a platform to prop up the disenfranchised. It was the kind of "clinical-strength egotism" that only someone with Asperger's could muster. But "Microcosm" seemed fitting. It was a word that I had learned from reading a zine the year before. First it was "Microcosm Distro" then "Microcosm Records" and eventually "Microcosm Publishing."

I had started publishing my own zines, *Stink in Public* and *Mullet* in 1993. *Stink in Public* contained my observations and criticisms of the punk scene along with hopelessly ahead-of-myself ideas such as creating isolationist economics within punk. *Mullet* was a humorous attempt

Performing with The Wimps, 1996

at sociology around the "business in the front, party in the back" hairstyle that had somehow lingered since the 1980s. While the spirit of xerocracy—democracy through photocopying—was alive and well in me, I liked the idea of making a zine more than I ever mastered the craft. I was still a kid, after all. It took a few more years to get the contradictions out of my head, get my politics straight, and get my feet planted firmly under me. In the meantime, I focused on building a catalog of work that reflected the world I wanted to see and challenge the things I found disgusting about the world I lived in. I believed that I could empower people to make changes to the world around them by offering them powerful rock-and-roll, skills, and information.

As a teeanger trying to make sense of books like *Refusing To Be A Man* and *Violence and Nonviolence* at Mac's Backs Paperbacks, I met Harvey Pekar and Joyce Brabner. The work of these two comic-book magnates had created a public appreciation for nonfiction, street-level autobiographical comics. They made it not only socially acceptable but also seemingly glamorous to produce independent and self-reflective memoir and political work. They believed that everyone has a valuable story to tell and art to produce from life experience. But for two people whose democratic thinking had been so influential and had inspired so many, they seemed worn down and tired. Harvey had just beaten cancer a few years prior, and they were having trouble finding publishers willing to take on their books. The declining health of the city of Cleveland seemed to be affecting them personally. I didn't realize it at the time, but Harvey had been living in Cleveland so long that he knew the city when it was at its peak in 1949.

Through Harvey and Joyce, I learned about Cleveland's rich publishing history. Jerry Siegel had created the character Superman in his own zines, *Science Fiction* and *Cosmic Stories,* published in the Glenville neighborhood of Cleveland in 1933. And the city had been a short-term location for Robert Crumb while he collected records.

I went to school with Jesse Bryson and Melissa Bonfanti, the children of Wally Bryson and Jim Bonfanti, members of Cleveland's hit pop band of the early 1970s, The Raspberries. After a single that sold over one million copies and four albums on the charts, the band broke up in 1975 because of arguments over who wrote what and thus who was owed how much. The difference between the lifestyles of songwriters Bryson and Eric Carmen was painful. Carmen's royalties continue to support his children to this day while Bryson (whose son is also a talented musician) put on weight and moved to a dilapidated home outside of the spotlight. It was a valuable lesson that selfishness and fighting over money could ruin even the greatest of creative partnerships.

The cover of Stink in Public *#1 by Brandon Williams, 1993*

Using the early FreeNet system that launched the Internet in the '80s I began stumbling upon early historical archives. Talking to the people around me filled in a lot of gaps. Wally Bryson was friends with

Cleveland punk luminaries The Dead Boys and The Pagans. Drawing on these roots and connecting these dots made me feel that I was part of something real and that adding to that legacy was my destiny.

I learned some lessons too: Like my local heroes, I could make up for a limiting lack of resources and a stifling environment with a healthy dose of passion, motivation, and vision.

Danny Nooman covered in newspaper on fire at Speak in Tongues, Halloween 1998. Photo by Ken Blaze

Outside of Speak in Tongues during Cleveland Fest, 1999. Photo by Ken Blaze

PAPER/WORK

I graduated a year early from high school a few months after I turned eighteen. I celebrated by moving out of my parents' house and getting drunk daily. I lived with four friends and worked nights while most of my roommates worked nine to five.

I had been dating someone for a few weeks when, at a restaurant, she told me that I was selfish and complained about the timing of our first kiss. We broke up shortly thereafter. I began dating the waitress at the local coffee shop. We went to a movie and got into an argument on the pier about whether needle-exchange programs support heroin use, and she told me that I had no empathy. Similarly to the comment about me being selfish, this was delivered in a matter-of-fact manner that I appreciated and found helpful. I asked both of them lots of questions about what led them to those conclusions. Unfortunately, it would be more than ten years before I understood that I literally lacked the cognitive processes that comprise empathy. According to Simon Baron-Cohen, empathy is "the drive or ability to attribute mental states to another person/animal and entails an appropriate affective response in the observer to the other person's mental state"—and I didn't have it. This not only made it impossible for me to predict the actions and behaviors of other people but also prevented me from being able to even feel an appropriate response to other people's emotions. While I was self-centered, at least it was clinical instead of willful.

Not knowing why I was this way left me depressed and lonely. I went to punk shows as frequently as I could motivate someone to go with me. I started staying out all night and going to bed as the sun came up. I began dictating my thoughts into a tape recorder. I struggled to accept the fact that I was a perennial loner.

I had a large, cold room without a door. It was furnished with only a TV and a fold-out couch, so, every time I brought a date home, the first question was "Is this your room?" There was an adjoining alcove with two empty closets so I set up a computer there, hung up a cork board, and turned it into the first Microcosm office.

I was making good money delivering pizza and I started to put $100 aside each week for Microcosm projects. My roommate's band, The Roswells, wanted to release a 7" record. I had spent the last few years researching how records are made. I proposed that we make the record be Microcosm #1 and they agreed. The band had high expectations of me, which was ironic for a bedroom record label's first release, but the pressure was a good way to learn many lessons at once and to try and take it seriously.

The band went on tour that summer but told me I couldn't go because I was farting constantly. At their insistence, I went to a doctor to get it checked out, but the doctor told me it was normal.

I discovered that most of the struggle in production work was finding creative ways of letting people, stores, or distributors know why they should care about a record and why I was so excited about it. I started making ads to photocopy and met a guy who worked at a Kinko's in nearby Kent. I would mail him my masters and money for postage, and he'd send back boxes and boxes of zines and advertisements. A friend insisted on making a website for Microcosm, which at that time consisted of roughly five items and a poorly drawn stick figure begging you to be interested in the items. I started purchasing ads in *Maximum* and sending out letters in which I talked endlessly about my vision for Microcosm. But the substance wasn't clear, partially because I didn't know exactly what my platform was. Perhaps it was because I hadn't yet had enough life experiences.

Judge Richard Swain, a local judge since 1975 who had been part of the original wave of eastward manifest destiny of whiteness running from Cleveland, was re-elected in 1995 and made a habit of giving maximum sentences with every conviction. In 1996 he made rulings that the sexual assault of several women was their own fault because of the clothes they were wearing. My friends and I were pissed. We made stickers that said "Judge Swain is an asshole." But, locally, not one store would sell them for fear of Swain's wrath when the owner received so much as a parking ticket. One night after a long shift at work a friend informed me that several police cars had been driving around with the stickers on their bumpers all day. I felt that we had done our part.

Wondering who was responsible for stickering the police cars in a diner later that night, I looked out the window to see three guys dressed as ninjas beating up Greenie, a guy that I knew a little bit, in the parking lot.

Unbeknownst to me, Greenie, had had a day as surreal as my own. He had just been released from a mental institution and was served a spiked drink at the diner that night. Drugged up, he witnessed some kids at another table being rude to the servers. He suggested that the kids should leave and flicked some ash from his cigarette into their coffees to make his point.[5] The table of three guys left in a huff, yelled some things about Greenie's mother, and drove into the bank parking lot next door; then Greenie left, and a few seconds later they came back and began attacking Greenie in the parking lot. In a 2015 interview, Greenie insisted that they were each dressed like Bruce Lee, but I remember their faces' being covered like ninjas.

There had been near-constant fights in my high school so it was a familiar sight, but something aligned in my brain right then. Greenie was undeniably the

5 Yes, you could smoke in restaurants in Ohio. We were barbarians who ensured the future of Cleveland's private health-care industry.

underdog in this fight, as these kids were ganging up on him when he couldn't defend himself. It was an unbalanced power dynamic. I could relate it to my own experiences and pain. I ran outside and the three kids dressed as ninjas ran away. Greenie was pretty bruised and bloody, so a few people brought him into the bathroom to get him cleaned up. I thought that I knew who the "ninjas" were, as it takes a very special kind of dork who would change clothes and go out in public like that to jump someone, but instead of revenge my thoughts were about assembling a life plan. I realized that I related to the underdog in almost all scenarios and that nothing made me emotional like witnessing that kind of systemic power imbalance. Sticking up for the underdog became my passion and ambition with Microcosm. In this moment I related my own pain to the emotionally charged situation that I had watched unfold.

I didn't feel ready to verbalize this new revelation to anyone. It felt earnestly dorky. Nonetheless, things were starting to go better. Microcosm's photocopied ads started to attract mail. *Stink in Public* was reviewed in *Factsheet Five*, which had a circulation in the tens of thousands, and I was flooded with hundreds of orders. I got offers for my zines to be distributed by Suburban Home Records and Vital Music Mailorder. I was sent other people's zines, with titles such as *Manual Resistance* and *Brainscan*, and I began routine correspondence with the editors of both. I started to write to hundreds of other zines and bands and ask if I could add them to my catalog.

I met a kid from upstate New York—I can't even remember his name—on the alt.punk newsgroup, and he suggested that we go in together on releasing a compilation CD called *Best of the Best* with bands from all over the U.S. I let him have free reign on selecting the bands, and it ended up including mostly Oi!, skinhead, and street-punk bands, none of which I had much interest in. Out of the 27 bands on the disc, only two women were represented out of 100+ musicians, which seemed strange to me. I thought punk was this great egalitarian equalizer! I didn't immediately realize how this lopsided representation of females might project an image other than the one that I intended to. But when they came back from the replicator I was still proud that I had been involved with it.

Fortunately, my friends thought it was cool, and other people must have liked it because I sold all 500 within a few years. It started to pay for other projects.

I began to develop a fairly discordant and eccentric catalog with zines from all over the world, as far away as Amsterdam and Australia. I felt that these people were trusting me with their most valuable creations. I took these zines to punk shows and showcased them in a milk crate or two.

I met lots of touring bands, traded zines with their members, and witnessed many shows from bands that toured the U.S. only once or twice. People like Joshua Ploeg, who set off flash pots indoors with his band Behead the Prophet, No Lord Shall Live, demonstrated a complete disregard for everyone's personal safety and inspired me with his embrace of theatrical performance.

Many bands performed for half a dozen people and put just as much into it as the bands that played for hundreds.

Maintaining the minimal level of relationship that is needed during a loud punk show turned out to be something that I could manage. I knew how to say hello, hand over a copy of my zine, make awkward smalltalk for five minutes; and anything that I did that was too eccentric otherwise was celebrated or at least understood within the framework of punk. I maintained relationships with hundreds of people in this capacity, showing up to their shows each year and building something that resembled a friendship. Of course, this also sometimes resulted in my coming home drunk with a record that I found unlistenable. But for every time that happened, I met someone whose zine blew me away either in terms of its graphic art or the ideas presented in it. I was always thankful when I was handed new issues of various fanzines by Lance Hahn from J Church, a San Francisco street car turned into a prolific rock behemoth. He was always up to some new kind of thinking and it was fascinating to get inside his mind, even when he was just writing about touring as a guitarist with Beck or about a TV show he was obsessed with but that I had never watched. In 1997 I recorded a live performance by J Church that became the *You Don't Have to Say No* LP, titled after the shouts of Jake Kelly and friends when Lance asked the audience whether they wanted to hear specific songs. In true punk fashion, the record sold out before the band sent me a copy and I was credited as "audience recording." Still, I was thankful that our relationship turned into routine letter writing.

I released records with bands that I had seen at Speak in Tongues or came in touch with through the ever-expanding Internet. In many ways, even though I was more interested in putting out books, I wasn't ready yet. I hadn't done enough reading to understand editing or producing books, and records were the cultural commodity of choice in my social circles.

Fifteen was another one of my favorite bands, partially because of the way they pushed the punk envelope and partially because of the way they talked openly about violence coming from parents, offering instructive steps for dealing with it: "I know, I understand. Mom and dad beat you up... Hitch the first ride; save your own life; stick your thumb out on the freeway." It was one of the few bands that spoke to so much of my experience that it scared me. Because of this, I started putting together a tribute to Fifteen in 1996. While working on it, I received an email from someone I had met on the alt.punk newsgroup in Illinois. Shamefully, I cannot remember his name, but he was putting together a tribute to Crimpshrine, a band that shared the same singer and guitarist as Fifteen. He suggested that we should work together and that, instead of going with my idea for two 7" records, it could be one CD. I didn't think this was a good idea, but I also didn't have the spine or wherewithal to object to it. In my mind, this was someone accepting my idea as good and wanting to work together, albeit in a way that I didn't approve of. Crimpshrine had suffered an ugly breakup and even eight years afterwards there remained bad blood between the members. Further, Crimpshrine had been a collaborative effort between two songwriters, and the internal tensions between them created results that were greater than the sum of their parts. By contrast, Fifteen was much more of a meritocracy, albeit not the most functional one. Members of Fifteen came and went and often had problems with hard drugs, causing inconsistent collaborations. Worst of all, the two bands really had little to do with each other and appealed to different people.

Putting them on the same disc was just going to rile people up—including the members of those bands. But I agreed to do it anyway. It turned out to be an important lesson. A few years later, a few members of Crimpshrine contacted me and expressed that they weren't terribly happy with how the compilation had been put together. I explained how it had shaped up that way and agreed to destroy the last few hundred copies of the pressing. It was the first time that it felt that there were broader, real-world implications for my actions. I began to understand how I was prone to making bad choices. Even my teenage actions could affect people far away. It was an important wake-up call.

Before long, my distro was so expansive that I had to bring a few people to help me carry it in Speak in Tongues, and it was taking up more and more room behind the bar there. I began to meet people who went there but didn't really care for the music and just saw it as a way to connect with the culture. They bought zines from me and we talked about the contents and recommended things to each other. I was still just a wacked-out drunk and eccentric old man in training. But I had figured out what my dreams and vision were. Or at least what they could and would be.

When a punk show was shut down at a nearby teen center and relocated to Speak in Tongues, I wrote a letter to the editor of the local newspaper. I explained that if you took away entertainment options from local teens, you could expect nothing but more delinquency and crime. The paper printed my letter, and I learned an important lesson about the power of the pen. Apparently only middle-aged grumps write letters to the paper and respond to them, because I was inundated with mail assuming that I was an adult homeowner who just didn't understand how bad teens are to deal with. One person lamented having to sweep up broken glass every week. I felt empowered by the experience.

I found an early website that Mike Hudson of The Pagans had made to tell stories of Cleveland's history and stories from his own band. I learned about how Dennis Kucinich as Mayor of Cleveland had led the charge to turn people's electrical service into a public utility but then lost it all when he needed to sell it back to private companies to get the city out of bankruptcy. I learned about how Mike had self-released Pagans' records and that hundreds of them had been dumped into the snow in his backyard during a Cleveland winter on the year I was born. It took a few days and a few phone calls for UPS to discover that the records were warping beyond playability in the moist snow. These were metaphors for the kinds of conditions that we were all undergoing in our minds, in our homes, and in our lives.

Through immersing myself in Mike's stories, the early zines where Superman was born, the Riot Grrrl movement, and Harvey Pekar's work, I honed my attitudes and ideas about publishing. I wanted to project my experiences and those of the people around me who I felt did not have a voice anywhere else. I wanted to incorporate humor and ideas of self-empowerment, demonstrated in the voice of the writer but especially for the benefit of the reader. I felt like my experiences and opinions had been disrespected or disregarded so many times in my life because I was a teenager. Just as my teachers had, it seemed like most textbooks talked down to me. So I developed a "style guide" as a publisher that our books would talk to the reader as an equal, be rough hewn, and try not to be too sterile or unemotional in how real experiences or events were discussed. It was important to me that it felt authentic and punk rock and that these intentions would be clear in both the look and feel of the publications, even if the content wasn't explicity about punk. I wanted the people framing the issues and expressing their concerns to be those who didn't have power in our society.

One thing I learned from watching documentary films, that I applied immediately to Microcosm, was the question of how a story is framed—and by whom. Even within the zine movement and punk scene, the same voices that were dominant in the larger society generally made the rules and dictated the priorities. Most were middle-class white male neurotypicals. Microcosm, through its catalog of zines offering people's experiences with and views of social issues, allowed people on the outside of any subculture some access into a small world while it offered people with little power in society a megaphone to simultaneously speak to both members of a social movement and the outside world. In *Dames on Frames,* the editors could talk about being sexually harassed on their bicycles while just trying to go about their lives. *Genderfailz* details what it is like to be a transgender person navigating the Canadian healthcare system. *Anti-immigrant Hypocrisy* outlines the misconceptions about and often downright impossibility of trying to become a U.S. citizen. In *Fat is Beautiful,* Crystal Hartman explains how society misunderstands and judges people who are "overweight" as well as the social stigma and rude comments that are imposed upon them in daily life. In *Survival Without Rent,* the editors explain the reasoning and lack of options that led to squatting abandoned buildings in New York City in the 1980s.

A dynamic relationship with the reader allows writers with marginalized voices to frame the discussions of the movement and social issues. Zines also allow them to be equal participants and stakeholders. Concerned readers with relative privilege can receive basic information and answers to questions like "How can I help support you?" in privacy and get real, unfiltered information. More to the point, when you read a zine, you can forge a connection with a stranger, write them a letter, and begin a real conversation. It's a learning experience.

Another thing I'd learned is that artists are generally distrustful of the businesses that handle their transactional stuff. Sometimes that's because they've worked with dishonest people in the past, sometimes it's because their brains aren't wired to understand all of the mathematics involved, and sometimes it's because they just have no way of knowing what a fair deal looks like because information to compare it to isn't publicly available. One thing that indie record labels had done to compensate for this was to offer a larger royalty percentage than what major labels paid. I liked this idea and learned that most book publishers paid new authors a 6-8% royalty based on the cover price of the book. I thought that an innovative and fairer solution was to pay 15% of the profits, offer copies of the work to the author at cost (since it was theirs after all), and immediately give them 5% of the printing. Years later, I also added a clause that if a book reprinted I would increase to 20% of the profits, since it had been a team effort and the labor costs of a reprint were vastly reduced. So, if we sold 5,000 copies of a work, the artist would receive about $5,000 over a span of years and the ability to make another $2,500 or more by selling their own copies. I kept cover prices to around $10 or less because it felt important to keep everything at a price that I could afford to pay, even when I was in abject poverty. After all, I was creating the kind of books that I would want to read. People like me needed to be able to afford them. The one thing that I couldn't offer was large advance payments as the major houses did, but I knew that showing transparency in our dealings and having a powerful mission would attract people who cared about other things more than money. As a result, we often pay authors more per copy than the major houses do. That plus the fact that the terms of our basic agreement haven't changed in twenty years continues to scandalize our peers and traditional publishers. But after all, Microcosm would be anything but traditional.

I began to plan ahead for growing Microcosm into a book publisher. Most book publishers reach their audience through a trade distributor, but, after reading about DIY record labels, my ideas for Microcosm were based more on the model of labels like SST Records and Factory Records. SST was founded by Black Flag guitarist Greg Ginn in 1978, when there was no infrastructure for independent punk rock. Previous punk bands had outside management and had worked with companies that were part of Sony or Warner Brothers. SST initially focused on putting out music from their local scene, challenging musical styles and conventions within the scene, selling their records for low prices, networking their bands into a community, and challenging people at bigger labels and cops who screwed them over. As Michael Azerrad puts it in *Our Band Could Be Your Life*, "Ginn took his label from a cash-strapped, cop-hassled store-front operation to easily the most influential and popular underground indie of the Eighties" through scrappiness, resourcefulness, and hard work. I also knew that SST was accused of dishonest bookkeeping practices and not paying royalties to their bands, which had cost them several of their highest profile bands. So there was a lesson there too: be honest and pay the people that you work with as you had agreed to.

I decided that, instead of signing with a big book distributor, it made more sense to handle the vast majority of our own mail order and relationships with stores. Ian MacKaye of DC's independent stalwart Dischord Records strongly advocated for this model, saying that distribution was the true marker of independence. There were many advantages to this model. Most notably, we weren't splitting the small payments with a distributor and we had a direct relationship with and a way to reach our fans. We knew who they were. We knew what they liked and didn't like. If something went wrong, we could correct it and didn't have to apologize for someone else's mistakes. And the work of fulfilling the mail order only takes a few hours each day.

Twenty years later, mail-order work is some of the most important labor in the industry. Most publishers don't think about it much and relegate it to someone else to do, seeing it as anything but glamorous. But it's ultimately the backbone of publishing: getting the books to the readers. It's far from what people romanticize when they dream of a career in publishing; it's done in dark basements or warehouses in the Midwest by people whose book handling would lead you to believe that they don't value or even hate the things—or their bosses make them work so fast that the books are heavily damaged on the conveyor-belt assembly line from one distributor to a wholesaler to a retailer. I cannot measure how many valuable hours are lost each week as distributors, wholesalers; and stores report damaged books back to the shipper, wait for replacements, and have to continue to inspect each one in a never-ending cycle. It's a major advantage to be in control of this aspect of the operation, and I found that I could take a ton of pride in getting twenty orders out the door each day. Sometimes it was the only task that felt tangibly accomplished after working a twelve- or fourteen-hour day.

I had always really hated filling out paperwork and applications. It seemed like most of them really only needed three or four pieces of information but stretched it out across two or three pages. Even when I was ordering books or records for our distro boxes at shows, I had to fill out applications and account paperwork just to make a purchase. It seemed like a waste of time and a headache for everyone involved. So my first time-saving innovation in this regard was the idea that I would sell things in our catalog at wholesale rates to anyone. There was no application; no paperwork; no processing. If someone's order exceeded the minimum invoice total and quantities and they selected wholesale rates, anyone could qualify. This reduced my workload as well and would eventually get our titles into hundreds of retailers who were always amazed that "setting up an account" was done automatically when you checked out on our website.

One of the biggest advantages of starting Microcosm as an eighteen-year-old was that I didn't feel any pressure to succeed or make it into a business. At the time I had few expenses. I seemed healthy. My ambitions were political rather than economic or structural, so I could focus on solving a different set of problems than most publishers.

Section

II

Telling People About
My Small World

WHEN I WAS A TEENAGE TICKLE WHORE

During my second-to-last year of high school, a friend's dad began paying me under the table to do deliveries for his Italian restaurant. Within a year it had turned into the best-paying job of my life. I earned $4 per hour to deliver pizzas and was making $10-20 per hour in tips on top of that. While the owner was a staunch Republican, the likes of which I hadn't yet encountered in my short life, he was hugely influential in my understanding of business management and finances. He explained every decision he made and every action that an employee took in terms of the financial cost to him. From a clinical distance, he would tell an employee to put only one dollar's worth of cheese on each pizza, as if they could visualize that as a measurable quantity as he could. He sang the praises of onions, which cost him only nine cents per pizza, while we charged the customer 99 cents. Then he raised the customer's price to $1.09, citing increased supplier costs.

He referred to my sexuality as "confused"[6] and would intersperse praise for President Reagan into a monologue about how we would get raises more quickly if we tucked our shirts in and then seamlessly segue into how we were all easily replaceable because we were so cheap to train. Despite these inadvisable ramblings that made us feel worthless he was a good manager, and when I showed interest in the financial operations of the business he would spend hours detailing to me how decisions were made. He would always use the cheapest suppliers regardless of quality, he explained, because most of our clients were businesspeople staying in hotels whom we likely wouldn't hear from again. I questioned his ethics frequently. Our disagreements were vital to my learning and also, I think, caused him to respect me for having a backbone. Within two years, he promoted me to manager of the restaurant. He began scaling back his involvement, and when a competitor opened on the same block, he began training to become a private investigator. I earned enough money that throughout the three years that I worked there, I could take $100 from each week's paycheck to invest into projects for Microcosm. All of the startup money for Microcosm came from working at that restaurant—about $20,000 total.

One day in the summer of 1997 while delivering food to a factory, the shop manager made the callous remark that I would someday have to get a

---

6 He never elaborated on where this conclusion came from, but my green Mohawk and dirty cut-offs might have reminded him of a cross between a character from *Suburbia* and a criminal on *Miami Vice*.

"real" job. The words stung so deep that I got up early the next day and filled out an application to work in the information technology department of a local company that made sterilization products for medical equipment. It seemed like everything in the building was pretty toxic and my roommate who worked there always came home with burns on his arms. He said that it was okay money but the job kinda sucked. They called me a few weeks later, I showed up late for the interview, and I spent the entire hour haranguing the manager about how much time I needed to take off for punk tours and explaining that I couldn't prove my income from my current job under the table. For some reason they never called me back, but I realized that I was making more money at the restaurant than I would at the sterilization company (or even at the factory where the manager had implied that my job was fake).

The following winter a car crashed into me head on in the middle of a busy intersection while I was delivering a pizza. My job didn't provide delivery insurance like they were required to, so I was pretty nervous and didn't notice that I was banged up, bleeding all over, and lucky to still be alive.

The paramedics got me out of the car and I could see that my car's frame was all bent up like an accordion. As I lay on the pavement, in shock, and fading in and out of consciousness, a small child asked me if I was okay, and her dad snapped "Don't talk to him!" Slowly, I deduced that they had both been in the car that hit me. They seemed to be in much better shape than I was. A few people came up to me and said that they witnessed the crash and gave me their phone numbers. I worried that the pizzas in my passenger seat were getting cold. Police arrived on the scene, took statements, and informed me that, given the damage, I was lucky to have survived at all.

A few days later I was lying in bed recovering from my wounds and got a call from my insurance company. The woman on the phone delivered a long lecture about how kids should drive only to and from work and school. Before I could explain that I *was* working at the time of the crash, they told me that they'd be in touch with the other driver's insurance company, would call me back after a few days, and hung up.

Months later I was still waiting for the incident to be resolved. Apparently the other driver was a "safety expert" by profession and kept bringing up this detail. He claimed that he had seen me having conversations with the witnesses on the scene and that they were my biased friends. I would call the insurance company once a month and was always just told that they would be in touch.

I couldn't keep working at my delivery job without a car, and money was getting tighter as I waited on my settlement. I came home after a night of drinking to find an email from someone named Terri DiSisto offering me a few hundred dollars to self-produce a home video of myself being tickled. It included such highlights as "Guys that interest me are YOUNG (basically, my age...18-23), HOT (....on the thin side...not too 'big-n-buff'....with absolutely no body fat whatsoever), and TICKLISH! No sex or nudity are wanted...Good videos feature exhaustion (which can usually last several days), pseudo-asphyxiation, emotional desperation, occasional muscle strains and pleading and begging...accompanied by truly desperate ticklish laughter..."

I don't know how she found me, but the enclosed photo looked like a college-aged Candace Cameron and the email described the person that I was making the videos for as "attractive." Many elements of this job offer seemed fishy, but this was before the era of Nigerian princes, and everyone in Cleveland had a scam anyway, so a person pretending to be someone else and soliciting tickling videos from strangers didn't raise a single red flag to me. It seemed like good fun for everyone.

I began enthusiastically telling my friends about this opportunity and tried to cut them in as the tickler, but their responses ranged from disbelief to abhorrence to questioning the ethics of it. My friend Ryan wanted to have a debate about the most ethical way to do sex work for a stranger. Having no interest in that, I turned the conversations back to money, "How about I pay you $50 an hour to tickle me?" He agreed.

I set up the video camera on a tripod, was tied to the bed with neckties while wearing only cut-off shorts, and was straddled by a friend, who tickled me for an hour according to the regimented timelines for each area of my body that Terri dictated. I mailed tape after tape to Terri and the money started really adding up. I was even paid for a shirtless interview on tape. She complained when I submitted a tape of myself with a beard and told me that it was not acceptable. I *must* be clean shaven.

There was only one problem: each time a friend spent an hour straddling me, s/he said that s/he wouldn't tickle me again. It seemed too weird to be in this supposed sexual situation with me for a stranger's benefit. I had one friend who loved it but, his girlfriend was freaked out about it and forbade him from doing it again. I was running out of ticklers.

Fortunately, after almost a year, the insurance company determined that I did not cause the accident. The settlement was quite large, as I'd been without a car for eleven months by then. I was too young for them to provide me with a rental car so I received a daily stipend instead. When spring came around, I'd begun a life as a dedicated bicycle commuter, riding my bike to a part-time, minimum-wage job at a dollar store in the same mall where I'd been caught shoplifting years earlier.

I loved cycling, especially at night. I began to get up at three in the afternoon to go to work, going to sleep at nine or ten in the morning after hanging out with my friends all night. I was directionless but no longer depressed. When winter returned, so did my car, and I went back to my delivery job.

Still, being a teenager with a severe accident on my record, my premium went up. I met with my insurance agent to ask whether there was anything that I could do about it. He said that there was a discount for having a high grade point average. So I enrolled in community college and took some business classes. The State of Ohio paid for it.

I told my teachers what I had been doing with Microcosm: publishing and distributing zines and records. They told me that it would never work, that I would need to raise prices and conform to more conventional models. "Wouldn't you rather sell one $10 item than ten $1 items?" they each inquired, thinking that it was such an original idea that it would shatter my misconceptions. The funny thing was, the more they kept yapping, the more I realized that they weren't running businesses. And I *would* rather sell ten $1 items. It serves a different goal that they were overlooking or perhaps was beyond their education: Many businesses employ the concept of "loss leaders," or selling something for less than it costs you in order to attract people to your business and advertise it by telling their friends about the great deals that they got. I was expanding on that concept. I knew that I couldn't afford to lose money, but I knew that I needed to get people talking about Microcosm, what it offered, and how great it was. Selling some things for $1 was a great way to do that. Stickers were like the pizza restaurant's onions: We pay nine cents for them but sell them for $1. The zines cost 50 cents each, so we weren't making much money but through creating systems designed to manage sending ten times as many packages as other small publishers, we would stand out from the crowd and be ready to fulfill those orders, get those zines and stickers into stores where new people could find them, and get people talking about us. I was young and pompous enough that I decided that my business teachers were idiots.

I took some accounting classes and discovered that I already had a freakish inherent understanding of all things financial. Everything that they taught me was already in my head somehow. I began to realize I had picked these things up through osmosis while growing up. My mom had raised my sister and me on very little income, less than I was making at the time, but she never complained about being broke and always knew how to shuffle the shell game. Despite the fact that her only income was social security and welfare, my mom suspiciously had enough money for "investments," such as a new minivan every three years and some elaborate vacation packages for herself. Many of my friends' parents asked how my mom could even afford her mortgage and taxes on such a tiny fixed income. I never asked questions and she never explained where the money came from, but I was thankful that I had picked up the skills of financial literacy and responsible decision-making.

A few months later, the parking brake didn't catch while I was running inside an apartment to make a delivery and my car rolled into someone's garage door. Six months after that, while delivering to a factory in an industrial part of town in the dead of winter, I stopped the car as I entered the parking lot and was hit seconds later by a snowplow going in reverse about 45 mph. The frame of the car had already been bent back into place once, and the car crumpled like paper under the weight of the plow. The impact of the crash finally stopped the plow inches before it crushed me, too.

As the frozen air surrounded me through the newfound holes that had developed in my car, I looked through the windshield and saw a giant machine towering over me, inches away from my body. I laughed like a lunatic. There was really no other reaction that fit the situation. It felt like a scene out of a movie. I couldn't tell whether I was lucky or indestructible. I was a teenager after all.

I didn't get another car. Driving felt too dangerous, and I had read a great article in a zine titled *how to save $7,000 per year* that detailed all of the merits of commuting everywhere by bike. Because of my punk-rock moral obligation, I rode my bike everywhere I went after that. In anticipation of another big settlement check, I bought a nice Cannondale bike that weighed less than a pound.

After the accident, I biked to work and worked only inside the restaurant from then on. As a fiscal conservative, my boss strongly approved of my decision to live car-free but seemed a little concerned about how this would affect him in the game of capitalism. He gave me another car that I drove for a while, but my heart wasn't in it so I gave it back.

School wasn't really working out for me either. It wasn't really engaging me mentally, nor was it meeting my intellect. Most of my classmates were either kids I had gone to high school with whom I hadn't liked the first time around or retirees who wanted to be landlords or fulfill such needs as opening a Christian bookstore inside the mall because the one across the street from the mall wasn't reaching enough nonbelievers. I was there only for the car-insurance discount, but my car was in the junkyard, so I dropped out, but first I took some graphic-design classes and changed my declared major to dentistry, if only to amuse myself.

Still, no amount of detachment could have prepared me for when my house burned down.

Joshua Tree performing at Speak in Tongues, 1998.
left to right: Lenny, Josh, me, and Brent

Tabling Microcosm behind the
bar at Speak in Tongues, 1998.

MORE THAN MUSIC

Throughout 1997 and into the winter of 1998, one of my roommates worked in a pet store and habitually stole animals. Before long we had dozens of pets living with us, and us upstairs residents began calling it "The Smelly House." We had ferrets, a flying squirrel, three big dogs, many things that I couldn't identify, an old cat, a snake, and numerous exotic birds. One day while everyone was at work, one of the big dogs knocked over a lamp. Eventually the bulbs caught the shag carpet on fire. The fire grew in intensity until it smashed out the windows and the neighbors called 911. By the time fire fighters arrived the blaze was too big to control: The house was totaled.

It felt like a good idea to get out of town and clear my head. So I went on tour with one of the bands on my label that spring. The tour was a disaster. Most of the shows were canceled. The transmission gave out in the van at our furthest point from home but not before one of the members constructed a lie that he won an award and canceled the rest of the tour. Still, I had a better time than I'd been having at home, which gave me real pause. I was twenty years old and had never felt more alive than those moments of being in fucked-up situations far away from home and having to resolve unexpected problems on the fly. It was the monotony at home that really was driving me crazy.

I had been growing apart from my friends for some time. My crass callousness was met with shaking heads and being ignored instead of the enthusiastic encouragement that I had gotten the year before. Many of my friends had kids during or just after high school. Some were getting lost in cocaine and heroin problems. I had never related with many other people about priorities or goals, and the gap widened as we all grew up. I drifted aimlessly. So when my house burned down, I had so few attachments left to the city that it actually wasn't that upsetting. It was more like a relief, an excuse to leave. In fact it might have been just the hidden motivation that I needed to make a deliberate change.

A few days later, I packed a bag and hopped into the car with someone who was headed down to Athens, Ohio. At first I was staying with a friend I had met at community college. The town was really small and there wasn't much to do. Rather than getting therapy or unpacking years of pain and baggage from the previous nineteen years, I grabbed my fake ID and spent every night at the bar.

I went to a party while black-out drunk, where someone that I had just met forced me into having sex when I did not want to. The next day I ran into the same person and they didn't seem to understand what that encounter had done to me. It was one stumble closer to the bottom for me. I moved into a squat for a few months but got bored, caught a ride home, and briefly moved back in with my parents.

I went with some friends to see political theorist Noam Chomsky talk at Cleveland State University. It was a 90-minute lecture to 300 people about the long-term impacts of American foreign policy and how it pisses off other governments and creates terrorism directed at the U.S. This was before 9/11, and some people were confused and skeptical of his examples of Granada's and Chile's popular leaderships' being deposed by the U.S. military. But my favorite question came at the end, from Ben Brucato, editor of the zine *Interbang* (and still in college seventeen years later), who asked, "I don't mean to be disrespectful, but if you are going to stand here and tell us about all of these global injustices, why don't you get an AK-47 and go to South America and fight with resistance movements?" Chomsky looked at the floor for a second and responded, "I'm not going to dignify that with an answer." Brucato, already well-versed in academic argumentation, couldn't accept that. "Honestly, why not? Doesn't it make you a hypocrite to know about this and do nothing to change it?" Chomsky retorted, "My part is educating people that these kinds of things are happening across the globe. There is no shortage of white people moving to Chiapas and taking up arms with the indigenous people there. I'm an old man who is more useful focusing on education and shifting perspectives than I am dying in war." These concepts stuck to my bones.

Another local band, Chalkline, was headed out west for three weeks that summer of 1998, and they said I could tag along and bring Microcosm. Their tour was much more organized than I was used to, but they picked on each other the whole time. I tried to stay out of it, but there's only so much you can do to ignore conflict when there are five young people in a Dodge Ram. Still, when people gave me a hard time for selling zines and records at the bigger shows, the band stuck up for me. Because of strong feelings and the politics of Big Oil, the person who arranged the tour had carefully planned daily drive-offs from gas stations. We would find a gas station near a county line that did not require us to prepay. We'd fill up the tank, drive off, and cross into the next county where, as he explained it, only state police could pull us over. I don't think we paid for gas more than once or twice. It made me pretty nervous but it was completely exhilarating.

We picked up a hitchhiker, and I was one of the two people in that van who didn't sleep with her. We all went swimming naked in the natural springs in Arizona. My emotions had become running counts of highs and lows, and the depression could be crippling for weeks or

Drinking at the Union, 1998.

months at a time, but on that tour it was all highs. I got to see Texas, the desert, California, and Oregon. I became closest with the person I had known the least well when we started. When the tour inevitably ended, I went home and sank into depression.

I went to More Than Music Fest in Columbus and spent several months hanging out there afterwards. I discovered many zines detailing people's frank experiences with being sexually assaulted, and it was comforting in a way to know that I was not alone. I wrote my own account but buried it before eventually submitting it in 2000 to an anthology, to be published under a pseudonym. On some level I was still ashamed and internalized it as my fault. I was hung up on how I could have prevented the situation. Writing out my experience and reading about what happened to other people was a major transformation towards my healing.

Cleveland had another blockbuster punk festival that summer that I came back for. I tabled for Microcosm at both fests and was inspired to discover lots of new zines and see the kinds of literary and political expression that were all around me. It was similar to what Cleveland Fest had been like in 1996, but the ideology was much more developed and Riot Grrrl had a much stronger influence in Columbus. It seemed that most of the coolest stuff that I saw and heard was coming out of Portland.

Heather, my pen pal and the editor of her own zine, was freshly broken up from a long-term relationship and came to visit me. We went to Wilkes-Barre Fest in eastern Pennsylvania together, and I tabled Microcosm there as well. Heather and I shared a tremendous enthusiasm for making zines. Our correspondence had fallen off when she continued sending letters to the house that was just a pile of ashes on the ground, but we were able to easily pick up the pieces where we had left off. We also shared an interest in punk in a way that I hadn't experienced with others before: Not only did Heather relate to the music and isolation that associate with punk, she also enjoyed the oddities and sociological parts of it. She liked to analyze and make jokes about the poses and outfits that people were wearing in the photos in zines and record sleeves. We made fun of bad album artwork and pondered some of the more cryptic choices that bands made. We argued about which punk song was the shortest while still being a "real song." The Descendents' "All" was a mere second, but it didn't qualify as it was really just one note. We eventually agreed on Weston's "Got Beat Up" at 36 seconds, though, while it was punk in subject matter, we agreed that it was not very punk sounding.

We talked for hours about topics such as how on the recording of 7 Seconds' "Not Just Boy's Fun," the band sings in falsetto during the bridge instead of having actual women sing on the track. It made us wonder how they made such a weird decision. Did the women cancel on the day of the recording? Did this decision not seem odd to the band? Did the band not know any women?

Heather and I proceeded to get drunk together, and she made me decode a letter that she received after her breakup. While I don't believe that I was able to give much help with that problem, we bonded that summer and she was one of the first people that I felt close to. She understood punk as a lifestyle without being into hard drugs or pressuring me to reevaluate my priorities. She was one of the first people I met who accepted me exactly as I was, and we could stay up late giggling about things that we had a hard time explaining to anyone who happened to stumble upon our private parties.

In an era of my life that felt directionless and terrifying, meeting Heather was a breath of fresh air. We related on almost every level, discussed the importance of ethical decision-making as a guiding beacon within punk culture—and what that looked like. I couldn't always tell if the plans that we jokingly made together were serious or not. I don't know if she knew either.

Eventually Heather went home to Salt Lake City and then moved to Portland. I resumed my somber existence. I tried to make the most of my environment. I showed up to a Halloween party in only a trenchcoat, G-string, and Gene Simmons mask. I had been drinking from a bottle of rum on the bike ride over. Unfortunately I was the first to arrive—even before the hosts—and I had to wait for them for an hour in my costume, raising my bottle of liquor to my lips every few minutes or so, alone on the driveway.

It was still daylight out. When the party finally got underway I entertained myself by grabbing malt-liquor bottles out of the trash, urinating in them, and putting them back into the fridge. After a frat boy took a drink from one, exclaimed "this 40 is *warm*," and continued drinking, I was implicated by the fact that I couldn't stop laughing. I was kicked out, and I impulsively decided to bike over to a Denny's restaurant and disconnect their electric sign while my friends watched and cackled gleefully.

In my continuing surreal existence, two Amish teenagers got caught in one of the biggest drug busts that the region had ever seen. It had happened just a few miles south, out into the country, and was all over the news. Both kids were named Abner Smith, but the newspaper said that they weren't related.

A few days later, I dropped off a roll of film at the grocery store where I worked part time. I knew that my friend behind the counter would develop it for free. When I came back a a week later to pick it up, neither the person behind the counter nor I could find it. We went through every roll of film in the box until we found it under the name "Abner Smith." My friends and I

CrippleKid tour, April 1998, left to right: Kevin, Nick, Jay, Jason, and I.

Bottom photo: Jay and Kevin in New York City.

found everything about the Amish drug bust story ridiculous, and my best friend started calling me Abner for no real reason in particular.

A few months later, a new manager at the grocery store emptied $60,000 out of the safe, walked out with the brand new copy machine, and was never heard from again. It was discovered that he had been hired under a false identity. I was asked to quit because my manager had found some empty packages stuffed into the corner where the security cameras had shown me working a few hours earlier. They had also heard rumors that my friends and I had contests for who could shoplift the largest value of items in a given day.

The same best friend who had started calling me Abner developed a cocaine habit. I didn't even notice until drug dealers started coming around to collect his unpaid debts. Eventually one of the dealers who had real muscle held a gun to his head while I ran over to an ATM to get money and pay the guy to leave.

By the end of the summer, four different people I knew were all moving to Portland. When they casually offered that I could come along, I had no objection to that idea. Everything seemed to keep tugging me towards Portland. We made a plan to move together in August of 1998, but the other people kept delaying our departure. I feared that if I stuck around much longer, I might not live to make it to Portland. I hadn't expected to still be alive at twenty years old—either because of nuclear war, my drunken antics, the toxic air and water around me, or another car crash.

One night my friend Robyn picked me up in her car. We were the last to leave a party and concocted a plan to brown-bag some bowel movements, set the bag on fire, and hurl them at the home of a guy whose dog had bitten her face, permanently scarring it. After executing our plan and cackling all the way home, a news story interrupted the music on the radio. There had been a mass shooting in Columbine High School. Robyn had brought a gun to school years before, but we had never heard of anything like this happening anywhere. This news set against the brilliant sunrise was too surreal to accept, and we were manic after our prank and from staying up all night. She dropped me off at my parents' house and I went to sleep. The next day I had to verify that the Columbine shooting had really happened. While I didn't agree with the shooter's actions, I related to how they must have felt in the months leading up to the attack and wondered whether I would have been capable of the same thing if I was pushed hard enough during high school. I still don't know for sure.

The move date was pushed back so many times that I had three going-away parties. Several friends, who were trying to remain close to me and were concerned about my downward spiral, sat me down to ask if I was really ever leaving. In the days approaching our next departure date, all four people backed out, and I made the hard decision that I would leave alone. My last two friends came over for final goodbyes, and we packed my few things into the big, empty truck that was intended to move five people. I departed alone in October.

A few weeks prior, the restaurant I managed was sold to some mob guys who spoke only Italian and asked me (through their translator) "What would it take to convince you to stay?" I replied "Nothing. There is nothing here for me anymore. There is nothing that you could give me to make me stay."

JUMBO KETCHUP

Despite the fact that Microcosm was in its third year, when I moved it to Portland, it was just six boxes of zines and records and shelves that Heather referred to as "ugly" so frequently that I began to take her word for it, even though I liked the way that they looked.

My original vision had been to augment the live experience of going to a show at Speak in Tongues. But I began getting more and more letters asking me for a copy of my catalog. I had been hesitant to produce a catalog, as it felt like a tremendous obligation to maintain. I was unsure if it was a good use of my time to print a list of titles that were mostly $1-2, write descriptions for all of them, and mail them out. After inventorying everything that I had in milk crates and handwriting a list of all of the zines that I had available at the request of two people who never wrote me back, I gave up and began producing a proper catalog twice per year or so. I designed it to look like a zine until there were so many zines to list on it that I had to conform to a more conventional layout. I had neglected the Microcosm website that my friend had insisted upon making for me. But online shopping was just emerging. Most people still ordered by mailing in some worn dollar bills or a check with an order form. Nonetheless, I began the arduous process of adding all of the zines and descriptions from the catalog onto the website as well.

I didn't exactly have a plan, but I wasn't intending to stay in Portland for more than a year and I figured it would just be another pit stop in my life so I didn't set my roots too deep. I received the last money that Terry Tickle owed me and I began looking around for a place to live. Along with Heather, Jesse Swan Thorson (later of The Slow Death fame)—whom I'd met because Heather had made out with his friend Tom—and Tammy, one of Heather's coworkers at the nickel arcade, I started to look for a place where the four of us could live together.

Before long, Tammy called me and insisted that she was too crazy to live with other people, and Jesse ended up moving into the house that he went to nightly parties at. Heather and I ended up moving around a bit before settling into America's oldest punk house, The Dustbin, est. 1970. It wasn't the coziest or prettiest place, but it was an old Catholic rectory, so it had plenty of space—two full kitchens and ten bedrooms. But everyone who moved in also brought along their date, so there were more than fifteen roommates and probably a few more whom no one noticed.

Heather and I started dating in the fall of 1999. It felt like a relationship of convenience and shared ethics rather than strong feelings. Here we both were in a city full of suitors and other wounded young people, but dating each other really felt like the path of least resistance. For my part, I latched onto the relationship hard. I had never before felt accepted for who I was, and Heather did that unconditionally. But we both had unresolved issues that we casually talked around, carving out existences in the comfortable space between things that reminded us of past hardships. Neither of us talked about our personal lives to our families. She once made me hide my things when her parents came to visit, which made me feel like a dirty secret. This was also more difficult than it sounds because we lived in a mudroom, a place to take off your shoes and hang up your coat as you entered the house. There were windows wrapping around the exterior of the house, and when the wind blew the room froze. We had far too many things to Tetris into that small space, so we spilled out into the hallway and a nearby closet. The rent was only $50 a month, and Heather worked at the nickel arcade during the day, so I used the time and my cheap rent as an opportunity to start making Microcosm into a real institution.

But having so much time alone returned me to the problems in my head. I'd been running from my problems for years, and nothing could affect my mental state like sitting alone with them all day. No one had ever suggested seeing a therapist, and the idea felt alienating and terrifying. There was a certain stigma to it. It seemed that something that only people with *"real"* problems did. I hadn't taken the proper time to reflect on what was going on in my head, how my fear and insecurity from childhood continued to direct me, and what my triggers were and why. I considered starting a men's discussion group, as that felt a bit more self-motivated and less disempowering but that also had a feeling of admitting that I had a "real" problem.

Portland was a little too comfortable in the '90s for people like me. I was in my 20s, surrounded by other people the same age who were all simultaneously

A scrap of paper from 1999 where I answered the questions from a book that I was reading about business.

1. How determined am I for this venture to succeed? Pretty determined
2. Am I willing to invest my own money & to work long hours for no pay, sacrificing personal time & lifestyle, maybe for years? Already do.
3. What's going to happen if this venture doesn't work out?
4. If it does succeed, how many employees will the company eventually have? 2-3
5. What will it's annual revenues be in a year? Five years?
6. What will be its market share in that time frame?
7. Will it be a niche marketer or will it sell a broad spectrum of good & services? Broad
8. What are the plans for geographic expansion? Local?
9. Am I going to be a hands on manager or delegate tasks on others?
10. Is this venture to remain privately owned and independent or will it eventually be acquired or go public? Independent
11. What initial investment will the business require? time, energy, duct tape
12. What are projected profits over time?
13. What kind of salary?

brandishing our battle scars in public or sometimes shouting from the rooftops about our pain. Instead of getting help, people were all too inclined to hold up their flaws as inescapable fact or as proof of their wounds. I identified as someone who could admit my faults and would work to improve them, but in reality I lacked the tools to deal with my problems. This turned out to be the greatest impediment to Microcosm's success.

I began a vegan diet, thinking that it might help with some of the problems that I was having with digestion while helping me make peace with my existence on this planet. I attended some street protests for things like police violence and youth rights and had the experience at several of them of being attacked by a wall of riot cops. When I had been thrown to the curb by the cops for swinging a plastic baseball bat out of a car window, at least I could see it as an exaggerated reaction to my behavior. But this was the first time that it really felt like the police attacked us simply for expressing a point of view and organizing in a public place. Instead of what motivated the protests, what stuck with me was the feelings. It felt horrifying and invigorating, and it filled me with motivation to challenge the way that law enforcement behaved.

I started hanging out at nearby Reed College and used their computers for scanning and layout. I began to think seriously about the idea of publishing real books. In my pompous brain, I felt that the things that my friends were creating were simply more interesting than most books out there, and I felt the need to tell the world about them. I really felt that my friends' zines were on par with "American Classics," imperfections be damned. It came down to the fact that I wanted other people to experience zines with the same kind of redemption and healing powers that they had provided for me.

I first reached out to my friends and pen pals who were the most skilled—rather than the most popular—writers. I thought of the Urban Hermitt, a little-known but self-promoting writer from Seattle with both literary substance and activist style who dissects gender and makes fun of how absurd society is. I wrote him a letter and got a fairly accepting—though understandably skeptical—response. We agreed to print 2,000 books, give 200 to him, and pay him $1 per book for each copy that I sold. He started writing a book for Microcosm.

I asked Mike Hudson to write a book. He seemed to know so much about radical Cleveland history, but he declined, saying that everything he knew was already published in the few articles that I had read and that he didn't feel ready to research and write a book (he's since published seven and is working on an eighth—about Cleveland history). So I looked closer to home, and in conversation Heather and I came up with the idea to do a how-to book about zines.

There already were a few books about zines. But these previous books were trying to box in what a zine was and repackage the edgy content into a presentable package. Even during the mainstream popularity of zines a few years prior, each one of these books flopped harder than the one before it. Each one reprinted pages from popular zines in a format that just didn't work aesthetically. You would be better off reading the actual zines. And, worst of all, these books made it harder for people like us to respect the author of such a body of work. While I see it a bit differently now, each book that came out during the heyday of zines seemed to cheapen them and upset the people making them rather than make them exciting to a new audience. It was interesting because it showed that zines represented a kind of dissent and were cultural artifacts that could not be commodified in the mainstream.

In contrast, Heather's book would be a nuts-and-bolts guide in a conversational voice about how to make your own zine. While it would have the look and feel of reading a zine, it would contain only original content rather than attempting to repackage existing content for a new audience. It bewildered me that there was no book out there like this already.

As my vision for Microcosm sharpened, I had conflicted feelings about success. I felt guilty each time that I succeeded, like this was somehow a betrayal of my roots. As the money coming in each month began to match the costs that I was paying out, I wondered if I should be embarrassed or even ashamed. I really wanted to do things the "right" way but was forever hesitant, and I lacked the confidence to put my best foot forward and be declarative of what the "right" way looked like. I saw this same feeling reflected all around me in Generation X, which made me determined to overcome it.

In a haze of depression and loud punk music, I started riding my bike downtown each night to a copy shop where I thought I was being subtle or clever by stealing thousands of copies. You inserted a blue magnetic copy counter into the machine, the counter kept a count of how many copies you had made, and you brought it to the counter to pay when you were finished. At first I would take two counters as I came in, run about 5,000 copies on the first one that I would then toss, and run a dozen copies on the second one, which I would pay for. Other zinemakers taught me that you could use a high-powered magnet to reset your counter to zero and not have as many opportunities to get caught, especially if you ran your petty-crime operation across a shift change. I attached buckets to the rack on my bike and arranged them so that I could strap a case of paper on top of them. I figured out that the maximum capacity that I could pedal home was about 5,500 copies, so that's what I carried home each night.

James Squeaky, former office manager of the sticker-and-T-shirt sloganeers Unamerican Activities, dropped me a line and said that he was moving up to Portland. We got to talking, and I suggested that he work with me at Microcosm. He was interested, but when he saw how little I was working with he lost interest. But he did leave me with a valuable idea: an online zine store. Other zine distros had online catalogs, but none of them had online ordering. You had to mail a check.

It was a good idea, and web commerce was just emerging. My friend Will Meek made me a new website that had a shopping cart built in. I spent months listing the hundreds of zines in my milk crates on my online catalog. I had to write original descriptions for each zine, as there was no boilerplate copy or description for each one on the Internet or even on the zines themselves. I could summarize contents and add a bit of editorial, but didn't know how to write, so the process was also one of learning brevity, figuring out what was valuable or useful to include, and understanding what kinds of zines people were interested in.

Because of trading ads with other zines and sending out catalogs, I continued to receive at least a few mail orders each week, and that was enough to give me a little more confidence and feel like I was on the right track. I maintained heavy correspondence with new pen pals, and I always included a catalog with my letters.

Whenever I encountered a zine at a punk show or a record store, I would always write a letter to the author. Practically each one would move to Portland a few months or years later. Portland had become something of a magnet for people involved in punk and zine cultures. It was pretty thrilling at first, but in-person relationships were the ones that I still struggled with. I still didn't know how to create emotional bonds with people or why I struggled with that while it seemed easy for others. So I stuck to what I knew best and felt confident about: working and writing letters.

I started working a few days per week for minimum wage with Heather at the nickel arcade. It was hard to go back to the bottom rung after managing the restaurant. Taking time away from Microcosm was making it harder to get it off the ground but I couldn't bear the isolation. For being shared with fifteen other people, our house was pretty lonely. I contacted Terri Tickle again to try and get back into the video-porn business, but I didn't hear back. Watching my co-workers at the nickel arcade living in the upstairs apartments and bringing dates to work and having their entire existence on one street motivated me to think bigger. The more I learned about their ambitions, I more I felt like I was 23 going on 40 and needed to get out. I quit the job.

Eventually, while reading a magazine in a waiting room one day, I saw an article titled "I was a Teenage Tickle Whore." That captured my attention. It turned out to be the story of another young man who had made videos for Terri. Apparently, a frustrated Terri Tickle was put on trial for shutting down a school's email servers after a student decided that he didn't want to make tickle videos anymore. Terri's real identity was found out: 39-year-old Long Island high-school assistant principal David P. D'Amato. While his actual convictions were comparatively minor, it ended up also costing him his job—and his tickling empire. Apparently, you can't be an assistant principal who is attracted to teenage boys being tickled, even if you claim to be a perfectly permed teenage girl. His arrest also meant that the best-paying job of my life was over.

I got jobs through an employment agency, which decided that I was qualified for white-collar jobs (the first of my life). I didn't know that there were jobs where you only had to dress up, show up, and sit there for eight hours—and you got paid even more money than most jobs where you have to do work!

They tested my typing speed and use of a ten-key system then asked me a few dozen questions and offered me a job at Visa making something like $15/hour looking for fraudulent debit-card accounts at credit unions. I had no college degree and didn't mention that I had no experience outside of food service. They didn't ask.

Of course the culture of the job sucked, but the worst part was that there was nothing to do. I showed up every day for the first four or five weeks and sought out my boss for instructions. Each day he told me that he didn't have time to train me yet and to come back the next day. I started bringing things to read and work on for Microcosm. After a month I stopped asking for work to do and used the eight hours each day to focus on work that needed to be accomplished for Microcosm. I produced elaborate goal charts, action items to get there, and began reading books like *Growing a Business* by Paul Hawken and *Small is Beautiful* by E.F. Schumacher. I got a little too comfortable and began using company equipment to produce the first paginated catalogs for Microcosm. I wrote zines about my experiences at Visa and printed them at work. Long-distance phone calls were still an expensive proposition at this time, but I had a phone next to my desk so I began to spend eight hours a day having phone conversations with every estranged friend in my phone book. A few weeks later, I came in to find a Post-it note stuck to my phone, proclaiming "No personal phone calls." I responded by showing up to work an hour late, outside of dress code. I asked if I could work from 11-7 instead of 9-5. My boss said "You'd be in the building alone with the cleaning staff after five." Missing what was probably his point, I said that was fine and began showing up at 11.

Try as I might, Visa wouldn't fire me. Each violation of company policy only resulted in more passive-aggressive Post-it notes. When there was an employee meeting over dinner and I wasn't invited, I listened all day long as people walked by the human-resources manager and jeered at her, asking what a vegetarian would eat at a fancy dinner. One by one, she told them that she ate fish and they all had a good chuckle together. This place was eating my soul. When someone stole company computers, the entire staff had to re-take mandatory drug testing. I considered quitting or self-sabotaging in more obvious ways.

After ten weeks my boss interrupted me while I was enraptured in a tense game of Minesweeper.

"Is this what you've been doing for the last ten weeks?!" he asked, horrified.

"Oh no; I've been doing a wide variety of things. Whatever anyone asked me to do."

This vague response somehow placated him. What was he expecting me to be doing? Sitting silently and still? He instructed me to send out 1,000 letters to various credit unions that Visa worked with. The letters informed the credit unions that I was going to begin investigating their debit accounts. This sounded suspiciously like work to me, but nonetheless I began neglecting my commitment to Microcosm and started to write and mail letters for Visa.

My solace was that each day after work I'd bike the zines that I'd printed that day up to Reading Frenzy, Portland's downtown zine retailer. I became fast friends with Amy Joy, the woman behind the counter. She would comment both on how consistent I was and how I was always in a good mood. I broke it to her that I was in a good mood because she was the first person that I saw after being bottled up all day, having to hide myself and my personality at work. I could relax and unpack my feelings as I headed to Reading Frenzy to have a normal human interaction. The synchronicity of having a way to produce zines directly into a receptive outlet really encouraged me at a time when it was vital to keep going. I made plans around those daily bike rides up to Reading Frenzy and starting looking to the future. Over time, Reading Frenzy was selling a lot of zines for Microcosm. It kept me sane but, more importantly, it created a pattern for me and gave me something to look forward to.

Back at Visa, I began sending out the letters. In response, I got phone call after phone call from credit-union managers *begging* me not to tamper with their system. Each time I insisted that it was my job and that I would go over their concerns with my manager and see if we could alleviate them. After I got off the phone, I crossed them off my list and never revisited their account. Pretty soon I was back to having a neglected workload—and a fully equipped office for Microcosm with no supervision.

I still heard the voice of the factory manager in Cleveland telling me that I would have to get a real job one day. But the more I attempted to conform to that reality, the more that it made me insane and eroded what little self-worth I had left. So I finished everything that I needed a computer for and then gave my two weeks' notice. On my last day at Visa I filled my bag with all of the jumbo-sized food in the fridge before bumping into a new hire in the kitchen. It was a young woman about my own age who was visibly pregnant. I panicked and shouted, "It's not sane here! Get out! They will make you crazy!"

I went to a party that night, had a great time, and a friend grabbed my jumbo ketchup bottle and jumped off the porch, tackling it against the front lawn. All 256 ounces of sweetened tomato covered him. It was a fitting and bloody eulogy for a place that had no life in it.

I got another job from the same employment agency doing polling for the 2000 Presidential election. It was fascinating and I excelled at it. I read verbatim from a script and recorded the long-form responses to such questions as "Why are you voting for George W. Bush?" If they indicated a candidate who was not running, most often incumbent Bill Clinton, I had to read a list followed by "Which of these candidates are you most likely to vote for?" I polled Missouri when John Ashcroft was running against Mel Carnahan, who had just died in a plane crash. Many people I talked to accused me of not watching the news or being insensitive. Each time I had to explain to them that the deceased Carnahan was still in the race. (And he won.) I heard impassioned speeches about how John Ashcroft had ruined his district and made obtaining an education much more difficult. It was the first time in my life that electoral politics felt real and impacting. I registered to vote that year.

Unfortunately for me, election day came and went and we reverted to doing customer-satisfaction surveys for utility companies. I quit shortly thereafter. My boss said, "I understand. You're too smart to be here anyway." I wasn't expected to be recognized for my skills and intellect. At most jobs and in school I would always get bored and quit trying, making my potential seem minimal. But my boss had seen something in me. Bolstered by that, I left corporate America, never to come back.

Heather and I in our home, The Dustbin, 1999. Photo by Erik Diffendaffer

NURSING WOUNDS

On Thanksgiving day in 1999 Heather and I had been riding bikes in the pouring rain to a potluck when I crashed into a traffic circle at the bottom of a hill. Heather later said that my collarbone was obviously broken, because my chest was sunken where I'd had the impact. I went door to door asking to use someone's phone but no one would let me. Heather picked up my book bag and complained that she had been carrying more than I was. When we finally found a ride and got home from the hospital, two friends came over and fed me because it hurt too much to move my arms. Heather interrupted to say that I had better not move the TV into the living room because she likes to watch it in bed.

So while my friends were at World Trade Organization protests in Seattle, I sat at home nursing a broken clavicle, watching them on TV. It was crushing to think that the fight for global justice in the streets was happening a mere 150 miles from where I floated helplessly on a beanbag chair full of pain meds.

A few months later, Heather, some friends, and I went out for dinner. We were sharing a meal that included grilled tortillas, which were delivered to us in tin foil. Not understanding that this was to keep them from getting stale, I unwrapped them onto a plate. A few minutes later Heather discovered what I had done. "Fucking idiot!" she snapped. Everyone sat in silence until we were finished.

A few weeks later, we went to a Renaissance fair. I thought we were having fun for a while, but she became frustrated with me and left me passed-out drunk on a heating grate. A cop found me and drove me home. Heather and I yelled at each other and I felt confused that she didn't seem to understand why I felt abandoned, unimportant, and upset.

The next morning, she grabbed a piece of my mail out of my hand, causing my hand to be slammed in the closing door, and shouted, "Mail!"

Checking the mail was one of my most vital daily routines, and Heather had massively disrupted it, hurting me along the way. When I explained why it was important and how I felt, she simply said, "I like mail!" One thing about having Asperger's is that I am not only upset if expectations are knocked out of balance but also that I can be incapacitated for the rest of the day or week by such an occurrence. It's all I can think about. It's not a want; it's a need. I can't focus on anything else. I'm left irritable and easily triggered. Heather didn't understand that, and I didn't know how to explain it.

I began to realize how much I had let my boundaries be bulldozed throughout my life. The habits and behaviors that I had been taught as a child for resolving conflict left me without the tools to deal with a disagreement. I liked Heather, but she often seemed disinclined to discuss a conflict or resolve it, while I felt the need to stay up all night and talk through it.

Another issue was that I wasn't yet aware of the range of feelings that I had, much less someone else's. I had a very hard time understanding or relating to the way that Heather would express her own needs. She would drop subtle hints that would be clear in hindsight—after she pointed them out to me. But in the moment I was oblivious. It felt like she was speaking another language, subtly talking around the matter at hand and expecting me to understand what she wanted me to do with it. It felt like she wanted me to be psychic in understanding her needs. It also seemed to me like she was just more comfortable pretending that everything was fine and not having those arguments, which is what our conversations always turned into.

I'd never seen a model of what a healthy relationship could look like, so our constant arguments didn't alarm me. My instinct was to keep trying. I figured that with enough practice we'd figure it out.

The Fla Flas, a band that I'd met on my first trip out west a few years before, got back in touch with me and said they were coming to Portland. I agreed to book a show for them if they could give me a ride to Columbus. I figured that some time and space away from Heather would be good for our relationship while some time on the road would be good for promoting Microcosm.

The Fla Flas agreed, and I booked a packed house show for them. But they had forgotten their money bag at the previous show and had to go back and get it. They arrived in Portland at 2 AM, hours after the show had ended. Nonetheless, they picked me up and we headed eastward.

Alfred, the drummer, started asking me questions when I got in the van.

"Have you ever been arrested?"

I paused and his tone escalated.

"Do you have any outstanding warrants?"

"Ummm. I don't think so."

"Are you carrying any drugs on you right now? We can't afford to get in trouble."

"No."

Jesus, the singer, interrupted the awkwardness to ask me whether I was in love with Heather. I honestly hadn't thought about it before, and I found the question pretty invasive. But after how the interrogation went a few seconds ago, I gave an honest answer.

"I think so," I said.

"So why are you leaving her?" he quipped.

"We haven't been getting along and I need to figure out my priorities. I don't know where I belong right now," I explained.

In reality I was running from my problems, and I think that I knew it, at least in the back of my mind.

The band complained that I had brought five boxes of Microcosm titles to sell on the tour. They complained that my feet smelled. But once we made it out of Portland, I had a really great time. I met dozens of my pen pals and discovered that I had mastered the theater of socializing, at least in very short bursts.

While most people with Asperger's are socially awkward or asocial, we are capable of learning social skills through repeated experience. Short burts of performance are feasible but exhausting. But the stakes always feel high. It is easy to get our feelings deeply hurt, since most of these efforts inevitably result in failure and hurting other people's feelings. In an effort to function better, I spent some time witnessing what worked for other people and mimicking their social behavior. At first, I would repeat phrases verbatim that I had heard other people say to great reception. But I tended to get different responses than they had, so I attempted to combine a variety of successful material by mishmashing phrases I had seen work for other people. Before long, I was adding my own flair and personality. It was getting to the point where I could hold court for up to five minutes before awkwardness would ensue.

If I tried to maintain the conversation for longer, I would sometimes trail off mid-sentence and stare at something that distracted me, or I'd lose my point as I stammered on. Sometimes I would stare at the person I was talking to, hoping that he or she would be the one to resume the conversation. I realized that people tolerated and respected me because of the projects that I applied myself to and the voices I was magnifying, not because they liked my personality or because we related on an emotional level. But I was okay with that.

The Fla Flas weren't having as much fun on their tour as I was. They were bleeding money and explained to me that ethics were great if you were a popular indie band like Fugazi with money to fall back on, which they didn't have. Hailing from El Paso, Texas, they were four young Hispanic men who were often treated with relative levels of suspicion. I witnessed Jesus being grilled about how to spell his name at a burrito counter. He explained that it's spelled like Jesus, which was treated as heresy throughout the Dakotas and Wyoming. After a small show in Des Moines and then a promising-turned-disappointing show in Chicago, the band informed me that their Cincinnati and Columbus shows had both been canceled. They would be leaving me in Chicago as they headed south. I made phone calls to my friends in Columbus to see if we could set up a show for The Fla Flas. I booked them a show, but it quickly came to light that the real reasons for giving up on the tour had more to do with the band's running out of money and its members' burning out.

Before they left town, we all went to a birthday party for our host in Chicago. But we were her only friends who came, and we had all just met her. Worse, her parents insisted that she had to make her own birthday cake because she was vegan. Her life seemed lonelier than mine. In her kitchen, I discovered a picture of Heather, whom she had met the year before when Heather was visiting Indiana. I thought we could bond over shared experiences, knowing the same person, and the pain in our lives, but she was closed up tightly. Perhaps I just didn't have the skills to do that. I resolved to develop them.

The Fla Flas left town and I took a cab across town with all of the Microcosm boxes to Liz's apartment, my friend with whom I had seen Fugazi during high school. She had just dumped her fiancé but didn't seem morose or regretful in the slightest. I stayed there for a week, taking solitary walks through Chicago's Chinatown each day and seeing Liz only for a few minutes after she came home from work each night. Liz and I had become close during school, at least as close as I could get to people, but Chicago seems to turn people into solo performers with their adventures in their heads. It was providing a lot of time for me to think.

While in Chicago, I found out that two years after my second accident I had received the settlement money from my car's being turned into an accordion by a snowplow. I decided that the most responsible way to spend it would be as a down payment on a house. I needed a new direction, some roots, and to get out of my rut. I wrote to Heather about this plan. She was understandably perplexed, as I had said that I wanted to purge all of my possessions *and* buy a house—on the same postcard.

Eventually, I found a friend of a friend driving from Chicago to Columbus. She was a full-time phone-sex operator who lived with her parents, who had no idea about her job. I had a lot of fun talking to her on our eight-hour drive, though when she began asking me questions the unique nature of my life came into focus.

"Where do you live?" she asked.

"Portland," I replied.

"How do you know all of my friends in Columbus then?" she asked.

"I grew up with them in Cleveland," I explained.

"How did you end up in Portland?"

"My house burned down and I... needed somewhere to go."

The conversation was clearly stressing me out so she switched to seemingly easier questions.

"How long are you going to be in Columbus?"

"I don't know. I guess until something else comes along," I replied

"You don't need to be home for anything at any point?"

"My life isn't really like that," I tried to explain.

I had spent previous summers in Columbus, and with my friends there it felt a bit like home. I moved into a house where ten friends lived together. The house had numerous attractive features for young people, including a recording studio, an opium den, a kitchen large enough to play "keg hockey" in, four stories, three kinds of mismatched siding, and a great location around the corner from storied punkhouse The Legion of Doom. It was within walking distance to an assortment of terrible restaurants.

The summer was getting hot, and I didn't have a room so I slept on a couch on the porch. I set up an office in the living room to run Microcosm out of. I borrowed a bike and shipped orders from the local post office, stopping at record stores along the way to devour as many zines as I could find. I wrote postcards to the author of each zine I read, offering unsolicited feedback to the ones that didn't appeal to me and distribution offers to the ones that I liked.

That summer, Matt DeWine and I were co-releasing a split record for two bands, Bedford and The Flotation Walls, and I suggested that we should organize a tour for them. The tour idea was a hit and within a week so many people were intending to come that we decided to buy a school bus and an ambulance. I took on the role of booking the tour and was de facto tour manager, being the only person with tour experience. I had a lot of enthusiastic conversations with the band members and their crew. But instead of preparing, we had parties almost every night, so frequently in fact that a rule was instated that bottles could be broken only if it was someone's birthday, or eventually, if someone's birthday was the day before or after, or if anyone in attendance knew someone whose birthday was coming up. It didn't bother me. Nothing in my life seemed to mean anything. I was 23 but didn't expect to live to be 25.

One morning after a particularly destructive party, the landlord showed up. I couldn't tell you what time it was but the sun was in full shine, reducing the wall of shade that could have protected me from his heated gaze. Looking at his yard completely covered in broken glass shards and shattered furniture pieces, the landlord stormed off and left a message on the answering machine. "When I get back there in an hour, I want every piece of glass picked up and I want the naked man off the porch!" I had been sleeping shirtless in a sleeping bag. I rushed to wake everyone up and get the mess under control. The landlord never came back that day but we discovered that a rival punk house had stolen all of the cushions off our couches and all of our cordless phones. We had to concede defeat in several wars that day.

Months went by. The more time I spent on the phone booking the tour, the more it seemed like the bands were less enthused to go. Some members dropped out and were replaced by temporary members for the tour. I worked hard on the booking, but it's difficult when the people you are doing the work for are less enthusiastic about their music than about going to parties after school every day. I had to "lend" some of my settlement money to one of the bands so they could afford their ambulance. I spent a week building beds and equipment lofts for the other band's bus.

After five months in Columbus, we finally hit the road that August of the year 2000.

ONE LAST DROP

The last few days in Columbus, after a week of walking on the roofs of parked cars and eating greasy food at 3 AM, I was rocking on a porch swing with two friends when I was struck by a series of realizations about how alcohol was eating my life. It was my crutch, my vice, and if I was going to build the life that I wanted to lead, I needed out. I was drinking only because that was what I did *every* night. And I suddenly hated it. I threw my 40-ounce bottle of King Cobra into the street. It shattered into a million pieces as I shouted, "Fuck this shit! I quit!"

A few days later, the tour started. Each day, the situation got worse. The bus broke down and never made it out of Ohio. I was sick from alcohol withdrawal and slept for days in the loft of the ambulance. The navigator wasn't calculating driving distances, so we arrived too late for the bands to play at the first few shows.

Going through alcohol withdrawal in an ambulance full of sober people would keep me from relapsing, but they weren't exactly the most understanding audience for my problems. The mood was somber bordering on tense by the time I was cognizant again on the fifth day of the tour. By that point, Bedford had turned on me and was questioning whether the whole tour was an elaborate ruse for me to get a ride home. If it was, it would have been the most expensive cross-country trip of my life! I called home and had several frustrating conversations with Heather. The way she saw it I was having fun cavorting around America. But in my eyes it was work. And every day I went to sleep exhausted.

The first show that they played on the tour was to two people. The second one had a packed house—until they started playing, at which point almost everyone filed outside to have a conversation and it became clear that the entire audience was there to see the headlining local band. To make matters worse, the solitary person who stayed began shouting requests—for songs written by a guy that had been kicked out of the band years ago. Then, as the band members tore down the equipment, the sole member of the audience turned on them and began to insist that they were actually imposters!

That night we had a very hard conversation. Two people wanted to cut their losses and go home immediately, and the other two were indifferent. I was the only one who was confident and optimistic about carrying on with the tour. As always, I was seeing the forest instead of the trees and focused on building something while others just saw it as long drives that ended with indifferent promoters and crappy shows. I saw it as a chance for Microcosm and the band to encounter new people, even if it was just a handful at a time.

I lost the vote by a wide margin. Feeling dejected, I decided to stay in Denver and cut my losses in other ways. It turns out that the show's promoter was a teenager who lived with her parents. Her dad said that I could stay there for a few days. Their house was far out in the suburbs and it took 45 minutes on the bus to get downtown. Two nights later, I was sleeping on the floor in the basement and woke up to find the promoter's mom standing over me, turning the light on. She had grown up in China and did not feel okay with a boy of no blood relation staying in the same house as her teenage daughter. I started staying downtown with friends of friends in an apartment after that.

After a few days of exploring the city and spending many hours in the public library responding to emails for Microcosm and contacting every band on tour that I knew of without any luck, I started going to shows and asking bands if they could give me a ride back to Portland. No one was as weirded out by this proposition from a stranger as they should have been, but no one was taking me up on it either. American Steel, a rough-edged pop band from Oakland that I liked, seemed to consider it for the longest before showing me that their van lacked the physical space for a fifth person, let alone the last three boxes of Microcosm that I was still toting around.

Heather emailed me an ultimatum: I could either come home right then or we were through for good. That seemed fair. I had gotten what I needed out of the trip. I bought the next available plane ticket home.

PATCHING THE CRACKS

Heather picked me and what was left of Microcosm up from the airport. The condition of the three cardboard boxes was almost comedic. Each one was so thoroughly covered in layers of duct tape and stickers of punk bands that there wasn't much box left. Sixteen years later, I still can't bear to throw these boxes away as they've taken on so much sentimental value even now that they aren't much good otherwise.

Heather had been understandably upset with me. I had selfishly traversed the country for five months while she was left to build a life at home without me. Our bonds were worn, but she was interested in continuing our relationship, only with stronger boundaries. That seemed fair to me; even healthy.

Still, some things concerned me. She was upset that I had quit drinking and insisted that I didn't have a problem with alcohol. Drinking was an important kind of bonding for her. But we were different kinds of drinkers: I drank malt liquor to get drunk and medicate my problems while Heather drank imported or craft beers to get to know people better and engage on subjects that people might be too self-conscious to talk about otherwise.

I was pretty closed off in general and didn't talk about what was going on in my head. Many people, including Heather, expressed that they felt shut out of my life. My first piece of professional writing was published that fall, a lengthy article explaining what Anarcho-Syndicalism is. Heather told me that she cried when she read it, because it made her realize how little she knew about me. It must have seemed like a lot of my actions at the time came out of nowhere. Perhaps it was a result of all of this and of wanting to know me better that made Heather take it as a personal rejection when I quit drinking.

But that wasn't what I had intended at all. Quitting was about becoming the person that I wanted to be and not losing more of myself or my choices to alcohol. Over the next few weeks, Heather and I had many long talks. I felt like I had convinced her that I had actually quit drinking and that, contrary to what I had said earlier that year, I was serious about wanting to stay in Portland and buy a house. Portland felt more like home than anywhere in Ohio did or could. I felt like this decision made me a better mate, but we were still always fighting.

I was finding my way. I had turned Portland into my adopted hometown. It was a magical time, as San Francisco must have been in 1960 or Cleveland in 1929: Things were about to explode and you could feel it in the air. Everywhere you looked, cultural holdouts were blossoming. Even after adding 21% population growth to the city over the previous decade, it was clear that Portland's wasn't just adding density: It was attracting like-minded people and a reputation for values and goals similar to my own.

The idea of a city that is beautiful inside and out seems too good to be true, and in some ways it is. But it's almost impossible to picture Portland if you are used to most American cities. Development hadn't yet pushed neighborhoods into hyperdensity, and there was lush greenery everywhere that you looked. There were multiple punk shows to choose from every night and different ones over brunch on the weekends. There were social centers where you could meet interesting and like-minded people no matter what you were interested in. The downtown street kids asking for spange were docile, creative, and humorous, or at least non-threatening. I could ride my bike everywhere I went all year round as long as I had a decent rain coat. The 24-hour Church of Elvis, an eccentric collection of weird ephemera run by a woman with an unpredictable personality who was constantly flirting with homelessness, was in full swing.

Portland felt like the kind of place where I could build Microcosm into something to be reckoned with. Or maybe I just found it to be a comfortable place to run from my problems and be myself. But my decision to stay and develop roots was the beginning of making truly intentional choices.

I began paying myself $400 every month out of the money that Microcosm was making, hired a realtor, and began looking for a home to call my own with what was left of the money from my car accidents. My friend Michael Ismerio, who owned my favorite local record store Q is for Choir, told me that if I was serious about buying a house I needed to act quickly. He was right—this would prove to be the last era of affordable housing in Portland. Even in the previous six years, housing prices had gone up by 150%. By the time I was looking for a house, reasonable options started in the $100,000 range, more than I wanted to spend, and we were in depopulated neighborhoods where gunshots were audible at night.

After a month or two the search was reduced to a handful of places. None of them was the dream home I had pictured: The giant collapsing frame of rotting wood from *Fight Club*. I figured that land and structure were more vital than condition, and I could learn whatever skills I needed and do the repairs myself. I was young, motivated, and industrious. But the houses just weren't there.

By the end of 2000, the realtor found three suitable houses. One was on a busy street in a sleepy residential neighborhood without much to do. The second was about fifteen percent more than I thought I could afford. And the third was located at the onramp to I-5 in a forgotten neighborhood in North Portland. Heather and I discussed the decision, and she rightfully pointed out that, while the third house wasn't beautiful, it was noisy, there was very little sunlight, the kitchen was tiny, and the floor plan didn't make much sense, it was the only house that could be adapted to have seven bedrooms. I put on a dress shirt, sauntered down to the title company, and bought the house. My realtor kept giving me nervous looks, seeming to wonder whether I could actually produce the money that I claimed to have.

The plan that Heather and I dreamed up was to move our favorite people with us from our current house, The Dustbin, and fill it up with our friends. The place looked better on paper than in practice and there wasn't a lot of privacy so when prospective housemates came over who were considering living there, they lacked the vision for the place that we had. The way I saw it, if someone didn't like the floor or the door, that stuff could always be replaced. One front room contained a beautician's sink, which weirded people out if they made it past the rottweiler slats on the "bedroom" door.

Most of the houses in the surrounding blocks were either empty or appeared that way. A few doors down and a few years later, the largest meth bust in Oregon's history would occur. The musical equipment belonging to The Decemberists, supposedly worth tens of thousands of dollars, was returned to the band more than a year after the theft. But other than that, the neighborhood was largely uneventful, and boxed in by four major streets that isolated it both in time and from the rest of the city.

The plan was to build another bedroom and an office for Microcosm in the basement. We had commitments from a variety of friends but some of them fell through after they saw the place. By the time we were ready to move in, eight people took residence: Steve (of *Journalsong* zine), Angela, Tom, Ann, Alan, Glenn Porter (of Alkaline Trio), Heather, and myself.

Most of the roommates were couples who didn't want to pay for two rooms so we still had an empty bedroom. We put up an ad at Reading Frenzy and let one stranger move in blindly. Perhaps it's just the nature of finding a roommate from a classified flyer, but she was so maladjusted that she really made the rest of us seem "normal."

Mell Niño had grown up in affluence in suburban Seattle and brought with her a trained show dog. Its bark had been removed, it did not know how to socialize, and all day long it whimpered from a cage. Mell couldn't share food with the rest of us because she claimed that she had a bad experience once. After spending all of her money on expensive convenience food like fake meats and processed grab-and-go "foods," she said that her roommates ate it all. She insisted that she didn't eat meat but her mom began delivering a monthly cooler full of fish that she'd sneak into her bedroom.

Once, when she had locked her keys in her car, she punched out one of the car's back windows. She explained this decision in economic terms: A locksmith costs $10 more than a new window from the dump. Whenever I saw her car during the following year, it still had a plastic bag over the broken window.

Mell once threw a party but no one came. She explained that it was because they didn't like the scene report I had written about Portland for *Maximum Rocknroll* earlier that year. I had been a little mean and picked on a lot of bands for being uncreative while being less than enthusiastic about the scene as a whole. I guess I did feel that way, and the scene was a bit insular and off-putting. It didn't make me any friends but I was still a cheerleader for what the scene could be and wrote with enthusiasm about the wide variety of local zines.

In my fantasy, Mell and I talked about our problems and let those pains make us closer. We never had an argument, but I got the distinct impression that she didn't like me. She moved out a few months later.

Microcosm organizing notebook, 2001

Microcosm business plan notebook, 1999

'STRUCTION

As 2000 became 2001, after the excitement of coming home and buying a house wore off, I was back to major struggles with depression and trying to find the motivation to not only get out of bed each day but also to do the work that needed doing, like finishing building the windowless Microcosm office in the basement that I had begun the year before and getting the mail orders out the door. My to-do lists got longer as I realized all that needed to be done. "Aspies" are prone to fits of depression because we just can't connect with people and feel isolated.

I had run out of money, I wasn't working, and Microcosm wasn't bringing much in beyond expenses and the $400 that I paid myself each month. I needed to build up the business but would gladly take any distraction instead and spend hours talking about my plans for Microcosm with people over breakfast.

As I finally got the office built, the mail orders were pouring in daily and I had to go to the post office two or three times per week. I became acquainted with all of the postal workers and began learning their secret codes of "bound printed matter" and "book rate." More and more zine makers were finding me and I was getting daily zine samples in the mail. It became a magical fantasy world of learning about all manner of lifestyle politics in extreme detail, from dismantling the cultural stereotypes of Asian women to mental health awareness to transphobia. I began stocking quite a few zines that detailed frank discussions about the experiences, trauma, and the aftermath of sexual assault. I knew how much zines about topics like these matter to the people who need them when they are as lost and lonely as I had been from time to time. I would send each zinester an encouraging postcard in response. Even if it seemed put together without much effort, I felt like they deserved a response. If it had an address on it, I sent a postcard.

But the isolation was getting to me and I asked Heather if she was interested in helping me read all of the zines that came in, as that was an interest that we shared. She agreed. She worked part time at the nickel arcade and would spent the rest of her time at home working on crafts and projects in her room while I worked alone in my office. I tried to draw her into my work but she seemed to see it as my thing. While friends and neighbors would often comment on how happy and successful I seemed, the reality was that I would often stay up late taking tests about depression and reading about how to overcome it before crawling into bed hours after Heather had retired. When I did have encounters with other people, I would often feel like we were missing each other.

One afternoon while dropping off zines at Reading Frenzy, the woman at the counter recognized that the photo of me in my zine was taken inside her former house in Los Angeles. We figured out that I had stayed there during my tour in 1999. Not knowing how to extend this into a friendship, I just said "Uh huh" and walked out the door. It wasn't that I didn't want to be friends. I just had no idea how to make that happen.

Understanding that what I was doing didn't work, I attempted a different approach. When I found out that one of my neighbors made a zine, I invited him over and told him that we should start a band. Within a few hours, I was playing him songs of my old bands and told him the story of how one of my close friends and former bandmates in Cleveland had been institutionalized for his schizophrenia. After he finished explaining to me that I was playing my own song in a key different from the one on the recording, pretty soon he was the one saying "Uh huh" and heading out the door.

My roommate Steve had his friend Pablo over one night. Pablo overheard me waxing philosophical about my dream of starting something similar to Cleveland Punk Fest for zines. The community aspects of congregating in this fashion had been so valuable to me as a teenager, both for learning what my values were and meeting older people who were living them. Heather insisted that it wouldn't work; zines weren't a social activity and congregating asocial people was against the spirit of the whole thing. She had a point but I had a vision. Pablo told his friend Nicole Georges, who had been involved in organizing the Midwest Underground Media Symposium in Kansas City and started making her zine *Invincible Summer*. Nicole called me to suggest that the Independent Publishing Resource Center, Portland's zine-making headquarters and social center, might be able to fund putting together something like that and that one of their board members was the event coordinator at Portland State University; maybe they could host. That phone call motivated me to take more steps.

Zine fests had begun popping up all over the U.S. in the previous ten years so it was not a unique or far-fetched idea that Portland should have one. Many other people in the scene had suggested similar events. Zine fests were generally awkward affairs but I wanted zines to occupy a cultural space in punk the same way that music and fashion did. Other people agreed that Portland could benefit from one and suggested that it could spark a new generation of zine publishing. Nicole suggested contacting some other zinesters that she had heard express a similar interest in organizing such an event. I got up "early" at 11 AM and began calling zinesters. Most of the people I called were still sleeping and seemed annoyed that I would call so early. Slowly, each person joined a chorus: "Call Eleanor."

The Eleanor in question was Eleanor Whitney, who organized the Radical Art Girls. A schism had widened in their group between the second-generation riot grrrls who were interested in being politically radical and the members who simply wanted to make art in peace and isolation. The group was slowly imploding and Eleanor was interested both in zine fests and in facing a new challenge in social organizing. Despite never having met me before, Eleanor was highly enthusiastic about my suggestion to work together.

Eleanor, Nicole, and I all had very similar backgrounds: punk rock with a great interest in identity politics, zine making, and community organizing. It felt right, and more importantly it felt like something to create the community that I desperately needed to have in my own life, based on mutual respect and shared experiences.

Soon, at Eleanor's behest, we had a rotating cast of two dozen or so people meeting every few weeks to put the event together. I asked Heather to join us and she did, quickly giving up on her skepticism, as everyone else involved was highly enthusiastic.

After several lengthy meetings, the group still could not come up with a name for the event. We had ruled out dozens of options for reasons like "that word makes it sound boring" or "attracts the wrong element." Eventually, Matthew Harris, who had been listening quietly for two hours, suggested the name "Portland Zine Symposium." I had no idea what a symposium was or what it implied, but others assured me that it didn't mismatch what we were discussing. The first year wasn't explicitly focused on zines, instead featuring a smorgasbord of DIY programming, with everything from electrical work to grant writing to bookbinding to instructions on how to steal photocopies to panel discussions on women in publishing.

As we spent more time working together, bonds were formed. The other organizers would invite me to their parties and I'd have them come over to our house. We were building a community, and I was proud to be in the middle of it. And for the first time in my life I was enjoying the *process* of something rather than the product. After a year of loneliness, the experience made me feel like staying in Portland was the right choice. At the same time, I didn't want the event to come and go, because I feared that my new group of friends would dissolve afterwards. Further, what if the event was a disaster? The safest thing to do seemed to be just planning and delaying something that would never happen. As the year lurched on, I was nervous about the event and what would happen to all of my new friends, but I implicitly trusted Eleanor's judgment about the right decisions for the Zine Symposium. When I got nervous, her confidence steered me back on track.

Microcosm Publishing
Spring Catalog 2001

Microcosm Publishing
Fall Catalog

Various catalogs that we produced in our first six years.

In 2000 we produced our first paginated catalog from my desk at VISA.

Previous to that, all of the catalogs looked like the one pictured in the lower left, with both sides of one sheet of paper listing an increasing number of items on them at decreasing font sizes.

Microcosm Publishing
Catalog Fall 2000

Microcosm Publishing
Catalog Spring 2000

THE STEAD OF HOME

The first Portland Zine Symposium happened from July 12-14, 2001. It was small, but mighty—and glorious. We estimated that about 400 people came from all over the U.S., and while some of the workshops attracted only a few people, others ran over the allotted time because there was so much discussion. Shockingly, my workshop on scams was so well attended that people spilled out into the hallway to listen. I had a table with prime placement for Microcosm with all of the zines. I found new motivation to convert my energy into working hard on Microcosm.

I had discovered a rave-flyer printing company in Miami that would print 5,000 full-color postcards for less than $200, an amount that seemed within reach to me. I also discovered that you can fit a *lot* on a postcard, including the first thought-out statements about what Microcosm was. It featured a sample listing of a dozen zines, a dozen records, a dozen political stickers I had designed, and a dozen buttons. On the reverse side I included the Greek word origins of Microcosm, an illustration of a person spray-painting the sign for anarchism, an illustration of a monkey, and a collage that Heather had made of two children with the word "share" emblazoned over it. When I printed more, I added "A DIY publisher that distributes radical ideas." I began mailing them out, 25 at a time, to other people to leave in their local coffee shops and record stores around the world.

That slim postcard caused my little office to be flooded with mail and online orders. One unforeseen problem that the glossy postcard created was the misleading impression that Microcosm was larger than one person working twelve-hour days alone in a 4x8-foot windowless basement office. The affiliation with the Zine Symposium, the postcard, and the website with an online shopping cart led people to a new and ironic adjective to describe Microcosm: "big." Unfortunately, the punk scene has some problems keeping things in perspective a lot of the time, and "big" is often not meant as a flattering remark but rather often one of jealousy or distrust. The connotations run deep, and gossip moves quickly in those quarters.

But there were positive results as well. I began receiving ten times as many zine submissions as I had previously, with something coming in every single day. It was magical but overwhelming while really helping me to select and distribute only quality work. Even if I didn't pick up a zine, I'd send them a rejection and include a copy of one of my own zines as a gesture to suggest that we were still peers and equals. Maybe we could work together in the future. My orders increased, too, going from an average of $25 per day to closer to $60 per day in mail orders and another $50 per day in online orders. I no longer had to go door to door to get stores to stock Microcosm things in Portland, though I did enjoy that part of the job and continued doing it when I had the time.

Despite Microcosm's being five years old, it was at this point that I went "all in" and began working 100 or so hours per week in my office. Previously I had spent a similar amount of time in my office, but now I made sure to spend the hours actually working. The camaraderie that I felt in my newfound friendships with the Zine Symposium organizers had motivated me out of my rut, and I believed that my vision for Microcosm could be achieved as my sole employment for the long term. I began relentlessly reading, reviewing, and ordering zines for the catalog when I wasn't sending out mail orders.

And I went "all in" in another way—I decided to purge all of the records from the catalog and focus just on the zines, books, and politics. There were so many record labels and distros that, while those things had excited me as a teenager, I realized it was too complicated and not distinctive enough, and that it wouldn't hold my interest as well as zines and books would for the long run. Even at 24 I was feeling out of touch with new music and from a business standpoint it was already clear that records were not sustainable.

And then I made a change that I didn't think was possible. I gradually pushed back my hours of activity all the way around the clock until I was getting up at 9 AM instead of going to bed then. I began to feel more motivated by getting up early, eating the same breakfast at the same restaurant every day, and

Heather, Nate, and I organizing the Zine Symposium, 2001

spending all of my waking hours either working in the office or running errands. Then after dark I'd work on updating the web catalog until I'd go to bed. I was so manic that I could easily work for twelve hours straight without eating.

One night after having worked since breakfast, I finally took a break to make dinner. As I was carrying my pasta, stacked into a little pyramid to fit as much as possible into the bowl, to the dining room table, my blood-sugar levels suddenly collapsed. I passed out, dropped my bowl, leaving bloody streaks of marinara across the floor, and I slumped against the doorway of the kitchen for a few minutes.

Heather noticed that not only had my focus changed but so had my mood. I wasn't intending to isolate myself socially, but the result of recognizing how much work needed to be accomplished meant that I saw her less and less. While Heather had previously focused on her own hobbies and interests, she began making dinner for me, checking up on me, and insisting that I come to bed each night around midnight as I protested that I just wanted to finish one more thing.

Despite the warnings of friends and my teachers at community college, it became clear that Microcosm was going to make it and become something lasting. I began keeping thorough records and started an accounting spreadsheet that showed what I had spent money on, what had happened as a result of that money, and what I intended to spend money on next. The numbers and results were my favorite part of the story so far.

My recreational solace each month was Critical Mass, a bike ride that radically re-envisioned what the city could look like as a huge parade. We had organized one in Cleveland in the '90s but it had never grown past a few dozen people until years after I left. In Portland it attracted hundreds of people and seemed to be growing. Years later I made a film about the bicycle activism back to the 1970s[7] and learned the inside nuts and bolts of the conflicts and difficulties, including illegal police spying, mass ticketing, and arrests at Critical Mass. But back in 2002 I was quiet and solitary at the rides and, while I witnessed some police behavior that was downright terrifying, I never had any problems. The ride was deeply uplifting and emotional for me. It was such a release that I would cry almost every time that I went.

---

7 *Aftermass: Bicycling in a Post-Critical Mass Portland*, 2015:, MicrocosmPublishing.com/Aftermass

My favorite part of each month was the final week. Critical Mass happened on the last Friday, and then on the last day of the month I would go out to breakfast and, through blurred vision induced by copious amounts of iced tea, I would sit for hours furiously adding up all of the scraps of paper from the month's mail and online orders and expenses into a total for each item. Then I would go home and add each one to the spreadsheet. It was a triumph to see that I was bringing in more than I was spending and that each month came out a little better than the previous one. I was still paying myself only $400/month and relying on each person's rent from the house to cover the mortgage. It didn't bode well when the furnace needed to be replaced or when I needed to do some construction or even fix little things. I spent many hours at the library, learning how to fix everything myself, from electrical work to wet rot to plumbing.

As I fixed each mechanical thing in our house, the social fabric began to unravel. The roommates complained about the sloppy, hand-drawn accounting spreadsheet that I drew up for dividing the bills each month. Some people assumed that the lack of legibility also indicated a lack of honesty and became distrustful of my numbers. Achieving my utopian vision would apparently require greater communication skills and more time than I felt capable of. Steve, Tom, Angela, Ann, and Glenn all moved out. Tom and Ann had a baby and moved closer to their families but Steve and Glenn both seemed to have pinned high hopes on the promised communal nature of what actually amounted to our collective volumes of dirt and clutter. Glenn told me pointedly, "If you ever put together enough money to fix this place up, call me." I did call him several times, but just to give him his mail.

Glenn had been in Chicago for months that summer dealing with family issues, leaving his bedroom unoccupied. Because of its location—a shortcut from both the front door and the upstairs to the kitchen—it became a high-traffic area in his absence. Disrespectful? Maybe. But once you watch a few other people trespass, it becomes the cultural norm. So by the time he came back and announced that he'd be moving in with his girlfriend, it wasn't really a surprise and I had become pretty attached to his room.

Instead of getting a new roommate, I decided that I'd move Microcosm out of the closet and up from the underground. The room was right next to the front door so when people came over I wouldn't have to walk them through our filthy house into a windowless dungeon. The room was also five times the size of the old office and had multiple windows and real natural sunlight. It felt like I needed to take risks like this, however small, to encourage and demonstrate the growth of the business growth. It's funny that during the first six years of Microcosm, when I was nocturnal, I couldn't seem to get anything done. When I adjusted to working with the daylight, things seemed to happen on their own.

Perhaps because of the relative success of the Zine Symposium or the work that I was doing with Microcosm, I was invited to be a guest lecturer for University of Oregon's *Zines and Democracy* class. A better reason might have been that I, a community-college dropout, had exactly the same name as a professor at Portland State University. The idea was hilarious to me to teach a college class and so I talked to the head of the department about what he had in mind. He suggested that the students would be interested in hearing about the compromises that I had made to achieve the things that I had, but I think what he really meant was that *he* was interested in their hearing about those things.

I packed up dozens of example zines and set out with a friend to ride our bikes the 130 miles to Eugene, Oregon. I loved the feeling of riding my bike these kinds of distances. I had done it years before from Athens to Columbus and the time and space provided the perfect opportunity to brainstorm design and zine ideas. I could write and rewrite sticker slogans in my head until they perfectly expressed what I wanted to say. Of course, we hadn't checked the weather and after a few hours the sky opened up and began pouring on us. We made it about 80 miles before my lack of stretching started causing my body to be less than cooperative. We pulled over to a truckstop and I put plastic bags inside my shoes. Eventually we rolled into Eugene soggy and cold—but in high spirits.

My first time teaching didn't go as well as it did in my dreams. The students stared at their fingernails and pencils and didn't want to answer even the simplest questions. I felt embarrassed when I realized that I shouldn't have expected the students to be as excited about the subject matter as I was and I should have prepared quite a bit more. I was a poor lecturer and didn't know how to be engaging. I had trouble maintaining eye contact. I went home disillusioned.

Back at home, Microcosm was thriving. I was selling so much that it would take four hours to add up the sales and expenses at the end of the month, so I asked Heather to help me. But even then, working full time on Microcosm, I still didn't like the feeling of being tied down. The zine people that I met were always quitting their jobs, dropping everything, and going on adventures. At the Zine Symposium I met some people who had bootlegged month-long Greyhound passes. You simply scanned a real one, changed it to contain your own name in **14-point Times New Roman**, made up a fake account number, printed it, and laminated the pass. I made one and began using it to go back and forth to Eugene, Seattle, and anywhere else that I wanted to go.

On one trip to Eugene I showed my fake Greyhound pass to the driver and was directed to stand in a group for an inspector to write down numbers on the passes. I did what I was told but got nervous after a moment. What if got caught? Could I be arrested? I got cold feet and wandered next door to the Amtrak station, where I charged the ticket to my credit card and discovered a love affair with train travel. I never rode Greyhound again. Amtrak's higher quality of service, spaciousness, and electrical outlets made me feel like I was upgrading. And I could do work on my laptop throughout the entire trip, having some of my most productive time.

Home office with shelves
that I had built out of
old televisions, 2002.

UNION DUES

In 2002 I went to the weddings of both my cousin Dave and my sister. After having been away for several years, I started to make sense of my family dynamic. My sister felt somewhere between a ghost and a skeleton. When I tried to talk about the things that we had experienced as children, she went cold. Her personality would demonstrably change near my mom. She appeared nervous in the house we grew up in. Hugging her was like hugging a robot. She had spent her life doing everything that she was told to, from playing basketball in order to put it on her transcripts to placing third in her class and getting a free ride to Case Western Reserve University. She became a chemical engineer who created temperature-control devices for chemical and biological weapons. She met her future husband on the job.

Her husband, Tim, wasn't prepared to deal with our family. They picked on him relentlessly and when it visibly hurt his feelings they made jokes about it. When he had a baby with my sister and carried the diaper bag, my family called him "Diaper Boy" and would laugh, as if this was not normal or responsible behavior. I felt bad for him and made futile efforts to ask people to stop. Tim didn't come around much after that.

Heather came with me to both weddings and my cousin joked during his ceremony that Heather and I would be the next to get married. Heather didn't really get along with my family or my friends. She would insult me in front of them while also arguing with my friends. But she was also supportive of me in ways that my friends were not. She believed strongly in me and my visions.

After the wedding we went back to what had been my childhood bedroom. As I closed the door, Heather said, "Your mom abused you." She said it so casually, as if there were nothing to feel uncomfortable about in those words. I just looked at her.

"Do you think so?" I eventually asked.

"It's obvious," she retorted, without needing time to think about her answer. I was silent for the rest of the night. No one had ever suggested such a thing to me previously. Maybe it was just the discomfort of saying it out loud. Heather wasn't loving or sympathetic as she said it. She behaved like the robots in the rest of my life in those moments. Maybe that's how she thought I needed to hear it to understand it.

Maybe she was right. I needed time for this revelation to sink in.

The day after the wedding ceremony we all gathered in one of Cleveland's Metroparks and I really had to poop. Of course all of the bathrooms were locked so I wandered slightly into the brush until I couldn't see the path.

I found some leaves nearby and wiped, thankful that the whole affair wasn't messier.

Instead of just going home, Heather and I got a job driving a van from Cleveland back to Minneapolis. I had met someone who tipped me off about a website where you could look up the availability of such driving jobs instead of riding the bus or train. We figured that we'd have a little adventure and see large parts of the country on the way. We got to Minneapolis before we'd heard back from Sam, the friend we were intending to stay with. Eventually we heard back from his roommate—Sam was in Europe for the month. Slightly forlorn, I called my pen pal Matte Resist whom I knew from his *Resist* zines. I sheepishly asked if we could stay with him and told him that we were already in town. He didn't seem surprised and said that it was fine. He even had an extra bedroom and spare bikes.

We didn't really have anything to do in Minneapolis, so I brought Microcosm stuff to sell to each of the local places and catalogs to leave at all of the coffee shops. When I saw The Hard Times Cafe, a worker-owned and -operated 24-hour hangout that truly catered to a wide variety of people, it felt like a place that Portland should have. A popular zine later put together an oral history of The Hard Times Cafe, which demonstrated that the hurdles and history were even more impressive than I had expected.

In a dusty used-bookstore basement, I flipped through book after book about the investigation of the assassination of Martin Luther King. I don't know what attracted me to this completely new subject, but I did become suddenly obsessed. I proclaimed to Heather, "One day I'm going to write my own book about this stuff!"

Half-paying attention, she seemed to respond without thinking. "You could just write a zine about it."

Yes, that was it. I will do that!

The more we biked around, the more my butt itched and the more I scratched it on the bike seat, the more the irritation started to inch down my legs and up my back. Before long a rash had spread all over my body and I realized what it was: poison oak.

So here I was, staying at a pen pal's house, covered in poison oak, and in a city where I was completely directionless and ostensibly had no reason to be there. I did what all weirdos would: I went to the grocery co-op and asked the person working in natural health to help. She suggested an oatmeal ointment and frequent showers. I went back to Matte's house and explained to him and his then-wife what had happened to me. Again, they seemed unfazed. They had two kids and had likely seen worse. After a week of treatment, it cleared up and Heather and I found a minivan to deliver to Phoenix where we had a friend we were excited to stay with.

While Minneapolis was a punk mecca, Phoenix felt like a sprawled out monoculture. There wasn't nearly as much to do. Nonetheless, our friends were fun and we went to some parties and talked endlessly about zines. After a week at their house we were subjected to a talk about how we were eating too much food. It was time to leave. I had already exhausted everywhere that I could promote Microcosm within biking distance, so we headed back to Portland.

I reverted back to my former self and Peter Pan lifestyle. I became an actor in a haunted house and joined an adult hide and seek league that played inside the mall. Having been a fan of Michael Moore's previous works, Heather and I went to see *Bowling for Columbine,* about how the relentless bullying of two students resulted in the school shooting in Colorado. The film connected a little too closely to my experiences and my emotions, and I couldn't speak for two days afterward. I was coming to terms with how intensely I felt everything—joy, frustration, hurt feelings, being misunderstood. I was trying to get these things under control but still didn't know how.

Even though Eleanor had moved to New York City, I still felt close to her. I called her to talk about how I fought all of the time with Heather. I wanted to salvage the pieces that I could of my life into something happy and sustainable. I had no healthy models for what that looked like, but in contrast to my own life, Eleanor's seemed downright peachy. She taught me a powerful expression: "When you do [this], it makes me feel [this way]."

The next day when Heather used the same familiar canned catchphrases to make fun of a record that she knew I really enjoyed, I tried it out.

"When you make fun of things that you know that I value, it makes me feel bad."

The results were staggering.

"I'm so sorry. I had no idea that it hurt your feelings. You don't seem to have feelings."

I was impressed with the results and continued to employ my new way of expressing myself with similar successes. It made her seem less callous when I understood that she had no idea that those actions hurt. One simple strategy created harmony in our relationship.

In the fall of 2002, we took a trip to San Francisco and joked about getting married. By the time we came home, the joke seemed to be serious.

Zine Symposium organizers potluck flyer by Shawn Granton, 2002

Zine Symposium Prom 2002

CROSSING THE TEAS

In 2002, I filed the paperwork for Microcosm to become a legal entity. It had been my more-than-full-time job for over two years, and I firmly believed in its future.

I hired Nate Beaty, the webmaster from the Portland Zine Symposium, to create a much more involved website and database that could manage sales, accounting, and inventory. I brought in Evan, a customer who seemed willing to work long hours for low pay like I did, and he became the first real daily employee of Microcosm. There was enough room in the office for both of us to sit down and he packed the orders all day, every day and left pieces of mail on my desk whenever someone sent a letter that needed some words of encouragement or a response beyond putting some zines and books into an envelope. I savored these moments to express myself and channel what I had learned so far to the people who were asking. Many people wrote in asking for advice or guidance or just to vent about terrible things that were happening to them. It felt good, like I could be useful for the first time in my life and help people with problems that I had gone through, whether that was how to copy their zine or how to hang in there when their parents were picking on them.

Finding myself with more free time, I stumbled upon another opportunity to teach. This time it was with gifted and talented high-school kids who were acting out and causing problems for their regular teachers. They were all put in the same discussion-based art class. We met in a beautiful building in Forest Park, which was then the largest urban park in the U.S. It had big canopy windows that overlooked walls of greenery while the kids would challenge my cultural awareness:

"Do you even know who Banksy is?"

"Oh, you like Banksy," I'd reply. "Here's some underground stuff that is even cooler. Check out these graffiti zines."

Perhaps not surprisingly, it was easy to relate to kids who behaved as I had in school, whether by acting out or pretending to be aloof or disinterested while testing me. I was starting to fall in love with the whole thing when the funding for the program was abruptly cut.

After that I spent my free time learning how to write articles and essays on the newly re-launched Microcosm website. I finished all of my regular work and then my reward at the end of each day would be writing an essay about whatever I had been thinking about that day. It was my outlet to express how I was feeling old and disconnected at 25, concerns about the Iraq war, fixing up the house, how punk fashion was its own kind of conformity, the subtly racist attitudes of people around me, the communication implicit in smiling at a stranger, my misgivings about accepting credit cards as payment, and the need for greater activism. It was an important step in organizing my thoughts and expressing my ideas while bringing my personality to the forefront. I had always felt the need to make my work public, but I also needed to develop a lot of writing practice since I honestly wasn't very good at expressing my theses yet.

Meanwhile, because of Eleanor's departure, I found myself in the pilot seat for the Zine Symposium in 2002. While the process was incredibly stressful and hard on my schedule, I felt ready for it. The event drew four times as many people as it had the year before. We were in a larger room, raised about $1,500 beyond our expenses, and created enough stability and protocols for the event to continue indefinitely into the future, beyond the involvement of any individual person. The event itself is much more of a blur, other than meeting many, many zinesters I had corresponded with and respected. The event attracted people from all over the world to come and engage in a creative exchange of their work as equals. I had never seen anything like it before.

We had dozens of guests staying in our house. A then-unknown Ben Snakepit, who went on to create the blueprint for writing a diary comic about every day of your life, slept face-first in the dirt in the backyard. I met a young Cristy Road, the prolific punk illustrator, as she danced barefoot and made inside jokes with her friends. I received a round of applause when I told one of my workshop classes that I had filed paperwork with the state for Microcosm. After the event I found myself with hundreds of zines to read and no capacity to do so. I started asking more and more friends to help me review submissions in order to stay on top of things and respond to authors within a few months.

The stars were aligning, and I was receiving far more submissions than I had in the previous six years. Perhaps my interests were in tune with the time and place. Perhaps I was finally projecting the right kind of image and people were responding to that. Perhaps Microcosm was influencing the kind of work being produced. Perhaps it was a result of finally having published submission guidelines. Perhaps it was a combination of these factors, but the zines had beautiful screenprinted covers, spoke in tones and language that I could relate to, and contained useful, practical information that I desperately needed for my own life. They spoke with the kind of urgency and meaningful yet didactic language that I did. These zines spoke to my life and experiences as I'd always dreamed with titles like *Trouble in Mind, Nosedive, Crude Noise, America?, Grundig, Cometbus, Arts & Crafts Revolution, As Soon As You're Born You're Made to Feel Small, Avow, Binocular Rebellious, Ten Foot Rule, 3 AM, Journalsong, Burn Collector, Emergency,* and *Chainbreaker.* Microcosm could sell hundreds and hundreds of copies of each. And most of the time we could actually sell even more copies of a zine than the creator could manage to print and send to us.

From all of her time spent alone in our room writing, Heather's zine was also creating a force to be reckoned with. She had honed her writing and art and found her audience. Unlike me, she had harnessed her ability to reflect how she felt about things into a literary device and channeled it onto the page with suitable graphics to match. Seeing how much progress she had made in just a few years motivated me further to pursue the work that I was doing with Microcosm.

One day over breakfast at the local café, Beaterville, we took notice of the Sweetheart Chainring on the bike hanging in the front window. Heather had always joked that I taught her how to be a bicyclist while she taught me how to be a pedestrian. The iconic chainring with its incorporated hearts seemed appropriate to symbolize so many things in our lives. We asked our friend Aaron Renier to draw a unique version for us with only one heart and we both got it tattooed that summer. Four months later we realized it also perfectly encapsulated Microcosm and I began using the same image as our logo.

In the months thereafter Heather and I started to fight again. She didn't understand or appreciate my jokes and I felt picked on all the time. I had an irrational fear of riding the city bus and preferred riding my bike. She took this as my judgment about her choice when she rode the bus, even though I don't believe that I ever disparaged her for it. I would simply explain the mathematics that showed that riding a bike is faster and more economical. A major downside of Asperger's is that I can't tell when something is hurting someone's feelings until it's dreadfully too late, let alone when someone I care deeply about desperately needs my support.

I also hadn't learned when to accept the way that other people do things, even if they are "wrong" to me. For example, to me it's "wrong" to sit in a chair while playing guitar. It's "wrong" to wait for the hot water to reach the tap, because it's a waste of resources. But Heather let the water run up from the water heater to the upstairs bathroom every night and would often leave the room with the water running. So I would turn it off or at least mention it. I didn't yet understand that there are plenty of things not worth fighting about.

Heather described my socializing as "distant and clinical." I tried to frame it a different way: I believe that people are predictable, with some margin of error. I could often make an educated guess about how someone would behave in a situation. I was mostly correct, but if I explained how I had accurately predicted what their behavior would be, it would always upset them—especially if they felt like they had been acting irresponsibly or out of character. I guess nobody likes to feel like a math problem.

I felt chronically misunderstood by Heather and eventually I told her that I did not want to get married. Somehow a positive moment between us had spiraled into serious wedding plans. No one had proposed or accepted, but the joke had become serious. But within a few months we were no longer getting along and I didn't feel good about our relationship. When I told her, anger flashed in her eyes. "My family is planning for this," she rebutted. "You can't back out now." I felt uncomfortable. Had I made a major faux pas? Trying to talk about my feelings was even less comfortable than just going along with getting married. I didn't feel good about it, but it felt like another case where I should fall in line. Perhaps this was as good as it got.

I made peace with the wedding but continued to be deeply unhappy about our relationship. The rest of my life was quite joyous—it was starting to become the life that I craved for myself. As the friends that I'd made in Portland began to scatter across the country and grow apart, I took solace in my work at Microcosm. I was jealous of the adventures in some of the zines. I felt like a square in my own community. Microcosm forced me to be increasingly stationary and stable. But it also allowed me to dive deep into the feelings and joys of the work.

Heather and I were married that fall at a Native American community center located a stone's throw from where we lived. I invited all of the friends that I had grown up with but those who had met Heather refused to come, putting their stamp of disapproval on our relationship. All of three bands that we had booked to play at our wedding canceled too. Matty Luv, a raucous and antagonizing punk rocker had suffered a heroin overdose after promising to be the 1,000th person to jump off of the Golden Gate Bridge, had his funeral the same day as our wedding, and two of the bands felt the need to attend the funeral instead. The drummer of the remaining band broke both wrists so they also canceled. Undeterred and stubborn, I invited more bands and more people. Most of my friends who made the trip were the ones that I hadn't seen in years.

On the night before our wedding, Heather and I managed to get into a fight. We were at the bar together and when we left she was so caught up in a conversation with a friend that she didn't notice I couldn't physically keep up with them. I felt literally left behind at a crucial time. When I saw her back at our house and mentioned it, she told me that it was my fault for not being able to keep up. I was embarrassed that the friends that came saw these parts of my life. I spent most of the time hiding in my office and working.

We got married. Matt DeWine was my best man and showed up adorned in dreadlocks and a T-shirt depicting a tuxedo. He had trouble operating the ceremonial fountain pen to sign the marriage license. During the ceremony I couldn't hear the judge reading me my lines through many years of punk rock hearing damage and asked him to repeat himself. The audience had a good chuckle because it appeared that the marriage agreements were shocking news to me. Heather and I retreated via bike trailer to a motel a few blocks away after inventorying the large volume of kitchen appliances that had been gifted to us.

The next day I felt unchanged and equally unhappy about the situation but resolved to make it work as well as it could.

One friend had come all the way from his military post in rural Japan to attend the wedding, but it quickly became clear we had grown apart. He insisted that the U.S. was involved in the Iraq war in order to free the women from the oppressive lifestyles of the Middle East. That seemed completely absurd to me in a war that seemed so obviously about controlling resources in a critical part of the world. I reluctantly got into an argument about it. He had always been reasonable before and could manage a debate. Instead, we lost touch and have never talked since. I felt like a real asshole. I have since tried to track him down without any luck and now wonder how much of my emotions were a product of everything else that was going on that week.

Wedding photos by Erik Diffendaffer, 2002

GROWING YOUR SMALL WORLD

Urban Hermitt's *The Flow Chronicles* and Heather's how-to book about zines were both published as paperbacks in 2002. I had no idea how to subcontract a printer so I called the other publishers I respected and asked them what to do. One suggested calling the local newspaper and asking about the heaviest paper that they have available. In hindsight, that's really bad advice. Another sent me to Hignell, a printer in Manitoba. I had no idea whether it was actually economical, because I had nothing to base pricing on and just assumed that all printers would cost more or less the same. This assumption proved to be untrue, and I paid about double what I should have. The cost was about $6,000, which was more than I earned in a year, I still had no idea what a reasonable first print run should cost.

Most titles that Microcosm had previously sold were zines printed in editions of 50-500 and we could sell through those sooner or later. Granted, both our costs and the retail prices were much cheaper than with these two books. I became very nervous as these were the first real risks that Microcosm was facing. I went with 2,000 and 3,000 copies of each, respectively. That felt hugely optimistic but I was making strides for the future. If this was going to work in the long term, I needed to have titles that sold for more than double what we paid for them and that would continue to sell over a long period of time. The biggest limitation to Microcosm remained that we could typically sell more copies of a title than we could get our hands on. Things were constantly between printings or going out of print. We'd put all of this work into reading, reviewing, listing, scanning, and promoting a title only to sometimes run out of copies within a day or two, then have to repeat the whole cycle again. The idea of such riskier, larger print runs was that we'd have these books for at least a few years and could reprint them as needed rather than having to have an extended negotiation with the author and a long wait each time that we needed more copies.

We didn't yet know about the long advance notice of publishing schedules or publication dates or how booktrade distribution worked. All of our previous effort had gone into building distribution channels that were parallel to the mainstream. We could publish a book as soon as we received copies from the printer with no advance notice. All we had to do was post it on our website. Instead of having to give 25% of each invoice to our distributor, we could lower the retail prices on the books by 25%.

So, instead of trying to convince an established distributor to take on our books and sell them through their institutional conventions, we put our nose to the grindstone to build a social movement around the ideas in the world that we were promoting. We built a set of values into a catalog and then built from that the reputation that our work was hard, fast, and reliable. Having read about Aaron Cometbus doing the same thing years before, I went door to door to stores and convinced many places to start carrying our titles even when they had nothing else like them in their displays. Often times ours were the only books in the store, which meant that they sold extremely well. Whereas most bookstores sell only one copy of each title in an average year, these stores could sell ten or twenty copies—and apologized that this was so few, assuming that we had bigger customers elsewhere.

I had spent the previous six months announcing that we needed to raise $6,000 beyond our usual expenses in order to publish these books. Our fans responded with larger and more frequent orders and we created an image of a thermometer filling up as we reached our goal. We raised the extra money we needed to print both books solely from these extra mail orders.

While we certainly missed the mark in the proofreading department on both titles, they were both well received by our fans, who seemed to order them as much because we had selected them for publication as because of interest in the subject matter. *The Flow Chronicles,* ironically, was a bit of a departure from what we had done previously. While most of our successes were built on titles that taught actual DIY skills, it was a coming-of-age queer memoir about trying to follow the path of liberal lifestyle choices such as working at a juice bar, going to the rainbow gathering, shopping at co-ops, and becoming a hip-hop performer but finding disrespectful and homophobic men barring each respective path to joy.

To celebrate the release of the book, we did what good punk rockers do: We agreed to go on tour together and sell the book by hand. I got on the phone and began calling all of the stores that ordered from us in Oregon, Washington, California, Arizona, New Mexico, Utah, and Colorado. I booked the tour in under two weeks this time, mostly because I wasn't depressed and there was a huge immediacy. Also, it was much easier to book because we weren't competing with dozens of other rock-and-roll tours this time. Our zine tour was notably different from most other events coming through these places. Public libraries liked to host us because, as they said, we carried an air of legitimacy and appealed to a younger audience than most book events.

I also put together a new zine to read from and sell on the tour. It was the first issue of *The CIA Makes Science Fiction Unexciting* about the incompatible evidence in the assassination of Martin Luther King and the involvement of the CIA and military. I spent that same month researching and writing it while I booked the tour.

Not one to miss out on the action, Heather also put together an issue of her zine and Microcosm published it. This tour now had a printing bill of nearly $10,000. The stakes were high but the spirits were too. When Hermitt showed up at our house with his date Harmony and saw his own book for the first time, the responses were ecstatic.

"Holy shit! It looks like a real book!"

Hermitt and I went back and forth about a financial agreement that could account for minimal or greater success. We were both starting to realize how big things could get. I reluctantly agreed to a flat $1/book sold on the tour, not sure if I could afford it with the cover price set at a measly $8. We loaded the four of us along with cartoonist and local historian Shawn Granton into Hermitt's small Toyota pickup and filled any remaining space inside the cap with boxes of books.

Most of the events were well-attended and people were super enthusiastic about what we were doing. A year before, we had caught wind that my pen pals in New Orleans had done something similar and called it "Y'Herd Me?" During the heyday of zines in the mid-'90s, some zinesters from LA had done a much more expansive tour but just showed up to a city and sat behind a tables of zines. No presentations or even a "hello." Reading about this inspired me to be more outgoing.

Among the five of us, our presentations could run three or four hours, not including the local talent who often joined us. In hindsight, it's embarrassing. One time my presentation ran 45 minutes and Hermitt re-emerged onto the stage to read another chapter, worrying that people might think I was the headliner. To be fair, I was a terrible performer. I couldn't focus and needed to reference my notes frequently. Sometimes I would turn all the way around and face away from the audience. Thank goodness for punk rock oddities because in a reasonable universe everyone would have walked out to get vegan ice cream instead.

We sold a lot of books. We crashed into a brick wall while driving in reverse. We made a lot of new friends. It was a complete success! So what did we do? We argued about money. But everyone made up and remained friends afterwards. Harmony pointed out the most important detail that everyone else failed to see: The tour had been very good for everyone's prominence. It had put each of us as a tiny dot on a tiny map.

While we received lots of positive press for the book and it showed an evolution in what Microcosm was doing, *The Flow Chronicles* wasn't the commercial success that I had hoped it would be. Fourteen years later, we still have a handful of copies collecting dust. The book is good, but that's not the point. I picked it because of the merit of the author, not because I understood how sales worked. And part of me still didn't want to succeed. I honestly thought it was more important for the book to have merit than for it to be commercial or even necessarily well received.

Heather's book, on the other hand, had sold out of its first printing within six months and we hustled it into an updated reprint of 4,000 more copies and fancier production values, which we clumsily called "the second edition." Portland has a heavy snow roughly every six years and of course it happened during the week that the truck was trying to deliver them to our house. There is likely a law of physics that the amount of time that a shipment is delayed is inversely proportional to how many pre-orders you have for it.

The tour and the success of the few titles that I had brought to life were being noticed. Zach Furness came all the way from Pittsburgh to interview me for both his academic book about bicycling activist history, *One Less Car,* and for the nationally distributed magazine *Punk Planet.* A few months later a woman got in touch and asked if I'd be willing to be interviewed for *Maximum Rocknroll.* Despite how much I had loved it as a teenager, it had never entered my wildest dreams that I might one day be featured in its pages beyond my cranky letters to correct factual errors they had made. Her questions demonstrated that she was really paying attention to the fine print and semantics of what I was doing. It was incredibly flattering to see not only that she was familiar with the project but had also given so much thought to what I did.

That winter I worked on my first feature film, *Do You Copy?,* a collaborative narrative about some employees at a photocopy shop who had imagined adventures in a Hello-Kitty-shaped starship. There was a crew of about 25 people who co-wrote, co-directed, and shared acting and camera duties on the whole thing. It was a truly awesome experience not only because we wrote, shot, and edited the whole thing in three weeks but also because it again made me feel like I was part of a new community of creative people who worked collaboratively rather than competitively.

Partly as a result of teaching about zines in the classroom, partly as a result of seeing it as a complement to Heather's book, partly because similar films were too short and lacked depth, and partly because I couldn't find anyone else to do it, I decided that I would next put together a feature documentary about the contemporary zine scene and culture. I began shooting four to six interviews per week on equipment I borrowed from people who worked

Copy & Destroy Tour, 2002

on *Do You Copy?* and getting excited about the stories and revelations that it could hold.

In 2003, Evan suggested that we bring in Heather to become a staff person at Microcosm and it seemed like a good idea. She was still working at the nickel arcade but was already occasionally wandering into the office and offering ideas or suggestions. The only reason that I hadn't suggested it sooner or myself was that when we worked closely on something we didn't see eye to eye on methods and protocols. We could both get excited about a common goal, such as producing a how-to book about zines and distributing it to a mass audience. But she wanted to photocopy it and hand staple each one. To me the inevitable result of that would be orders for yet another zine that we couldn't keep in stock as fast as it sold. Most of our aesthetic disagreements were related to the fact that I always thought bigger in terms of scope, but it seemed that we always found a way to disagree about my way of doing things no matter what. She didn't like my organizational systems because she said they made no sense. She made fun of me endlessly when I began organizing my records by geography but I thought it helped someone pick better a selection based on their mood.

As John Elder Robison, author of *Be Different: Adventures of a Free-Range Aspergian,* puts it: "We will always be perplexed when we gaze at people who aren't on the spectrum and they will always struggle to understand our unconventional way of thinking." But I was not yet diagnosed so we did not know that this was the problem; we just knew that there *was* a problem.

Soon after I hired Heather to work with Evan, I finished shooting my documentary, now titled *$100 & A T-Shirt* after a quote from zinester Moe Bowstern in which she describes the difference between a zine and a magazine: when you write for a magazine, you get $100 and a T-shirt. When you write for a zine, you don't get a token payment, but you get satisfaction and belonging in a community.

I connected with two friends who had rented out a concrete basement to become a video-editing studio. They let me use it for $10 an hour, including all of their equipment. I was paying for it out of pocket so it felt like a fortune, but in hindsight it was a screaming deal. The proximity of working closely with Evan and Heather stressed me out, so I preferred to work alone and learn a new skill. So Heather and Evan were left to work together alone in the office while I spent five days a week in the studio across town and would often sleep there after twelve or fourteen-hour days of editing. Over the next four months I became obsessed, and, while I didn't enjoy the process of making the documentary per se, I loved learning how to do it and what was involved. The experience opened me up to the tremendous possibilities that were possible for storytelling with documentary film.

Knowing that I would have a meltdown if they questioned my systems, in my absence Heather and Evan slowly untangled all of the systems that I had created, making them make sense to other people who didn't want to work 100 hours each week. When I came home, I would start to notice more and more changes that they had made around the office. We had monthly meetings where we talked about administrative changes, new ideas, or creating policies. As their requests for more and more changes mounted, I became resistant. What was wrong with writing titles that needed to be reordered on a bulletin board each day? Why did they insist that everything needed to be alphabetized? That was a tremendous loss of space. Why can't we just store everything where it best fits and memorize each location? They began to discuss proposed changes with each other in advance and delivered them as a unified front.

Their changes upset me at first because I *needed* to have everything a certain way. But gradually I understood that if Microcosm was going to grow beyond myself, I had to let this happen and understood that most of the time the reasons for these changes were important. People often tell Aspies that they should let go and adjust their habits. Wouldn't it be easier and faster not to have certain hang-ups? Unfortunately, it doesn't work that way.

Each day would begin with Evan's printing off a sheet of the orders. I would interrupt what I was doing to make sure that the orders fit into columns on the sheet with the greatest efficiency possible so no order was split between two columns and all of the orders fit on as few sheets as possible. This process could take over an hour. As each order was filled, the packing slip would be cut off of the sheet with a pair of scissors, leaving a constant pile of scrap paper on the packing table. I would have to periodically interrupt whatever I was doing to remove the tiniest scraps of paper from the table and put them into the recycling basket.

"You're such a freak!" Evan shouted at me. "You're going to have a heart attack before you're 40!"

It's not that I couldn't stop myself from doing it. It's that not doing these things upset me so much that I couldn't focus on anything else. If you had asked me, I would have told you that the purpose was to save one sheet of paper per day, but really the point was the grounding that participating in this routine provided me. Several times when Evan questioned this habit or even physically tried to stop me, I would have a meltdown.

In certain ways, I liked to have two more people around to bat around ideas with. Of course, not every groupthink idea was brilliant. When we were planning to publish two cookbooks, Evan insisted that they should be made into one book with each half facing a different cover, like a split record. Each side goes to the halfway point before you reach the second half, which, if you're reading sequentially, is "upside down." So you turn it around, turn it over, and read the other half. While, on paper, this seemed very clever and punk rock, the authors weren't thrilled to be partnered together as they were both doing very different things and had mismatched aesthetics. Most people who picked up the book assumed that it was a production error. It stymied distributors, reviewers, and the middle-aged vegetarian home-cooking community alike.

Perhaps the most telling thing about the situation is that I thought the idea was charming and went along with it, not realizing or caring how people on all sides of it would feel. And it wasn't helping that I was more and more absentee from the office and didn't have email or a phone in the studio.

FIDELITY

As soon as I read about vasectomies in a zine as a teenager, I knew that I was going to get one. Heather was on the same page already. We both felt there was no need for biological kids, if there were going to be kids at all. So I got snipped that winter of 2003.

Kids were not something that I had time or money for. But on the other hand, I had something inside of me that felt the need to prove that I could be a better parent than my parents had been. A friend's girlfriend, Vanessa, told me that she had an interest in fostering a child and that she wanted me to help take care of the kid. She referred to me as "patient," but I'm not sure why she chose me; perhaps it was my flexible schedule and seeming availability of time. Vanessa worked for a medium-sized nonprofit that provided healthcare for street kids, so she looked like a good prospect for being a foster parent. After months of paperwork, home investigations, and preparation, eight-year-old Casey was released into Vanessa's guardianship. I picked her up from school and she immediately began calling me "Dad." The caseworker had warned us that Casey had serious attachment issues. Her biological mom had a drug problem and was heartbroken to have Casey taken away.

To say that I had never felt this way about someone before was an understatement. When Casey peed in her pants at school and I was called in to the office, I was proud when the counselor assumed that I was her biological father. When Casey was picked on at school, I yelled at the little shitheads and meant it. I knew what being treated that way feels like. And I knew what it meant to Casey for me to stand up on her behalf. Of course, she was also a little manipulator and would often attempt to tell me bald-faced lies.

"My mom lets me stand on the kitchen counter."

"I'm allowed to eat ice cream for dinner."

"I'm allowed to ride on the back of the bike... as long as you don't go too fast."

"I don't have to do my homework if I go to the park."

After she fooled me a few times, I figured out that if I stared at her silently for five seconds, she couldn't hold up a lie to me. On her ninth birthday, when I showed up late because I had run into a fascinating garage sale on the bike ride over, she stopped playing with her friends to excitedly yell "Daddy!" and rush over to give me a big hug. Words can't describe how good that felt.

But it was not to last. After leaving her alone one night, Vanessa came home to Casey's beating her elderly dog with a jump rope. It was too much to bear. A kid can't be expected to manage her feelings after all of the untold experiences that Casey had undoubtedly gone through. Vanessa returned her to the state's custody and her biological mother got clean enough to get her back. It was explained to me that because of her attachment issues, it was better to give her distance. But realizing that she is now an adult, I would like to reconnect with her if she can be found.

At work, we continued to publish around four books per year. Every book that we published paid for the next one. My spreadsheets were very good at predicting our financial health and letting me know who was owed what when. We had relatively low expenses and could publish things as our finances allowed it but still generally, as soon as we received a completed manuscript in the mail, we'd package it up and send it to the printer right away, often without even proofreading. We would generally even let the author design their own book cover. Most of our authors had previously published their own zines and could navigate the editorial and design process without our help. We were focusing more on creating a unique experience for authors and readers than we were on the traditional work of a publisher.

We trusted our authors to deliver a quality work so often that we wouldn't even read it until after it was at the printer. In hindsight it's hard for me to understand how this seemed reasonable. Most publishers would have someone in acquisitions review the work and massage it into what they wanted it to be. They would hire a marketing team to do an industry analysis of what competitive titles are available, figure out how to distinguish the book from them, and package the book in line with other

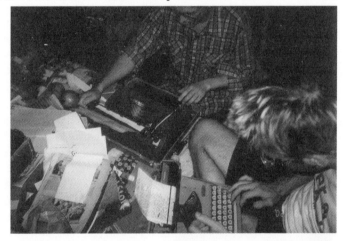

Marc Moscato (Microcosm's future publicist) and I work on writing zines of our own on typewriters, 2003

Right: A portrayal of myself, Heather, and Evan by Clutch, 2004

books on the same shelf while still standing out. Then they'd hire a designer to create a cover that evokes the feelings they want to convey and captures the spirit of the book. They'd hire an editor to make sure that the book delivered on those promises, read coherently, and didn't leave the reader feeling shortchanged or confounded by typos. If, after all of this, things weren't penciling out, they'd scrap the book before it was published in order to cut their losses. But somehow our insane system was not only cost-saving but also was remarkably reliable and I was really excited about where we were headed.

I realized that Kyle Bravo's *How2* zines were incredibly popular and we couldn't keep them in stock so we suggested that he could put them together and we could make a book out of it. He was into the idea and put together nearly 300 pages of DIY projects, ideas, and inspiration about all manner of topics. The book sold out of its first printing in under four months, but we ran into an unexpected problem: The author had used other people's work without permission. He explained that he didn't think the people whose work that he had used were active in the scene anymore and he didn't know how to reach them. Of course, when the book exploded and appeared everywhere, those people were immediately in touch with him, wondering why he had reprinted their work. Worse, people tended to blame Microcosm for this mistake and we heard about it for ten years afterwards. We gave everyone free books and big discounts if they wanted to buy more copies, but trust is a hard thing to recover.

At the same time, I was finding credibility in a very different world. On the two-year anniversary of 9/11 I was invited to be a presenter at the San Jose Art Museum for the opening of an exhibit about zines. I screened a very early excerpt of my zine documentary and convinced the curators to bring Heather as well to answer questions after the film. Unfortunately, I was credited in the program as being the author of Heather's book. I called and tried to get the museum to correct it but Heather was pissed anyway. I mentioned that she was frequently credited as the founder and owner of Microcosm, to which she retorted "there is a huge difference between what teenage girls think and what a major art museum is saying!" It was an interesting debate to me. In my mind, the viewpoint of teenage girls, who largely made up Microcosm's audience and were the future of our world, seemed vastly more important to me than one aging institution who didn't speak to people who were familiar with Microcosm. Heather was seething and seemed to think that I was taking opposing side with the museum against her.

On the day of the event, zines were hung on the walls in plastic protectors through which no one could touch them or do much but gaze at the covers. As the presentations began, Heather yelled out to interrupt every time anyone made a factual inaccuracy. From the moment that the presentation began and the curator claimed that they had the largest collection of zines on the West Coast, Heather screamed out "No you don't!" and I had the awkward position of explaining that the Zine Archive and Publishing Project in Seattle had over 10,000 zines. When anything was claimed to be the "first" or "biggest" or "best" or any other superlative, Heather's voice broke out, telling the moderator that she was wrong. After the panel presentation was over, Heather hid under the table and refused to talk to the museum curators about what had upset her so much.

We went home and I went back to my rigorous editing schedule. When you edit a documentary, you watch each interview dozens of times, sometimes in slow motion. You try to make clean cuts between statements and words that sound smooth in transition. After cutting about 60 or 70 hours of interviews, I noticed that people made facial expressions when they were about to speak and even had different facial expressions that added further depth to what they were saying or sometimes even betrayed how they felt about things. I had always been so literal, just listening to the sequence of words people said and seeing no depth or communication beyond that. It was such a huge revelation that I locked the doors, walked to the payphone, and called Heather.

"I just discovered that people express emotions when they talk and you can tell when someone is about to talk by looking at their face!" I shouted into the phone. She seemed annoyed.

"Ummmm, of course they do."

"...I just wanted to tell you that I discovered this..."

"Okay, I'll talk to you later." We both hung up.

Dave Roche came over to our house as he did every week to drop off copies of his zine, *On Subbing*. He told us about some of the students in his class who have Asperger's Syndrome. I had never heard of it before and it fascinated me. The idea that there was a medical explanation for one obsession that you celebrated along with other symptoms like emotional distance, inflexibility, and missing social cues all rang a little too close to home for me. I began joking to Dave that I might have Asperger's. After he left, I brought it up to Heather who pointed out that the traits were all stereotypically male. She brushed it off.

We had begun going to marriage counseling during the previous summer and this seemed to tie into one of the things that we had talked about: Her not feeling like I understood what she was nonverbally communicating. Once she repeatedly stomped on my foot to try to convince me to pay the restaurant tab for someone that we were meeting with. Another time before we were headed somewhere together, she wordlessly went outside to try and pressure me to hurry up. I looked all over the house for her and when I couldn't find her I went back to what I had been doing earlier.

At one point the counselor asked me to pick a few feelings that I experienced in the course of our relationship. When I couldn't do this, she asked me how I felt right then. All of the words I produced were thoughts instead of feelings. I struggled to come up with one feeling. Perhaps it was the entire point of the exercise—that they had both predicted that it would go this way—but it was a massive illumination for me. I didn't know what a feeling was. I mean, I felt things very intensely but relating my feelings to other people or even putting them into words was nearly impossible for me. It was like the volume knob was too high to make sense of all that I was hearing.

I began to feel like Heather was asking too much of me. I mean, how could I possibly be expected to decode her strange language of raised eyebrows and positioning her mouth in a certain way? Why would that mean anything and why couldn't she just say it instead? At minimum, if we were going to make it work, I felt like she would have to meet me where I was capable or at least closer to the middle, but instead she continued to expect me to figure out what she meant and seemed to give less context and fewer clues as time went by. I understood verbal communication literally and I was pretty convinced that this was normal. We fought constantly about that and our marriage counselor tried hard not to take sides but to rather attempt to mend the fence.

Nonetheless, we were getting invited all over the U.S. to appear at book and zine fairs and we went on a second big zine tour in 2003 from San Francisco to Boston. All along the way we met more and more of the people who wrote the zines that we had in our catalog as well as plenty of people whose work we later went on to publish.

It was an epic year where I discovered what it felt like to have fans. Melissa Hostetler, an editor at *Friction Magazine* wrote that year: "Joe Biel is cool. Joe Biel is a good guy. I know, I've met him. He is the brains and the driving force behind Microcosm Publishing, a super-cool DIY project that produces CDs, T-shirts, buttons, and cool zines. You should support projects like these if only for the fact that it's people like Joe—someone who can make a living off his beloved scene and do it with style—that keep the rest of us firm in the thought that we are fighting the good fight."

Outside of our show in Detroit, a man about my age wandered up, almost bumping into me, and stared at the ground while he addressed me.

"I really appreciate the work that you do." he mumbled.

"Thanks man. It's really important to me too. What's your name?" I asked.

"I really like that one zine, *Skeleton Key*. I think you should do more like that."

"Yeah, I like that one too." I replied. "But we can't get more. I think the editor had a baby or something. In any event, she disappeared and stopped sending us more copies."

"Oh, that's cool." He said. "I really like your zine too, *I Hate This Part of Texas*."

"I really like that zine a lot too. It's one of my favorites. But I don't make it. It's made by John in New Orleans."

"I know but you should make the next issue. I like that *CIA* zine but it doesn't go far enough. There's a lot of stuff out there."

This whole phenomenon was entirely new to me. I loved the attention, but found the dynamic totally strange. If people were so excited about my work, why did our interactions never resemble a conversation?

At the Allied Media Conference, Joyce Brabner approached me, claiming that HBO was making a biopic about her husband Harvey Pekar and their family. She insisted that I should make her and Harvey special guests at the Portland Zine Symposium that year and that HBO would fly them out and put them up. I thought she was pulling my leg. Sure, they were influential people in the world of underground nonfiction comics, but why would HBO make a film about their family? They were like every other family that I knew—totally normal. I didn't believe it.

Cut + Paste Tour, 2003

SEEING THINGS THROUGH

At the third Zine Symposium we encountered some of our first drama. A writer with a long-standing place in the community, with several books, and who tours regularly was quietly accused by dozens of women of making unwanted sexual advances, up to and including groping and sleeping with them. I felt like the situation was cut and dried so I contacted his publishers and asked them not to release his next book at the Symposium. They fought me bitterly and dug in their heels. Gradually, the situation escalated and efforts were made to push the man into an accountability process, a way to resolve concerns raised by members of his community so they could feel like they trusted him again.

Trying to ensure the success of accountability, for many months I made weekly trips to his apartment, ate soup at his kitchen table with him, and tried to level with him about the gravity of the situation. But it became clear that he would only talk circles around and poke holes in the accusations and requests made of him. He wasn't ready to honestly look at what he could take fault for, acknowledge it, and move on. People would stop and accost him on the street, screaming while he calmly refuted their points. The accountability process had been an utter failure but I didn't understand why. I spent months going over and over what had happened and how to do it better next time.

One night there was a knock on the back door of our house. It was Tony, a guy who did martial-arts training with one of our roommates, and an apparent fan of Microcosm.

"Hey. Would you ever consider moving Microcosm out of the house? I work on this radical community center project called Liberty Hall and we really need some tenants to move into our offices. You can even borrow my van to move." He continued to make the case, explaining that my friend Michael Ismerio, the record-store owner, was the mastermind behind the new space.

"Ummm, I've never really thought about it. But we'll talk about it. That might be cool to get some separation between home and work."

"Okay, well we need to know...soon."

Evan, Heather, and I talked about it. I was trying not to be in charge and attempted to give them space to make the decision, explaining that I'd be in the editing studio and then on tour with the film. Heather loved the idea but Evan had moved right next door to our house so he could walk to work in his pajamas and pack the mail orders each night from 8 PM until 2 AM. The thought of living next door to us but having a commute to work annoyed him.

Nonetheless, Heather won out and we began sweeping out years and years of rat poop and historic garbage from our future office. We painted the walls orange and even replaced the hollow and thin office doors with some heavier used wooden ones. We packed load after load into Tony's van and drove each one the 30 or so blocks. Evan's roommate worked at a clothing store that was throwing away some industrial racks and they gave them to us for free. The new office was actually smaller than the room in our house but Tony agreed to give us crawl space storage for all of our books as well as a closet.

Our spirits were high. It felt like a new era and a further evolution for Microcosm. The move strengthened morale and resolve among the three of us. It felt like we were growing, which made us feel good and, in turn, work harder, which helped us to grow even more. A sense of steady evolution of the organization also kept everyone from getting too set in their ways or their rhythms. I would frequently bring up future changes that I wanted to make, such as adding books from a different publisher to our catalog or increasing our selection of comic books or political documentaries on DVDs. These suggestions would always be received with some grumbling. "There's no more room for more zines" or "I don't like that subject so I don't care. I'm not interested." But as the change happened, it was accepted. I was still the boss and this was understood. And as I watched, Heather and Evan's enthusiasm would slowly grow around each change. And their help on the nuts-and-bolts work allowed me more to explore how I felt about relevant issues. In a 2003 interview, I asked Travis Fristoe, editor of *America?*, "What motivates you to make zines and produce things in general?" He responded, "Anti-depression... we're creating work that speaks for itself rather than having an academic come in years later to validate and interpret. Or waiting on museums to catalog and sell our sweat... Zines & records make my life better and worth fighting for." These words strongly resonated with my own thoughts and helped me put a frame around how I saw my own work at Microcosm. I spent more and more time in my head privately reflecting on these topics.

Having Evan and Heather around allowed me to get a little too complacent and less focused on Microcosm at times. Partially because they were both insistent on having things be done their way but also because my digestive problems were starting to be bad enough to distract me from my work. I had tried to ignore my health problems since they had started to appear when I was a teenager, perhaps a little too similarly to how my dad had tried to ignore his stroke. But by this point, it was hard to ignore the fever and migraine that would leave me incapacitated on the couch once a week.

I had tried for years to see doctors about the pain I had whenever I ate anything, but they typically would just feed me a line about how my body was growing or that it was stress-related or just all in my head. After having enough experiences like that and not having insurance, I gave up and lived with the pain. I had been vegan for five years and sober for four years, figuring those steps were healthy and would help. But the more time went by, the worse things got. Perhaps I had been testing the limits of my body for too long.

I started to see Evan's doctor, who went by "Dr. Steve." He was a naturopath who charged a scant $20-30/hour. I went in and detailed my problems to him. I would find slices on my hands where I didn't remember cutting myself. I was tired all the time and falling asleep earlier and earlier. Dr. Steve concluded that my problems were glandular and most likely in an unbalanced thyroid. His treatment was to read his poetry out loud to me, and to prescribe two pills, one to cut through the "mental fog" that I experienced and the other to stabilize my thyroid.

As soon as I began taking the pills, I found that I needed to sleep only for a few hours each night before I cartoonishly sprung out of bed around 3 or 4 AM. Rather than being alarmed, I found the pre-daylight hours of the morning to be the perfect time to catch up on my to-do list before the phone started ringing. Having four or five extra working hours each day allowed me to catch up on years of backlogged tasks within a few weeks.

For many years, washing the dishes had been a contentious matter in our household. I had always had the wherewithal to traipse into a kitchen full of dirty dishes, wash the pot, bowl, spoon, or knife that I needed, and then return it afterwards to the top of the sculpture of dirty dishes, content to tell myself that I had not contributed to this problem. But now that I had extra hours each day and knowing how much the state of the dishes upset everyone else in our household, I applied myself to washing every dish in the sink each morning. My roommates somehow complained about this too, insisting that they felt guilty and were going to get to their dishes after their shower. I suggested that they might use that time to clean the bathroom or living room instead.

The sheer amount of focus that I had and the number of hours that I committed myself to my work began to freak out my roommates. They investigated what was in the new pills I was taking and discovered one mysterious ingredient: organic sheep brains from New Zealand. Unfazed, I continued to be excited that I could get even more accomplished in a day. My roommates insisted that I had to call my doctor.

"Umm, Dr. Steve...what's in those pills that you gave me? I mean, I love them. I have so much energy and I wake up before the sun but I read the ingredients and..."

"According to Chinese medicine if a part of your body is not working properly, you should give yourself more of that body part. In New Zealand it is against the law to give hormones to sheep so many manufacturers import parts of those sheep because they are pure."

I was satisfied with that answer. I wasn't about to question my doctor or my medication. Upon explanation, one of my roommates found a place where he could order the same pills online and began taking them with similar results. After a few months of this, his girlfriend freaked out and demanded that he stop.

Meanwhile, I was not only caught up on a lifetime-long to-do list but I was also accomplishing tasks as I could come up with them. I came up with a time-management strategy that serves me well to this day: If a task can be completed in under fifteen minutes, do it immediately as it comes up. Do longer tasks at the end of the day or delegate them to someone else. In the long run, this method has saved me tremendous amounts of time. My inbox is always empty, my stress is much lower, and people always marvel at how fast I can turn a task around.

But my production-management skills were light years ahead of my health. One day I noticed a sharp pain in my foot and when I investigated closer I discovered a small abscess. According to my time-management strategy, I immediately called Dr. Steve, who told me that he could see me that day. I biked the five miles to get there through much pain and showed it to him. He recommended soaking it in a hot salt bath, taking some antibiotics, and then applying some blue drops to it afterwards. He swore up and down that this had worked on every one of his patients who have had this problem. I added this routine to my schedule but three months later all I had to show for it were blue stains on some of my favorite pants, water damage on the floor under my office desk, and the discovery that antibiotics really interrupted my sleep.

Heather went on a trip by herself back to Salt Lake City, where she had grown up, ostensibly to do research on the radical history of the place. We talked on the phone periodically and I told her how restless my sleep was on the drugs, but for some reason she didn't believe me. She seemed withdrawn, distant—even more than usual.

One time when I called, I talked to her friend James, whom she was staying with.

"Uh, she's not here... She didn't come back last night."

"Oh, okay. Do you know where she is?"

"Ummm."

"Well, do you know if she is okay?"

"Yes."

"Okay, tell her that I called. Bye."

By the time Heather returned from Utah, she admitted to me that she had purposefully tracked down her ex-boyfriend of three years while she was there. They had talked through their problems, rekindled their feelings for each other, and she had begun staying at his house.

I was upset. It felt like an insult, a betrayal. It was the same guy who had written the letters she had asked me to decode when we first met. Worst of all, I had foreseen this moment. The first question I asked her when we started dating was if she was over him. She looked confused at the time, seeming to wonder what might prompt such a question, and had insisted that she was.

My nights were already restless, but now I actually had something to worry about.

I returned to Doctor Steve's office and showed him my now-large abscess. He looked concerned. I was confused; I had followed directions to the letter. Why hadn't it worked?

Steve called the hospital across the street and asked if they could see me. They wanted to surgically remove it, and I made an appointment to get that done the morning after Heather got home. She grudgingly joined me on the bike ride to the surgery and validated my experience, saying that she had talked to a friend's girlfriend who works as a nurse and she now believed that antibiotics do affect a person's sleep.

The surgeon took out a gigantic needle as I begged and pleaded for her to just cut out the abscess without anesthetic. She looked at me as if I were insane and said "that would be like torture."

"That's fine." I said. "Just put that damned needle away."

She fought off my protestations, and the whole thing became a non-event as soon as my whole foot was numb. Heather and I biked home in silence. The next night Heather and I watched *American Splendor*—the film that I'd had such trouble believing HBO would produce about Harvey Pekar and Joyce Brabner. Much of the story focused on how they had problems and bickered constantly with each other. The next night we watched *End of the Century,* a documentary about The Ramones, forefathers of punk rock, from New York. Again, the film focused largely around the relationships within the band, how everyone involved was totally insane, and how even their relationships with their spouses were dysfunctional. When I explained to Heather that my takeaway was that in the context of these two films that our relationship is really quite normal, she just shook her head at me.

Tabling for Microcosm, 2002. Photo by Chris Boarts Larsen

PERMANENT INK

I made a rule when I turned eighteen that I would get only one tattoo per year. I was afraid I would run out of real estate on my body before I had *really* good ideas later in life. For the first few years I would plan out the next four or five tattoos. Ideas rarely got scrapped but sometimes got refined. Most of the concepts were paper-thin and the executions weren't much better. I took images that were meaningful to me and put them on my body—things my friends had drawn or artwork I found on albums that I liked or things to represent commitments to my politics—"One Less Car," "Revolution Between The Lines," or "Break Free From Gender Roles."

After the better part of seven years of walking around with permanent ink, I started to feel a little on display, expecting to be judged, or maybe just a little tired of explaining what these things mean over and over. In the social circles that I was a part of and to fans of Microcosm, art was expected to have intense, didactic meaning, and it was fair game to ask for an explanation, perhaps turning a stranger into a friend.

But I was beginning to tire of this. So I put together a concept piece. It might have been someone else's idea; I don't remember anymore. But I loved it: an image of a wooden table and two empty chairs. One of the chairs would be knocked over, like an argument had just occurred. There would be no text. I would get it tattooed over my heart. The absolutely meaningless image would appear to have deep, intense meaning, both in its execution and in its placement.

I've always found joy in being a troublemaker, and I thought this idea was hilarious. So did the tattoo artist and her friends from art school. Unfortunately, Heather did not agree.

"You can't claim that something has no meaning. That is ridiculous and offensive!" she berated me.

"Well, I don't know...I'm sort of riffing on and poking fun at people who have this idea that images carry all of this weight and meaning."

"Well, I'm one of those people and I think it's a stupid idea! I don't even like the cross-hatching on those chairs. Why didn't you get wooden slat-back chairs?"

Everywhere I went for the next few weeks, people would ask to see my new tattoo. I would lift up my shirt and show it to them awkwardly. Each and every one of them responded with some variation of, "Whoa! That's intense! I didn't know you were getting divorced!"

To which I would foolishly respond, "Oh no, it's a joke. I was trying to think of the most seemingly intense tattoo and then put it in the most intense place. I even gave up on getting the outline of the state of Ohio tattooed there instead."

Everyone gave me skeptical looks and continued to insist that I was getting divorced, like they knew something that I didn't or could trust my tattoo better than my words.

Maybe deep down in my subconscious I did know what they saw. By that point Heather had been making regular trips to go visit her ex, and their relationship had become a constant source of argument in our household. I was jealous of the emotional proximity that they seemed to have. Heather and I had been dating for five years and married for one, but we barely knew each other. We knew all of the details about each other's lives but we each really had little insight into what made the other tick. Part of not knowing me also led her to constantly misread my words and actions, as well as to come to distrust my intentions.

When Heather was applying for a job that she suspected two other friends of ours also had their eye on, she asked me to write a reference for her. I was flattered to do so but afterwards she somehow got the idea that I probably wrote one for our other two friends as well. I hadn't done so and told her as much. But she was saddened and hurt, and she kept pointing to ambiguities in my speech that convinced her that I was lying about my true motivations.

The same thing that made it fun to talk about the double meanings of words with Heather led her to believe that I meant every potentially insulting double meaning in everything that I said. When I bought a T-shirt depicting a person with his ass on fire and sticking his head into a bucket of water with the caption "voter," Heather got upset and took it so personally that she told me she would not be seen with me wearing it in public.

Heather often claimed that people treated me differently from others as a result of my confidence, which grew as a source of resentment between us as well. She said that people were more likely to do things for me than they were for others. So gradually I changed my behavior to accommodate this, losing a bit of myself in the process. Whenever I had an exciting piece of news and would tell her, she would immediately post it on the Internet. When I would run into friends, they would already know all of my news, having read it as it happened on Heather's blog. I asked her if she could stop. She instead asked people to stop mentioning that they had already read the stories when I told them about things. It seemed that she could even take my achievements and stories away from me. As our interactions got more and more awkward I started keeping the things that I was excited about to myself, which didn't help matters. More and more of my time and emotional energy were taken up by explaining that what Heather had gleaned from a conversation wasn't representative of how I felt at all. I would ask her if she understood what I was saying and she would always say that she didn't.

Months later, after many more conversations like this, she said that, to her, saying that she understood what I meant was the same as saying that she agreed with me, which she assuredly did not. So she would say that she did not understand rather than saying that she disagreed. I knew that our perspectives were different and we were both prone to unique views but this conversation absolutely floored me. The way that Heather belittled my feelings, called me names, insulted my perspectives, and declared that I had no friends during these arguments destroyed my confidence and self-esteem. She would buy me presents and then not give them to me if something that I did upset her. I was watching the only stable relationship in my life unravel. I clung harder to the relationship even as my dwindling confidence began to erode my ability to do things that I had always been good at: math, remembering names, and planning out a logical course of action. Sleeping for only three or four hours each night was likely not helping matters.

One of my pen pals, Bree, had moved to Portland, which was exciting, as she was one of the few people in my life that I was close to and could relate to at the moment. Bree commented on my constant drive towards self-improvement and how much effort I put into understanding how I could relate better with others. She had just turned eighteen and I was in my mid-twenties, but we related as equals. We had a room vacant in our house and I asked Heather how she felt about Bree moving in.

One night Heather insisted that I had a crush on Bree. She continued to bring this up and make reference to it often as the days went by, so much that I began to question my own version of events. Did I have a crush? Did I have romantic intentions? What if I did but I didn't know? Reluctantly, I made a deal that I would not make a fuss about Heather's having a romantic relationship with her ex if Bree could move into our house.

Shortly afterwards, Heather declared to me with a sneer that, while she had agreed to the deal, she had never agreed to be nice to Bree. She would lash out regularly. One night as I sat on the porch talking to Bree, Heather appeared to bring us each a delicious plate of tofu scramble, biscuits, and gravy. It was a mixed gesture as she handed them to us with such hostility that Bree and I just sat there silently afterwards. Bree moved out shortly afterwards.

I was lost and lonelier than usual. So I planned a trip by myself to Bloomington, Indiana for the Plan-it X Records ten-year anniversary music festival. I had numerous friends there that I had met at zine conferences, and I figured that a convergence of hundreds of friends would help me firm up my self-image and decision-making skills. Bree was also going to Plan-it X Fest, which greatly upset Heather.

I headed to Cleveland and met up with my old friend Drew, and we drove out in his car to the Allied Media Conference in Bowling Green, Ohio. We had a really great time. He had declined to come to my wedding, but we hadn't really talked about the particulars much before this.

"Why did you get married to her?" he asked me.

"I don't really know. It seemed like the right thing to do at the time," was the best I could muster.

Drew was a good friend and he supported me even if he didn't approve. We drove from Bowling Green to Bloomington and arrived a few days before the fest. We stayed with my friend Christopher, whom I'd met when he lived in San Francisco. The two people that he lived with and who owned the house were constantly fighting and screaming at each other. It felt like every little thing the other one did hit a nerve. It was so similar to my life at home that it made me feel like my relationship with Heather was normal, maybe even healthy.

The festival was probably pretty great but I spent the whole time moping outside or dragging my sorry mess of a story around and telling everyone I ran into about my heartbreak. I figured that sharing in this way would create the kind of emotional proximity that I so desperately sought and might create close friends instead of a sea of distant acquaintances. Instead, most people with clear boundaries seemed freaked out by it. They nodded and fled. The people who did engage me were as lost in life as I was in that moment. They were there for reasons similar to my own: To find their way by

To unwind, I went back to the hairstyle I had ten years earlier.

being open to whoever offered them the time of day long enough to ensnare their lives together.

Christopher asked me "What is it like to be a celebrity here?"

"You'd have to ask one." I replied, trying to dodge an unanswerable question.

"No, really. What is it like? How do people treat you here?"

"It's a little weird. People engage with me as the person that they perceive me as rather than the person that I am. It doesn't exactly create a lot of room for exchanging ideas as equals."

With permission, I had been setting up tables of zines and books on the sidewalk outside of the shows. The reactions were pretty mixed and some people were outright offended that we were asking for money in return for books and zines. I met a lot of people wearing our T-shirts who were huge fans of Microcosm, and they gushed about what they had taken from some of our titles and asked questions about things that they couldn't fully understand on their own. It was overwhelming to feel like all of our fans were in one place and all had the opportunity to engage with me in real time.

Although most of my interactions in life were made less overwhelming because I could stem the tide through email or by talking to one person at a time on the phone, being in Bloomington opened up the floodgates for people to ask me all kinds of questions. Because much of my own writing had been about my personal life, fans felt like they knew me and could ask me anything they wanted about my personal life. Whereas I had overshared with people that I didn't know very well, fans seemed equally uncomfortable being given this information. Sometimes the awkward pauses that I would leave after someone asked a question were so long that they would just walk away while I was still forming my answer. Being that my personal life was in shambles at the moment and I was deeply unhappy and insecure, all of this socializing unfolded into a bit of a nightmare.

I didn't watch many bands perform that weekend, but looking back, I did feel excited and inspired by the trip. Bloomington felt magical in the same way that Portland did, and seeing it while hundreds of people from out of town invaded made it seem larger than life.

The highlight of the trip was getting to spend so much time at Boxcar Books, a store that also housed Pages to Prisoners, the oldest program for sending free books to people in jail who request them in the U.S. The store was started by two friends of mine based on their experiences of being involved with another anarchist bookstore, Secret Sailor Books. They thought they could create something more stable and lasting while keeping the heart and soul of the place. Boxcar really impressed me because it was built from the ground up by people I knew. They had really dug deep to source books from all kinds of publishers and all of the sections in the store were really fleshed

out, not just the usual titles on the usual politics that you'd find in radical bookstores all over the U.S. I picked up quite a few books for myself, but, mostly, as Drew and I drove back to Cleveland, I carried inspiration home from Boxcar itself. It let me know that my dreams for Microcosm had lots of different directions that they could still grow in, even after eight years.

Plan-it X Fest, 2004

SINKING THINGS THROUGH

I finished editing *$100 & A T-Shirt* in October of 2004 and released it on another cross-country tour with two Microcosm authors, Dave Roche and Nicole Georges. I chose not to include Heather on the tour as we were really not getting along and I was trying to focus on some other faces from Microcosm. Nonetheless, Heather and I went on a little vacation to the coast on the days leading up to the tour. I was having more and more trouble staying awake past dinner, which frustrated her while she was trying to get quality time together before I would be gone for a month. Nonetheless, we had an okay time until the trip back to Portland.

On the trip home, I explained my boundary that if we were going to have a relationship, she could not also date her ex-boyfriend. She explained that it wasn't the appearance of her ex in our life that was driving us apart. She was unhappy and he was only the catalyst. After an hour of arguing about it, we got home and sat in our living room. I tried to put my foot down that she could not have it both ways and she had to pick one of us. At that moment, the phone rang and she started to walk out of the room to answer it. Angry and feeling disrespected, I stood up, blocked the doorway, and pushed her. She pushed past me. Of course, it was her ex on the phone. She talked to him for 45 minutes before returning to the living room to continue our conversation as if nothing had happened.

Heather told me that I was not allowed to mention that she was dating her ex to our marriage counselor. I insisted that if I wasn't allowed to then she must, as it was undermining our relationship and was a good jumping-off point to talk about underlying issues. But for months we continued to see the counselor and Heather refused to bring it up.

Instead, we followed the counselor's lead. She asked us to define what love is. After some faltering, I recited the Fred Rogers quote, "Love isn't a state of perfect caring. It is an active verb, like struggle. To love someone is to strive to accept that person exactly the way he or she is, right here and now."

Heather was quick to object to this. At first I thought that she meant that we did not agree on that definition for the purposes of our therapy but Heather went on to explain that she did not approve of that being *my* definition for love. But conversation broke down right away. Instead of working through our mutual understanding of fundamental issues, Heather always wanted to ignore our disagreements and just focus on having a good time. But I wasn't able to do that. Hoping to rectify the growing void between us, I stayed. To me, it felt like the illusion of getting along was far more dangerous both to our relationship and to my self-image. I couldn't respect myself if I didn't at least try to advocate for my needs.

One night as Heather and I were leaving the office together, I assumed that we'd hang out after work, but she had plans to go drinking with Evan. The moment got awkward, as it was apparent that we were growing apart. We sat down to talk through it.

I kicked the toe of her worn Doc Marten boot and said, "You're so capable." Heather would later write that she believed that I was realizing in the moment that she didn't need me. But, while it was hard to watch our lives diverge, I just meant it at face value, as a compliment. While I was rapidly losing my self-confidence and ability to care for myself, I wondered how she could both take care of herself and make plans to socialize. Heather told me that the problem was that I did not have friends. I knew this wasn't true but I watched Heather go out almost every night and appear to have a good time while I wallowed alone at home. To the detriment of everything else in my life, all I could do was focus on the divide between us. Heather and I went our separate ways that evening.

Before I went on tour that year, Heather and I had agreed on rules for having an open relationship. I thought it would be a way to form new bonds with other people while maintaining the skeleton of a life that Heather and I had together. We had to use condoms with other partners. We would call if we weren't going to come home. If one of us dated someone that the other felt uncomfortable about or didn't like, the other could ask for the relationship to cease. But when I felt this way and asked her to stop, she said no, explaining that she was unhappy in our relationship. I understood that but I didn't understand why she tried to sit on the fence. I felt like a sucker.

The stress started to have physical manifestations. One morning while having breakfast with Bree and her brother I felt like someone had been repeatedly punching me in the stomach. For the first time in my life, I couldn't finish a meal.

A day later I left on the tour. We rented a compact car, filled it to the ceiling with books, and did about 50 events in almost all of the lower 48 states. The events were bigger, people were familiar with each of us as performers, and the dynamic between Dave's reading, Nicole's comic slide show, and my film balanced the audience's attention in a way that five readers hadn't in years past. I always remember the worst events on tour or the funniest interactions, like the woman in Detroit who explained each of Dave's jokes to her son while he was reading; or driving overnight from Fort Worth, Texas to Tucson and having my glucose crash as the sun was coming up; or all three of us crowding onto one dirty fold-out couch and being given a VHS copy of *Hairspray* to watch along with a bag filled with hundreds of oranges, but this tour had many memorable moments for other reasons. We did events in respectable college lecture rooms and at historic punk venues such as ABC NO RIO in New York City where our heroes came to watch us perform.

I came home triumphant and excited to return to my life. I'd had several awkward phone conversations with Heather while staying at people's houses, but I was determined to make things up when I got home. At my insistence, we drove overnight after our last show in Arcata to get home the following morning.

When I arrived home, Heather was still asleep. The first thing that she told me when I woke her up was that she was moving out and our relationship was over. She was tired of my disrespect for her feelings and she was breaking up with me.

In order for Asperger's to be defined as a "disability," and often for it to be diagnosed and recognized in the first place, a person must be experiencing "failure" in some aspect of their life. Normally this is manifested as failing out of school or at the workplace. I had been a C average student in high school and had been a social misfit all of my life, but I had always found ways to make things work. The collapse of my marriage was the first failure caused by my Asperger's disability.

I wandered around like a homeless puppy for most of the following year, not ready for the reality to sink in. I figured that Heather would change her mind. Surely she'd broken up with her ex for some reason the first time around and we could mend our differences.

Nonetheless, Heather moved in with one of our newer co-workers and began having a relationship of sorts with him as well, making things more awkward at work. She published a zine about her perspective on our relationship, shortly after we broke up. It was the third in a series; the previous two issues had detailed her perspective on her breakup with her ex. I saw a potential pattern in the works, and this gave me further faith and evidence that Heather and I would rekindle our relationship.

I went on with my life. Heather moved back in with me six months later but we didn't get back together. It was the road of least resistance, not the road to recovery. When my glasses were stolen from inside our house, she was supportive and made the trip to the eye doctor with me. I learned that my extreme nearsightedness put me at risk for glaucoma and I needed eye surgery. I could only see an inch away from my face without my giant coke-bottle glasses. Heather went with me to various suburban labs and through four eye surgeries and follow-ups. But our communication became increasingly fractured as she spent more time reuniting with her ex, whom she communicated well with. Seeing how apparently happy Heather was with him made my limitations clearer to me.

At work, Heather complained that I had left some loose ends to be dealt with while I was on tour, forcing her to coordinate a few deliveries and tasks that I normally manage. I explained that there were simply limits to what I was capable of doing and organizing, especially while preparing for a tour. She just looked at me and eventually responded, "It doesn't seem like it." Later that week, while she was logging into my email to see if I had yet read a message that she had sent me, she accidentally deleted my entire email account and all of its history. I recalled everyone that I had emailed in the previous week and wrote to each of them again.

The boundaries and expectations in my relationship with Heather still felt blurry to me. When I took an unexpected trip out of town on short notice and didn't let her know, she got upset and told me that my co-workers and housemates were worried about me. Confused, I explained that I had told the staff and my roommates about the trip and even forwarded her the email where I had explained it to them. I apologized for hurting her feelings. She accused me of lying about the trip and "rewriting history." She claimed that I believed myself to be "the ministry of truth."

Every sincere apology I offered each time I hurt her feelings was met with yet another explanation of how she saw it as another dismissal of her feelings rather than a valid admission of guilt. I felt responsible for my actions, but when I looked up "guilt," I didn't feel that I had "compromised standards of conduct or violated a moral standard" because I had never meant to hurt her. We began treading into increasingly strange and dangerous territory.

By the time I recovered from eye surgery in 2005, Microcosm had achieved more success than I ever thought possible. We had a staff of six plus a handful of interns. We were now publishing six new books per year. People who had never before been comfortable working with a publisher were approaching us with ideas and projects. People really appreciated what was unique about us. Our authors were also our customers. People felt like they were part of a community. After almost ten years of operations, I gave myself a raise from $1/hour to minimum wage.

Our success was so extreme that I started to feel guilty and even bad about it. I had felt like a friendless failure for my whole life but my hard work and unwavering determination had delivered Microcosm to a healthy place. Coming to work each day was always unique and exciting—and a blast. There were heartening phone calls. We opened our office up for the public to shop, and everyone who came by in person was adorable. It's not just me saying that; other tenants in our building commented about it all the time too.

Having a brick-and-mortar location was like a lightning rod for attracting people who focused on the kind of ideas that we were projecting. People began to visit us from all over the world, sometimes just because they were fans and wanted to meet us. People would come in and spend hundreds of dollars on themselves. Every day held a new and exciting surprise. Even so, I was afraid that other people would react negatively to the kinds of success we were having, as if it was somehow disingenuous with the goals we were expressing. I think this attitude was visible to the public in the way that I talked about things. I apologized for my success, which forced people to get defensive on my behalf.

For instance, once when someone cornered me at an event and told me that they saw *On Subbing* "everywhere," I got sheepish and worried aloud if it crowded out other deserving books. She told me that I should be proud.

The staff was really rising to the occasion. Everyone was very self-motivated. They were showing up to work, answering dozens of emails each day, shipping out every order, leaving cute notes for the next shift, reordering everything that we had run out of after writing it all down on the bulletin board with a check mark next to it, and reviewing the mountain of submissions with rigor.

Each day as I showed up for work there were charming pieces of original artwork left to brighten my day; new ideas flowing in that Microcosm was equipped to turn into a reality in short order; and a strong commitment to the ethics, ideals, and even productivity of the company. I really liked each staff person as an individual but collectively I felt like they had exceeded my wildest dreams. My hiring criteria was often based more on each person's enthusiasm, showing up on time consistently, and commitment to similar politics to my own rather than any kind of experience in publishing. In fact, no one had any background in publishing, not even myself. We continued to hire a larger and larger staff, bringing the total up to eight workers including me. Each person brought new ideas and perspectives to the table, though often just from their own experiences of what enticed or alienated them when they are considering what they want to read and support.

I had read a healthy amount of labor history by this point, which was one reason that I was uncomfortable being the boss. I wanted the organization to thrive but my stress levels were through the roof. Remembering how Evan joked that I would have a heart attack before I turned 40, I thought that forming the employees into a collective to manage the organization could re-shape the culture in such a way to increase people's feelings of investment and allow me to relax and step back a bit. Heather agreed strongly with this idea. Together, we approached the staff about it on a rainy Sunday. Only one other person showed up for the meeting, which could have served as an indication that this was not a great idea. It took nearly two hours before we got to "turn organization into a collective" on the meeting agenda. The other employee who showed up said, "Maybe this isn't the best time to open this can of worms." I had always been energized by long meetings and expected this piece of news would excite any young worker turned manager with the option of ownership.

The lack of response or even enthusiasm disappointed me. When I would ask people if they had any interest in becoming an owner, no one did. There weren't even that many questions. Nonetheless, the collective was formed a month later in early 2006. Perhaps because of the lack of excitement, we did not create a set of bylaws. We didn't even crudely define what the collective meant. Some staff people were confused and thought that it meant that they now owned the company or that I was leaving. Perhaps I hadn't explained it very well. Even Heather seemed to have differing ideas about it than I did but they were unspoken until conflicts arose. For some staff people, including Heather, being a collective seemed to mean that they could do whatever they wanted on the clock or make whatever changes that they wanted to the office without consulting anyone beyond those present when they wanted to make those decisions. Nonetheless through thick and thin, through bumps and annoyances, I wanted to let the experiment play out and see how it shaped up.

Top: Jack and I in Chapel Hill with the promoter, Niku, and her husband. Left: Nicole and I at a gas station. Right: Gas station art outside of Boise.

Section

III

Introducing Bureaucracy

A CHANGING CLIMATE

I still wanted to get back together with Heather. Her parents and sister still welcomed me during holidays like I was a part of their family. I was like a sad and forlorn puppy during holiday meals, hoping that her family still believed in me. Trying to appease Heather, I would get drunk when she asked me to. She would make fun of me for not understanding which fork was used for what or how to set a table or that I could rest my forearms on the table but not my elbows. She would reward me when I did what she wanted and punish me when I did not. And reliably, once I was drunk, she would use sex to hold power over me in a way that made me very uncomfortable. She was violent towards me during sex, even after I asked her not to. I began to wonder if this new behavior was the result of habits she'd picked up sleeping with her ex. At work she would tell me that I was "stupid" or an "idiot" or an "asshole" in front of the other staff or even customers so frequently that I eventually felt comfortable only working on days when Heather was not in the office. When I explained this decision to her, she denied that it was a problem and it only made her more upset.

By June of 2006, Heather and I had been separated for eighteen months and I gave up and started dating other people. But I was still processing the break up and so each effort was short-lived. I didn't know how to move on.

A friend had heard about our split and he sent me a letter, pointing out that when the punk band Hüsker Dü had broken up in 1987, the public felt like they had to take sides between creative partners Grant Hart and Bob Mould. Their collaborative work was greater than the sum of its parts, and after the breakup Hart's solo albums and tours were not nearly as interesting or well-received as Mould's. Hart told endless sob stories about how he'd been wronged, so at first fans took his side. But over the years Mould continued his creative path prolifically and challenged himself to new heights, eventually changing people's minds. Later in Mould's memoir, *See A Little Light,* his self-hatred gave more perspective on why his actions were so hard to interpret. It's hard to conceive of how it all looks from the outside sometimes, my friend pointed out, but it's important to continue doing what I did best: being prolific and communicating where you are at to your fans. The thought stuck with me.

In December I was part of a group bicycle-art show at City Hall in Portland. I showed off some of my design work, and it felt like a real honor to be included as part of something like that. It felt like a recognition that people knew where I had come from. A blonde woman with glasses approached me with a checkbook. She barked her requests at me. I grabbed the shirts that she wanted and attempted to make flirtatious smalltalk:

"So, what are you up to?"

"Are we all done here?" she responded gruffly before walking away. Next to her name—Elly Blue—on her personal check, there was a man's name printed. Although I found her attractive, she clearly wasn't single.

My decision to attempt to move on and date other people really upset Heather, who tried to impose rules, saying that I couldn't bring people I was casually dating to the office. She had been upset about it the year before when I had said that her boyfriend couldn't hang out at the office with her all day. I felt that it would impede her motivation to do her work. I pleaded to get divorced, but Heather was in no rush to do so, saying that it was not a priority for her. I called the county office, asking them for a divorce application. The woman who answered the phone laughed at my request and said "Oh honey, if only it was that easy." I called the library's information line and asked how to get divorced. The librarian explained that Heather and I would need to create an agreement to determine how dependents and property were to be divided and that most people need a lawyer to do so. This was upsetting news as I had not foreseen this outcome let alone the hassle it would inevitably produce.

I needed a break from my routine, so I talked to my friends in Bloomington and arranged to do a month-long learning internship at Boxcar Books. I hadn't really considered that arriving in Indiana in January would not be comparable to the mild Portland winters that I had grown accustomed to or that my friends there might not drop everything this time to hang out with me. There was a lot of snow on the ground and the social climate had changed quite a bit compared to my visit during the festival in 2004.

The first few days were odd. Boxcar Books sold textbooks and it was the first week of the quarter. I spent my first sixteen hours there doing nothing but ringing up students with bad attitudes asking for a textbook when they didn't know the name of the book or the professor or the class. They were annoyed that they had to leave campus in the first place. This wasn't what I had signed up for. But over the next few days it got better, and it was pleasant to have so much personal time with each of the staff members and to get to know each one and how they impacted the dynamic of the store with their personality, their music, how extroverted they were, and how many friends would visit them during their shift.

I had a few wake-up calls too. At Microcosm we basically acted like our store was our living-room clubhouse and we'd blast punk rock out of a trebly boom box and make jokes and tell stories about our Dungeons & Dragons games to each other like no one was listening. When Boxcar's director came in during my shift one morning, she leaned in close and said "Your music's too loud. Turn it down." I wasn't used to being addressed this way but it made me respect her more. She went on to explain that it wasn't the punk rockers who spent money in the store so blasting The Minutemen wasn't going to accomplish anything besides rattling people who came there looking for a gently used copy of *Harry Potter And The Sorcerer's Stone* or William Zinsser's *On Writing Well*. If I forgot to turn off one set of lights or the open sign, I would get a phone call an hour later as someone rode their bike past the store, stopped in to say hi, and found no one there with the lights on. For reasons like this, Boxcar was a respectable establishment, accessible to a pretty diverse audience of leftists in a conservative state. Their attitude was that punk rockers had access to the same wealth of materials elsewhere, so the store did not focus on catering to them, though it did have a good collection of zines.

By contrast, Microcosm was in the basement of an unused church building, with no sign, located near Commercial on Ivy street, the most dangerous intersection in 2006 in Portland. We were located on a dead-end street off of a one-way street in a neighborhood that most people in Portland didn't know existed. We constantly had to give the same person multiple sets of directions as they would call, we'd explain how to get there, they'd get lost, and call back over and over. The building was most famous in the news because of the high volume of break-ins and gang shootings that occurred within its walls. Teenagers would text everyone that they knew to create flash mobs and wreak havoc on the street. If we unlocked the doors before 8 AM kids would skip school and hang out in our building all day. I had thought about details like this, but only as it related to my own physical safety and the likelihood of having to deal with problems. Learning about how these issues were handled at Boxcar made me start to evaluate property based on criteria beyond cheap rent.

In some ways it was comforting to see that Boxcar had similar interpersonal conflicts to Microcosm's. During meetings one person would always leave upset or even crying because another person was consistently blunt or downright cruel. Nonetheless, I managed to be friendly with everyone and I learned quite a bit. Mostly at first I studied the curation, finances, and ordering practices of the store. I had always wanted to open my own bookstore, as any good nerd is prone to. One thing that was interesting to me about Boxcar was that the fact that it was a legal nonprofit and all of the staff were volunteers allowed the vast majority of their cash flow to go into inventory. If a book sold out, another copy was ordered. When any new topical book was published that fit into any of the 60 or so shelving categories, at least one copy was purchased. I inquired frequently about these habits and got the impression that ordering seemed to be on autopilot. Staff members could make requests if the store didn't have something that they wanted, and diligent efforts were made to follow through. The system was functional. Everyone was relatively invested.

Heather sent me some thoughtful care packages while I was at Boxcar, further confusing me about our status. While I did spend some time on the phone with her, I mostly tried to enjoy myself by reading, socializing, and meeting people with whom I shared common interests.

After a month behind the counter I made my way back to Portland's mild winter and my uncertain personal future. Microcosm, however, was thriving. Having some time away from me had given some staff members the feelings of agency and responsibility they needed to manage the company. Other staff members had less motivation to do the best job possible and were trivializing and flippant when talking to customers about their problems, but these matters could be resolved by talking it over as a group. It was an interesting experiment. The staff had swollen to twelve people, but most of them wanted to work part time while still maintaining managerial authority. The staff created a system of weekly email updates so all information would be shared and nothing would be privileged. People complained that my weekly updates were too long, that I completed too many tasks each week.

The result of collective management was that people had different levels of commitment but wanted to have equal levels of input in steering the organization. We still lacked bylaws and were slowly seeking out models for how other organizations had handled situations like this. In the meantime, we had four-hour monthly meetings that turned into bi-weekly meetings where we discussed the next year of upcoming publications, any changes to policies, problems that people were having and how to solve them, procedural questions, reviewing submissions, or frustrations with organizational aspects that people sometimes just wanted to vent about. The problems that this model posed were two-fold: While collectively managed businesses tended to employ profit-splitting, publishing was essentially a break-even endeavor at best. We had no profits, partly because I had designed our finances so all leftover money was used to support our mission, mostly for publishing projects that would otherwise not see the light of day. So in order for profits to exist, we'd have to cut the budget elsewhere in our finances. As a result, it was hard to convince people to take on ownership roles in Microcosm or even to realize the stakes involved in decisions that affected our finances. Nonetheless, feelings of personal commitment to our reputation, the agency of decision-making, and pride from doing a good job often led the staff in decisions that were also responsible for Microcosm.

After learning that it was a condition for the San Francisco Public Library to buy books directly from Microcosm, the collective voted to pay for and implement workplace healthcare once we had paid for the four books that we had at the printer. Unfortunately, the most expensive book of the bunch, *Sounds of Your Name,* which cost us over $18,000, had serious printing issues and the printer dug in their heels to say that "we don't see anything wrong with it" and that they would not reprint the job correctly. I fought and fought with them until they offered 30% off a reprint. Lacking the tools to properly negotiate a free reprint, I relented and $12,000 later[8] we had books that were correctly printed. But we had to delay healthcare coverage for another month. Heather was furious, saying that she needed the money now. Other collective members tried to explain the situation to her but she seemed to still believe that I was somehow being duplicitous about the matter.

While it was great to have the whole team's opinion and feedback held at equal value, this slowly diluted Microcosm's vision and our public expression of that vision. It confused our fans who wanted to know if we embraced electoral politics or radical politics. They wanted to know what our views were on every issue, as if Microcosm were a single person they were talking to. In some ways it was a relief to have hard conversations from the position of being a collective: I no longer had to deliver bad news from a decision that I had made; everyone could put the responsibility of the decision on the shoulders of the vague and anonymous "collective." At the same time I often found myself having to deliver bad news resulting from a decision that actually had gone against my better judgment and the history of how I had handled things. We started to get angry letters in response to rejections from people who felt like their friend, Microcosm, was rejecting *them* rather than their work. The copies of my own zines that I had included with the rejections were no longer treated like I was saying that I was a peer and an equal with the creator of the work we were rejecting but rather were perceived as an arrogant notion that I was suggesting that my work was a superior model for them to learn from.

Our fans were invested on every level which was proving dangerous and volatile. Worse, word started to trickle back from people who had heard

8 *In late 2012 the printer finally relented and made up for the misprint by giving us discounts on new jobs.*

of my breakup with Heather. Our readers felt like they knew us personally and they wanted to know why we had broken up. Explaining that the relationship had never been very good or healthy for either of us was hard for people to understand, as that wasn't how it looked from the outside. Worse, the idea that sometimes two well-meaning people can be incapable of loving each other the way they need to be loved can be hard to understand, especially because our fans were often very young and held didactic politics firmly in their fists. Everything was either good or evil, helpful towards activist goals or opposed to them. There wasn't a lot of room for grey area in this framing of the world that I had created.

Because of the the amount of work that the collective was handling, I began working only 7 AM to 2 PM each day. At first I used the rest of the day to work on film projects or other work-related "hobbies," but my roommates quickly took notice of this and had something of an intervention.

"Don't you have any friends?" they asked.

While these words had been used to taunt and jeer at me throughout my life, they were coming from a place of concern this time. And truth be told, most of my friends from the Zine Symposium had moved out of town as I fell out of touch with the rest. I was part of a boardgaming group once per week and even if I felt like I annoyed some of the members by constantly being distracted, I met people there that I thought I could be friends with. One night after our game I went out with the group to a chain diner and tried to remember how to make friends.

Quietly, I looked around at my tablemates and realized that while they were all nerds and probably had relatable lives once we got talking, I was the only one who was a punk rocker. The dozens of patches sewn onto my pants, my mohawk, and my sleeveless T-shirt allowing my tattoos to spill out into the open air probably made me stand out in the group, at least in the eyes of my companions. I thought about how refreshing it would be to have friends who wanted to talk about something other than which punk bands they thought were ethically bankrupt or the politics of buying gasoline or the hand-wringing struggles of being in an open relationship. So many years of my life had been consumed in conversations about these things that I had forgotten that most people never talk about these things.

"So what do you guys... like to do for fun?" I asked.

"Fuck shit up!" April responded enthusiastically, flinging a packet of sugar across the table and knocking over the pepper shaker.

I laughed. I liked her.

"I'm shooting a music video for my band, The Unit Breed. You guys should all be in it. I need a *lot* of zombies," said a different Joe. In looking solely at his appearance, I had misjudged him. He was a punk but was wearing slacks and a teal velour button-down shirt.

"Rad." I said. "I'd love to."

The next weekend we all piled into Joe's living room and got into costume. It was the perfect opportunity not only to be a part of something cool but also to form real bonds with people and make friends. Not only did I play the lead, "Death," on the grounds of being tall but I got pushed by zombies while sitting in a hearse and got enveloped in a pile of zombies while making out with myself.[9] It was artistic in the best way because the actors all had fun even if we couldn't explain what the meaning being conveyed was from each or any scene.

After feeling dislocated for the previous year in Portland with my old friends gone and managing my emotional instability from the fallout with Heather, I finally figured out what healthy friendships looked like and I cultivated them. I invested in people who laughed at my jokes and expressed concern when I was going through something difficult. It was vital to see other people invest in me and comfort me when I was upset. It felt good and I suspected that other people felt the same way when they were comforted at appropriate times by people they valued and trusted. These experiences formed the beginning of a new blueprint.

Future Microcosm author Dawson Barrett was one Portland resident who understood and appreciated Microcosm's vision. Unfortunately he was moving out of town, but first he was putting on *Steal This Festival,* a blow-out punk gathering, to express how much he had appreciated Portland as a home. While the flyer featured a veritable who's who of hip punk bands, I was much more excited to see that they had convinced former Weather Underground member Mark Rudd to fly out to Portland and speak about his experiences of being a radical social-justice activist in the 1960s. I had loved him in Sam Green's *Weather Underground* documentary a few years earlier and his charisma and story in particular had motivated me to action. The group's story felt like the exact merging of politics and aesthetic that Microcosm championed. Above all else it was exciting to see someone else organizing in the way that I believed in. We set up a table of Microcosm books at the event and I excitedly clamored to listen to Mark Rudd talk. It was the only performance that I watched that day.

Unfortunately, Rudd was a total downer. He talked about his regrets. He talked about how his strategy would be different today, and not because of a changing culture. He talked about how his politics and perspectives have changed over the last 45 years. The presentation was structured to assume that most people would be familiar with Rudd's work and that he was offering advice to young activists. I left feeling disenfranchised and fearing that I would regret the decisions that I had been making up until that point in my life. Mostly I learned from his performance how *not* to engage an audience and the importance of establishing your tone and what you want people to take away from your talk. It helped me as a speaker and to understand the importance of connecting with the people who respected me and meeting them where they are.

Plan-it X Records had been one of the first labels whose zines and records I had distributed through Microcosm. The label's story of two young friends expressing their ire and frustration about global hegemony and the personal politics of their work inspired me. In the summer of 2006 they hosted another festival in Bloomington and I heeded the call. I spent a third of my time hanging out in the parking lot playing four square, a third of my time watching the bands, and a third of my time working on a documentary film about the festival with Eric Ayotte. After being bitten by the film bug in 2004 I had developed an interest to make a film about the story of Plan-it X, and Eric's idea to document the festival was the perfect opportunity. The results are captured in the documentary *If It Ain't Cheap, It Ain't Punk* and even after Eric had a death in the family during the fest and had to leave, I worked with a dozen other people

---

9 I dare you to watch the finished four-minute video at http://bit.ly/longlongeverlasting

to interview all of the bands, capture the feeling of being there, and explain the dynamic of what makes DIY punk special in a world of commodities.

Similarly to all treasured social groups, DIY punk really feels special because it's an exclusive club complete with secret handshakes and an endless expanse of community that wraps all across the globe. I felt like I was part of something important and unique, and I wanted to challenge the bubble of where the limits to that social circle and its cultural practices existed.

While I was in Bloomington I also began a casual relationship with Stefanie. We had met earlier that year when I interned at Boxcar, but we hadn't gotten along. But this time I learned about her passion for books. I had always wondered who bought new books in hardcovers, and it was people like Stefanie. She was supportive of my feelings and my constant and delicate moods, and went to great lengths to make sure that I was happy. She always got presents for me and laughed at my jokes in ways that Heather never had. Whereas Heather would go to great lengths to make fun of music that I held dear, Stefanie supported my choices even if she didn't appreciate them herself. We bonded over liking the same bands and appreciating punk-influenced literature even more than the music itself, going home from shows early and writing long letters to each other.

I made five short films about passenger trains, a homeless dog, bicycle lane decorations, board game arguments, and theories about decorative patches and screened them on the *Thinkin', Stinkin', & Rarely Drinkin* tour with Joshua Ploeg, cooking; Dave Roche, reading form his *On Subbing* book; Cristy Road, showing her art about growing up queer and Cuban; and Mary Chamberlin, curating a selection of books for sale.

Our tour ran down the East Coast that fall. Repeated van breakdowns only added to the legitimacy of the experience. We missed about a third of our shows but I spent the whole time in my head, focused on how future generations would continue to stretch, twist, and distort the boundaries of what people could do with the punk art and touring circuit. After our final breakdown and the van's demise in Florida, Joshua and I reconvened in Detroit and continued the tour via Amtrak. Seeing how Joshua structured his food tours was a big inspiration because he was already doing what I had envisioned: Creating a worldwide network of people who would support any interesting project that passed through town in the same way that punk music promoters did. I spent most of my hours on the train writing zines to go in the DVD sleeves of my new documentaries. The zines were about the tour and how eye-opening it had been and my new vision for my work. Joshua's background went back to the early '90s. He was a pioneer of the queercore movement, who had pushed similar boundaries for acceptance of LGBTQ rights to be expressive within punk, saying "We can do it too. You'll watch us. You'll like us. But we'll do it our way." Joshua's work spiraled into an international movement now commemorated in the song "Ode" by queer hardcore group Limp Wrist. We made a plan to publish his cookbooks through Microcosm. I felt on top of the world.

While we were on tour Heather was given some grief while making a deposit for Microcosm at our credit union and was incorrectly told that she was not listed on the account. Our credit union remains very small and is sometimes disorganized, but she took this as a personal attack at her from me. Minutes later, when she attempted to pick up the mail for Microcosm from my house, she discovered that the locks had been changed after a recent robbery, and she didn't have the new keys. I had told her about this but she had apparently forgotten and again took it personally. Heather responded by sending an email to the entire staff that said "I quit" and then separately explaining to me that my actions were again insensitive to her feelings. She said that she felt locked out of the things that had once been important to her, which made sense to me, but when I apologized she responded with "Thanks for admitting that you were wrong."

The following week she came back to work to set up our new shipping hardware and software. When she left, she took our new laser printer, button machine, and some financial records with her. Soon after, she founded her own button making business. Frustrations mounted in the collective when she appeared on a panel at Stumptown Comics Festival as a representative of Microcosm a month after she had quit.

Aside from the frustrations of having to deal with the fallout of our relationship, the staff took a blow to morale when they lost Heather. While she had only worked at Microcosm for three out of our ten years, she definitely represented and reflected a lot of the spirit of the organization and what it meant to people. She had worked closely with all of the staff and her involvement had preceded everyone working there at the time. She was a force to be reckoned with, worked hard, and inspired other people to step up. Her spirit, communication skills, and convictions made other people see her as a leader. Many people remained under the impression that she had founded or co-founded Microcosm.

My own managerial skills were still sadly underdeveloped, or as Heather put it "You have terrible communication, you withhold information, you straight-up lie and you are a horrible manager because of these things." I could agree with about half of that. I knew that I was a terrible communicator and a horrible manager. Sometimes I withheld information to protect someone from getting involved in an unpleasant situation, like a poor experience that a customer or an author had with us, but most of the time I had a really hard time understanding what information was relevant to share. It was largely based on perspective, I guess, but it was clear that my interpersonal skills still left a lot to be desired. I had exerted myself to establish systems rather than creating a healthy interpersonal workplace dynamic.

Even at 28 years old I remained underdeveloped emotionally, which is typical for adults with undiagnosed Asperger's: You know that you don't fit in anywhere but you don't know why or how to fix it. The result was that I often hurt other people's feelings. I was generally so absorbed in what I was doing and so annoyed to be interrupted that I wouldn't have noticed if our building was on fire. Of course, this did not improve my skills as a manager, especially when I tried to have meetings with other staff to answer their questions while continuing to do my work and stare at my own computer screen. Staff members began requesting that I not multitask while we had a conversation or meeting. Others told me that I was impossible to talk to because they never knew precisely the right questions to ask to get the information that they wanted. When they would complain about this to me, I focused so singularly on the specific examples that they gave that I could not see the big picture of how this was such a frustrating dynamic for them.

To help with the loss of Heather, we hired two interns to take on paid positions. The more promising of the two, Juliette, was so hard-working and committed to Microcosm that I worried that she might be a COINTELPRO spy sent to undermine and destabilize us. Even when she was a volunteer she showed up from nine to five Monday through Friday and was constantly engaged in asking questions and learning about how things worked. Once it became clear that she was not a plant from the FBI, Juliette and I sat down, I told her how much I appreciated how hard that she worked, and we made an agreement that she would not quit and we would not fire her—even though that wasn't really something that I could promise.

Even though I wasn't sure whether or not I wanted to have a proper relationship, Stefanie and I would have nightly phone conversations. She would tell me about the funny things that happened to her each day in the kitchen where she worked and I would express whatever I was excited about. Lately and without me noticing, I had made a bit too much of a habit of telling her how excited I was about Juliette's enthusiasm at Microcosm. After a week of this, Stefanie exploded at me and told me that she'd rather not hear about how I'm excited about another woman at work when she is half way across the country. I took her point and learned from it but we kept running into conflict. I had no attraction or romantic feelings for Juliette, who was married and younger than I was but it became impossible to convince Stefanie that they weren't competing for me.

On Thanksgiving, Stefanie called me at work, freaking out that she didn't have any money or food and felt bad attending a potluck empty-handed but was afraid of what she might do if she stayed home alone. She was having a real meltdown but called me at work while I was in the middle of something, which I had explicitly asked her not to do. I told her to make peace and show up at the party anyway. When she continued to stammer on about her feelings that I did not understand, ignoring my advice, I hung up on her. She called me right back, screaming. She explained that she just wanted me to listen and say encouraging words, not to give advice. This was a new revelation to me and I paused to make a note: "Learn how to be a better friend." This annoyed her too—she felt like I was making fun of the situation.

After a few months of similar arguments, I was fed up. But more than that, I was feeling the weight of my failed marriage and wanted to do everything that I could to make this new relationship work. I didn't want to be alone forever or always at odds in my personal life so I made a promise to myself that I would learn how to communicate with others. This resolution slowly turned into a new to-do list with advice like "Listen, don't give feedback until requested" and "Acknowledge what people are saying. Don't jump to conclusions."

To preserve institutional memories at Microcosm, some of the veteran staff members began writing a manual on how Microcosm functions. It contained information regarding accounts, policies, passwords, procedures, and sample communications for handling various situations. Many excerpts were entertainingly unique to Microcosm: A rude sample email to a customer who was complaining about import taxes, involved instructions for advising authors on matters in ways that were against Microcosm's interest, dueling arguments within the text about the proper way to issue credit to a customer, the most forgiving tardiness policy you've seen in any workplace, six paragraphs on how decisions are made, evaluation forms about how committed each person was to the collective process, and elaborate mathematical formulas that tell a staff person how to determine their pay after tabling at an event.

Heather had moved in with her boyfriend but when I came home from touring, I found that she had told one her friends that they could live in my room. Suspiciously, Heather was also at the house, brandishing a tape measure. When she saw me come home, she tried to ask me to leave by saying, "I don't feel comfortable around you." This seemed very strange to me. I suggested that if she didn't feel comfortable around me, it might make sense not to come to my house. She yelled at me and left.

While Microcosm continued to send out dozens of orders and add a handful of new titles every day, my health continued to decline. I was often short of breath and weak, huffing and puffing on a short walk with pain in my gut and my legs. I had recently talked to some friends I had grown up with who ended up developing cancer before they were 30. The thought terrified me. I wanted to live and I had so much that I wanted to accomplish. I doubled up on my visits to the doctor. Answers weren't forthcoming, but one doctor suggested that stress was likely a factor and that I probably shouldn't continue living in the same house that I had moved into with my ex.

It was sound advice. Plus our house had repeatedly been robbed that Fall. When I came home from work to learn that my video camera and computer had been stolen, Heather's sister could understand that I was distraught and asked, "How do I comfort you?" I suggested a hug and she obliged. We'd known each other for six years but when she stepped away, she said, "I never understand how you are feeling or what would make you feel better."

A few days later, across town, the lock was cut and my bike was stolen. Having my space violated in this way messed with my head. It made me paranoid all the time, it made me feel uncomfortable in my own home, and it made me worry about what would happen next. I started asking around about a place to live. One friend connected me with one of the original members of Citybikes Worker Co-operative, who had literally written the book on how to operate a self-managed business. She lived in a tree house, and allowed me to stay there for free while she was in New York City for six months.

Before I could move out, I went back to my old house after a long day at work and found that Heather had taken a number of my things, claiming that she appreciated them more than I did. Despite putting a lock on the door to my room after the experience of being robbed, I felt increasingly unstable and insecure. Her sister told me that Heather had appeared angrier than she'd ever seen her. Heather demanded to be let into my room and began taking things. She later ran into my stolen bike on the street and sent me a photo of it but wouldn't lock it up or tell me where she had seen it or the circumstances. She bought a T-shirt of my favorite band for me as a present and then told me that she was still deciding if she wanted to give to me because she had decided that I was "poorly behaved."

One day Heather asked if I would accompany her to a student counselor. It seemed important to her, so I agreed. She picked me up in a rental car. When we arrived, the reason for my presence was still pretty unclear, so I asked. The counselor told me that "Heather and I have been talking through her feelings for a few months and we have some questions that you might be able to help with." That didn't make any sense to me but also felt obvious and condescending, as it was all implied by the scenario. I didn't push the matter and Heather again asked me the same question that she'd asked me half a dozen times, "Did you tell me that [my ex] was not welcome at Microcosm?" I again calmly explained, "While in hindsight you clearly understood that from what I said, I didn't actually say that. I said he was not allowed to hang around the office all day alone with you because I didn't think that you would get any work done."

Heather scowled and made a face that even I could recognize as disgust. The counselor took me back to the waiting room where it dawned on me: Did Heather really bring me here because she still thinks that I'm lying about this and that I would see her student therapist as the sort of authority figure that I couldn't lie in front of?

When they finished she drove me back into town in silence.

Two years after we had separated Heather finally agreed to get divorced. We used the last of the money that we had received for our wedding to hire a mediator to negotiate the terms of how we'd split our property. The mediator wasn't terribly patient or helpful. When Heather would have outbursts or insult me, he would tell her to resolve her feelings elsewhere and that he couldn't help with that.

After numerous sessions that went nowhere, she sent me an ultimatum: She wanted to either keep the house or Microcosm.

We had agreed that we wouldn't hire lawyers to advocate for us but I later found out that she had done so in secret and was being coached on how to handle the negotiation. It turned out that Heather's visit to the house had been to measure the rooms in order to figure out its relative worth on the real-estate market. A month later, she would tell me that she didn't want the house; she wanted to take it away from me. While it was obviously meant to be callous, I was puzzled. Why would she talk to me this way? Later still, I would learn that our marriage had been so brief that I could have kept everything I went into it with by simply filing for divorce with the court. But I didn't realize that at the time, and, as usual, felt entirely at her mercy.

So I capitulated. I didn't need to think about the decision. I had tried to love Heather but it was Microcosm that loved me back every day.

Portland, Maine on tour in 2006. Photos by Dave Roche

SOLITUDE AT LAST

I had always been happiest having exactly the same thing for breakfast every day. If that wasn't possible, I would be upset all day long. Bonus points if it was from the same kitchen and produced in the same predictable manner. So living alone in a tree house was truly ideal. I could create exactly the environment that I wanted. No one was there to move things from exactly where I had intentionally left them to "where they belonged" and no one criticized rituals I had, like sorting all of my medications into caps in neat rows that would count down the days until the next time I left town. After socializing, I could retreat exhausted into my solitary confines and recuperate, excited to eat the exact same breakfast the following morning alone while reading my book.

As the divorce was finalizing I realized that I was afraid of Heather in the same way that I was afraid of my mother. The way that she had treated me over the last six years had taken an extreme toll on my confidence and on my ability to go out in public without apprehension. I was feeling increasingly estranged from the city I lived in. Near our office in Liberty Hall there was a plan to build new condos that would literally cast a shadow over a grade school where most of the students were Black. The way development was happening in Portland offended me on every level. Worse, Microcosm was growing in such a way that we needed to move into a larger office and warehouse, at the same time that real-estate prices were climbing out of control. We had been looking at places that we could move into and each place that I called was snatched up within 24 hours, sometimes sight unseen. Our neighborhood that was so unknown five years before that I had to argue with people to convince them that there really was a "North" quadrant in Portland was now being overrun by people from the suburbs. I was beginning to understand the effects of hyper-development and gentrification.

The only places that we could find available were up on the Washington State border in an industrial neighborhood or way out east near the airport—some of the only parts of Portland where you really need a car in order not to defy death on a daily basis. None of our staff had cars. I was at a loss about how to move forward. I found someone who would lend us money to purchase a building but he had two conditions: He wanted to remain anonymous and he wanted it to be a personal agreement with me rather than with the collective. The collective did not agree to either of these terms. Things went south from there.

If we were a more traditional publisher most of our sales and warehousing would have been handled by our trade distributor. But our success had been based on building relationships with businesses that didn't typically sell books and often *only* sold Microcosm books. This had created an important financial independence but it also meant that we had to warehouse our entire inventory. Most publishers who went bankrupt did so because of withholdings on payments or financial trouble happening at their distributor. That monthly check from their distributor was relied upon to pay all of their bills. I had heard *that* story so many times that I doubled down: Microcosm would focus our strategy so that we would maintain direct relationships with anyone who would work with us directly. This meant we could collect small checks every day of the month for stability's sake. Sure, it was more work and we relied upon each staff person to diligently do their job, but it was much more reliable. We were paid faster. We could pay our authors better and faster.

I had a natural advantage as well: I could complete complex algebraic calculations in my head in split seconds. So I could look at our printing unit cost for a book and extrapolate from that how many we'd expect to sell, at what discounts we'd expect to sell them, what our other costs would be, and how much money that would yield to calculate how much money we could spend on the project and what the price needed to be. This was so second nature to me that it confused and frustrated me when other people couldn't do it. I would memorize how many copies of each book we had sold to date and from there could determine which books that made money had paid for which other books that were still struggling to break even. This level of mathematical awareness allowed me to know exactly what we could afford. And I was not seeing properties that we could afford.

At the same time the lease for our building had shifted from Liberty Hall to a labor union that was not as invested in creating a comfortable place for Microcosm to thrive. After a few months, things that we shared in the common areas of the building began disappearing and when they didn't pay the bill for the Internet and we were unable to work for days without it, they told us that there would be no compensation. As the situation was becoming untenable for Microcosm, Juliette was sweet enough to come with me to a meeting with the leaseholders. They were rude and insulting to us, but to be fair I referred to their office manager as disorganized and inept. I thought these were factual statements and didn't intend them to come across as insults. When I explained that their actions had made it impossible for us to work, they pointed to our sublease, which said that we would pay for Internet but did not say that they would compensate us for Internet failure. In a world of mutual support, this attitude of antagonism was completely foreign and capitalist to me. I tried to explain how tenuous our financial situation was and they called us a business. When I explained that we didn't make money by design of our structure and mission, they said it was because we were "bad at capitalism." It became clear that our days in the building were numbered.

We succeeded in signing an agreement for a spot in a commercial condo in a long-abandoned call-center building. It would take a few years to build but we'd pay only 1% interest. But, as the excitement wore off, the situation started to seem less rosy. Our costs there kept going up while more and more rules were imposed on us. For example: We had to report graffiti that we saw to the police, lock our dumpsters, and pay for a janitor to clean up after us. Our maintenance fees on the building were as expensive as our mortgage. It would cost about seven times what we were currently paying, the neighborhood wasn't great and had no foot traffic, and I wasn't sure that we could afford it, especially while I was losing my financial stability in the divorce. I backed out.

Downtrodden, I gave honest consideration to what it would mean to move the mail order and warehousing to Bloomington while still having staff and a store in Portland. I investigated. In Bloomington we could have a nice location for about half of the price and three or four times as much space. The idea was scary, and if the collective couldn't agree on terms to take out a loan I had a hard time agreeing on moving part of the operation out of state. Nonetheless, I sat down with each collective member individually and explained the situation to them.[10] For what we needed in the long term we were being priced out of the inner city of Portland. Everyone understood and no one tried to raise objections. In many ways, Microcosm had outgrown our office and the writing was on the wall about Portland's real-estate market. Several staff members suggested that it would be appropriate to give the management of Microcosm back to me, but that's not what I wanted at that time. I was more interested in keeping the finances under control. The plan was that employees could keep their jobs even if that meant some of their duties would change. My plan for my own life was to go back and forth between Portland and Bloomington every three months. This seemed reasonable and logical to me.

I loved Portland dearly, but it was already clear then what direction things were headed: in favor of developers and people with deep pockets. In March of 2007, I was pictured on the front page of the daily newspaper, *The Oregonian,* with the headline "Rents soar. Creatives edged out. Who will keep

---

10 This is considered poor form in a collective situation, as it "stacks the deck" when you make the decision later in a meeting. The prior discussion influences how people feel about a choice and reduces discussion about the pros and cons. Nonetheless, I felt desperate enough that the situation seemed to warrant this behavior.

Portland Weird?" The article implied that I single-handedly kept Portland weird and detailed the Portland that was to come: Increased rents were pushing out the interesting and creative operations that had made Portland so attractive in the first place. The reporter talked to me for over ten hours while working on the article. That same week, between phone calls, we packed up the entire office and warehouse into a truck and moved it to Bloomington. While some people scoffed at my analysis and predictions at the time, almost nine years later, a near-identical cover story appeared in The *Williamette Week* as rents and a lack of vacancies had further spiraled out of control.

Some of the staff members felt a loyalty to Heather and her involvement with Microcosm and wanted to remember her contributions, as they felt that the organization hadn't properly honored her departure or done any management work around the transition. I was honestly too frustrated by the way that Heather was treating me at the time to find this conversation helpful, but in hindsight they were right. While Microcosm credited Heather's departure and contributions in our newsletter and on the "about" page of our website, we didn't acknowledge her departure in a way that the staff or public were able to process this information and move past it. The situation continued to leave quite a few people inside and outside of Microcosm feeling like there was a gaping wound without so much as a band aid on it. I could have been more respectful about the situation but Microcosm had so many problems already.

Two staff members quit on the day before the move. They saw this as an end of era, which it was.

Me in the Liberty Hall basement offices, 2007

WHERE WE STARTED TO CRUMBLE

We made very few management changes when we opened the location in Bloomington. One problem that Microcosm had in Portland was that most of the staff wanted to work part time, so in Bloomington, new hires were required to work full time. This allowed us to have a full-time staff of four in that office rather than eight part-time people. The wages that we paid were also much more competitive in Bloomington than they were in Portland.

Stefanie began telling everyone who would listen that the reason Microcosm had moved to Bloomington was because of our relationship. She became upset that this was not the story I was telling. It wasn't my truth but I understood that this hurt her. During the weeks leading up to the move, we had jointly purchased a bottle of shampoo to share and I could track our relationship breaking down faster than the bottle was emptying.

While Stefanie was probably more qualified than the other people that Microcosm had hired and had artistic and social skills that few others possessed, I didn't want to work together. She continued to bring up the issue, and I explained my hesitations about hiring her and the situation that I had just gotten out of. She responded that, given the choice, she'd rather work at Microcosm than date me. I wasn't giving her an option and the barb of rejection stung deep. Was I really only desirable as an access to Microcosm? Slowly and reluctantly I agreed that she could work at Microcosm. She would put constant pressure on me for what she wanted until I would relent. I couldn't seem to stand firm behind my boundaries and form a backbone. I feared rejection and a repeat of my previous relationship.

With Microcosm's help, Stefanie had purchased and lived in a former rooming house. We both had put a tremendous amount of effort into restoring its condition, refinishing the floors, and painting the place for Microcosm to move in as well. Part of the brilliance of the arrangement was the barn-style double doors that opened onto the street so that we could roll pallets straight into the basement "warehouse." Stefanie and I lived upstairs together, and Microcosm operated on the bottom two floors. At 1,716 square feet it was the largest workspace that Microcosm had ever had. But the home/work boundary was tricky to navigate at the volume we were now operating at, especially as fans started to visit unannounced on the weekends. I had concerns about immediately enmeshing our lives and finances together. I was making many choices that I was immediately regretting. I wasn't taking the time to step back, set boundaries, and make the right choices for myself.

The new people were highly motivated, showed up on time every day, worked hard from nine to five, and were immediately and clearly invested in Microcosm's future. At the same time, the three staff members who remained in Portland started to feel left out of conversations, like they were less important, and began to have bipolar morale barometers. When they had successes or good things were happening to us, they were on top of the world with enthusiasm. When we had bad news or something fell through, I heard only doom and gloom about the future of Microcosm. So much of business came down to feelings. It irritated me immensely. We were trying very hard not to behave as a business. And dealing with feelings was my achilles heel. Many of our staff got involved in order to be a part of something, to have their opinions valued, and to create something that could be held up as a model of both product and process. While we were succeeding at the former, we were failing at the latter.

Heather continued to assert herself into Microcosm. She claimed in an email to the entire staff and then on her blog that I was violating agreements that I couldn't find anywhere in our divorce settlement or remember agreeing to. She wrote another longer, more in-depth zine about our relationship. In this zine, the conflict and drama climaxed as I spilled ice cream on our couch and then instead of cleaning it up I complained that she had picked out the couch cover without talking about it with me first. She detailed how a friend of mine had sexually harassed her when she offered to fix his bike. Heather submitted the zine to Microcosm. After the staff spent time reading, reviewing, discussing, and approving it, Heather said that she would have to think about it. It was clear that she still wanted to be a part of the process. She complained that her contributions and influence were not being acknowledged. This was really hard on the staff, especially the new people, because they didn't know her. Juliette pointed out that she was listed on the "about" page of our website and that we had sent a newsletter to 8,000 customers acknowledging Heather's departure and contributions. Ironically, the newsletter actually overstated Heather's tenure, saying that she had worked at Microcosm for eight years, when in reality she was only involved for three years working full time and three more years when she had only peripheral involvement, maybe one hour a week at most. Heather would introduce a subject without explaining the backstory, and the staff would have to ask questions until they could understand what she was talking about while she got increasingly upset. Then they would be dragged into a conversation with her about the conversation that had just upset her.

After the move, Microcosm stopped offering to design and produce custom buttons and stickers as a service for our customers. This service had little to do with the publishing direction that we were increasingly headed in and it meant that we would not compete with Heather's new button company. One button customer whom we referred to Heather told us that she lived down the street from Heather but would rather work with us. At a loss about how to respond to that, we fulfilled her order. The next day Heather emailed me, angrily assuming that we had done the work as a personal slight against her.

Microcosm owned the rights and had it in writing that we would sell the last 500 copies of Heather's book. But Heather got in touch to say that she no longer agreed with this arrangement and wanted us to return the remaining books to her. The staff discussed it and agreed to uphold the existing arrangement. We explained this to Heather and she responded with an angry screed detailing a laundry list of things that she was still upset about from our relationship.

Zine World published an article called "Microschism," full of inaccuracies about Heather's departure and the staff's actions. When we got in touch to talk about it, the editor explained that she did not have time to give the piece the attention that it deserved but felt morally obligated to include something about it in the magazine. Strangers began contacting Microcosm about rumors that they had heard that we used people's work without permission and that we had agreed to stop using our logo but hadn't. Neither was true but it was further proof of the need to create a united front, with both healthy emotional dynamics within the organization and clear communication with the public. I had thought that by making decisions transparent and respecting others internally that these problems would go away. After several discussions about it, we decided to try not to publicly engage with Heather as each time would only leave her more upset than she was already.

Two years after I'd first seen her at City Hall in Portland, Elly Blue called our office in Bloomington to order a few hundred stickers for the Towards Carfree Cities conference that she was organizing. I tried to keep her on the phone for a few minutes but again she hung up in a hurry. "Very Type-A," I thought. Still, it was a bright spot in the dark and a connection to home.

Within my first few months in Bloomington, perhaps as a result of all of the stress, my health took a major downward spike. I would fall asleep on the couch by 6 PM after work every day. I had constant digestive pains and heartburn. I would have a migraine once per week that would leave me splayed out on the couch all day until the sun went down. Living in Bloomington was so easy that I stopped trying to approach complex problems. It was like I was limiting my thinking to a fifth-grade vocabulary. The city and the punk scene there were focused on throwing a collective wrench in the works of the establishment and complaining about injustice. Actually engaging power structures and creating social change just seems so difficult when life flows so easily. I stopped challenging myself and my personal development and grew cozy.

After seven years of sobriety, I started to drink again. I was drinking regularly within a month after I arrived in town. When drunk, I would turn into a different person. When someone that I'd met during my Boxcar internship handed me photos to look at, I accidentally dropped them in some beer that I'd spilled. When he complained, I said "Well, you just handed photos to a drunk!

What did you expect?" Very basic activities like getting dinner, taking a shower, or locking up my bike felt like oppressive inconveniences. I felt tired all day long every day. My excitement about Bloomington and this new chapter of my life quickly turned into malaise.

I sought out a new doctor and found Dr. Montague, a British gentleman who patronized Boxcar Books regularly. He had a different kind of background from the dozens of doctors who had told me that my problems were in my head or solely stress-related. He spent most of the time during our appointments asking me questions and wrote things down for hours. He created an elaborate set of charts and began recording my diet. He discovered that my vegan diet had led me to mostly eating wheat, protein bars, soy, and sugar. He explained that even a Clif Bar had too many carbohydrates in it for me to manage, not to mention the fact that Stefanie and I liked to eat a whole pizza or two every night. He did some tests and discovered that I had an extreme case of hypoglycemia. The cause is still unknown. "Hypoglycemia" means that the body can't successfully manage its own blood sugar and as a result levels are often too low. When blood sugar is too low, he explained, the body begins shutting off non-vital functions in order to stay alive. This is why people feel groggy before they eat breakfast. Conversely, digestion was also difficult on my body and consumed a lot of energy during the process to turn food into energy. As a result, I was constantly tired. I either had low blood sugar caused from not eating for a while or all of my blood sugar was being used to digest my food. I couldn't win. He discovered in our testing that I would have stable blood-sugar readings that would suddenly drop without a seeming cause or warning. He surmised that I was probably born predisposed to having trouble managing my blood sugar and it was worsened by my stress and eating habits.

By mid-2007, after 30 years of poor eating habits, I started to regularly pass out from having low blood sugar. Being conscious or aware was a non-vital function and when my glucose got low enough I couldn't remain conscious. I learned that my migraines were the result of the fact that my heart was flooding my brain with too much blood in an effort to supply enough blood sugar to my brain. The swollen blood vessels would pinch my nerves and cause muscle cramping and migraines.

This was the first diagnosis that completely made sense to me. Dr. Montague further concluded that the months that my previous doctor had left me on antibiotics had probably destroyed a lot of the healthy digestive flora in my gut and allowed it to be replaced by infections. He prescribed a new collection of pills that I put on display in caps on my desk, lined up in rows counting down to my next trip.

Juliette continued her commitment to Microcosm, but her husband lost his job that supported her and she told me that she was sinking into depression. The physical distance between us seemed to also hurt her morale. She said that it was hard for her to feel like part of a team when she was mostly working in isolation. She came out to visit the location in Bloomington but tensions between her and Stefanie flared. I appreciated the brains, commitment, and hard work of both of them, but the tension became centered around the way that I doled out praise. Perhaps because I often brought up the precarious financial situation at Microcosm, there was often a feeling that no one could never be doing enough. I worked hard to ensure that I meant the things that I said and that I was sharing information in ways that were relevant, understandable, and helpful for people to use to make decisions. But in the span of a month, without realizing it, I had apparently told both Stefanie and Juliette individually that each was the "most" interested staffer that we'd ever had in wanting to learn the nuts and bolts of the publishing process, the "best" at her job, and the "hardest-working" person that we'd ever had on staff. Of course, they discussed the fact that I delivered the same superlatives to each of them. They both concluded that it was I who was trying to drive a wedge between them. I apologized and explained my mistake but there was difficulty moving forward as I kept committing blunders. When Stefanie accidentally threw away a check, I lost my patience and yelled at her about it. Money had grown quite tight and my stress was at its peak. Even though I was no longer the manager of the company and on paper we were all equals, people explained that they still looked to me as a father figure and my volatile moods and shifting levels of confidence really hurt morale and made the careless things that I said sting and feel personal.

I felt isolated in a new city and was usually homebound by my new, weakened condition. Most of the friends I had in Bloomington had moved away in the months before I arrived and others didn't get along with Stefanie and thus I didn't see them. My social anxiety worsened. The city wasn't the same as it had been in years prior and there was a certain gloom there that I hadn't noticed on previous visits: frequent tornado sirens and a lack of streetlights; and it was in the poorest county in the state at that time. I became increasingly socially isolated, partially because I was older than most of my peers and they didn't understand that my health problems were real, crippling, and worsening, and that they often dictated my social schedule.

I tried to make new friends. But in Bloomington, the success that I had created with Microcosm brought a lot of small-town gossip and expectations about what I would be like. Some people were intimidated by me in various ways, or they were trying to knock an assumed chip off my shoulder. I had always lived in big, urban areas and so it was a huge transition to adjust to this life. If I ran into someone that I knew on the street and didn't stop to make smalltalk and share gossip, they would throw a fit, even if we didn't get along in the first place.

I had never felt this isolated or lonely in my life. A certain part of me felt like it was a suitable punishment for myself for screwing up my relationship with Heather but the wiser part of me usually reminded me that it was Heather who believed that punitive measures were appropriate ways of reconciling hurt. I was excited to get back to Portland but my health and the responsibilities in Bloomington prevented it. I didn't make it back to Portland for over a year.

DEATH COMES LIKE A THIEF IN THE NIGHT

In April of 2007, when I was 29, another, younger man named Joe Biel went AWOL and shot up his military base before taking his own life, after years of living with PTSD. I found myself in some morbid moments reading weird news stories about the event.

By that summer I was receiving a phone call each week about the death of other old friends. I began to lose count and dreaded answering the phone. Some of them had chronic health problems and it was expected. Some were suicides and it was crushing. Some were people I had felt close to even if we hadn't talked in a year or two. Others were completely shocking and devastating. My friend Dan, the one who I had become close with on my first-ever trip to the West Coast, committed suicide after a lifelong battle with clinical depression. He was still in his twenties and had begun dating my friend Robyn. Things had seemed to be turning around for him.

The week after hearing about Dan, I got the phone call that my dad was not expected to live for more than 24 hours. I canceled my trip to the Portland Zine Symposium and rented a car. Stefanie and I drove to Cleveland and stayed with Drew. I still hadn't worked through problems from my childhood or my feelings about the father that I barely knew. I hadn't been able to have a conversation with him for over twenty years, not out of lack of interest or empathy but because both his brain and vocal cords were fried. I continued to manage the situation, even my own feelings, with some clinical distance. I had long ago made peace with the situation of my upbringing and had intentionally made the decision to leave distance between my family and myself. I didn't feel understood or respected. They didn't even know what I did for a living, but not because I hadn't explained it to them dozens of times. I had moved on.

I didn't understand how much my mom had influenced my perceptions until I was standing at my dad's funeral, greeting my remaining childhood friends. Seeing the array of photos artfully hung in the funeral home, I learned that my dad had been in the military, stationed in Alaska after World War II. I remembered that he had been funny. My only living memory of him before what we referred to as "the accident" was him driving me back from some otherwise boring errand in his tiny hatchback and teaching me how to hum along to the Pink Panther song on the radio. Even though he was 49 when I was born, he knew how to relate to me as a child. He effectively wasn't part of my life for most of the time that our lives overlapped, but when he was physically capable he had known exactly how to make me feel wanted and involved in what was going on.

I realized in those moments that my childhood hadn't been ruined by my dad's selfishness but rather by my mom's control and dictation over how every situation should play out. I realized that my dad had always been downright pleasant even if he was emotionally pretty cold. I realized how much I had fucked up in falling for my mom's perspective as the only one, the "real" one. My dad's choices had affected my life but my mom's framing of the situation had affected my life much more intensely and unpleasantly.

Nonetheless I stayed with my mom for a few days. The house that I had grown up in was in a horrible state. The basement was full of black mold. The dog we had adopted when I was a teenager was incontinent and couldn't walk backwards. She would get stuck behind a chair and lose control of her bowels, so all of the furniture in the house was pulled away from the walls. The carpets stank of urine, the basement smelled of wet rot, and the fridge smelled of rotting food. The composite scene looked like it was created out of schizophrenic logic. I wondered if things had been this bad when I was growing up and I just didn't notice because I didn't have anything to compare it to. It was the first time in my life that I realized how alone my mom really was.

My mom tried to feed us but the food wasn't appetizing. No one else would come over. My sister stayed away because my mom had become so morbid and my sister's husband had felt uncomfortable around my family. My mom's sister stayed away because she believed that my mom was in denial about the situation and would likely have a nervous breakdown at any moment. My mom's brother didn't seem to care much about anyone but himself or at least how to express it if he did, though he showed his face at the funeral. The social fabric that I had been raised in began to unravel. The violence, the deceits, and the things that were withheld from me had always caused so much frustration and anger in me. But it wasn't directing me anywhere good and I was always blaming the wrong people. It just left me blathering, unhappy and alone, even when surrounded by other people.

Even though we'd slowly grown apart over almost ten years, my friends still showed up to my dad's funeral to support me. Some of them had been out of my life longer than they'd been in it and others didn't know that I'd long ago moved to Portland and thought that we just never ran into each other. After not seeing each other for ten years, they didn't take it personally and told me to stop by when I was in the neighborhood. Of course many of them understood what I was going through because they had gone through it their whole lives too. It's why we were close. My dad taught me in his final lesson in post: Despite all of the hardship, we still have each other.

I left that night and completed the eight-hour drive in six hours. I hypermiled: I drove the whole way using techniques designed to put less strain on the engine and save fuel, to stimulate the mathematical part of my brain. By the time I got home, I realized that I had forgiven my mom. Not because I owed it to anyone—I did it for myself, so I wouldn't be carrying around that baggage and that anger anymore. This didn't mean I planned to let her become a part of my life. But it meant that I would no longer let her have control over my life.

I sent Heather her final royalty check. Without thinking, I wrote a one line note with it that simply said "I forgave my mother." When I thought about it later, I realized I'd included it because she was one of a handful of people who knew about the lifelong dynamic between my mother and me. I thought she would like to know and would see it as part of my healing. But Heather read the note as a demand that she should forgive me. She was livid.

I hadn't realized that Heather's opinion of me had worsened quite a bit over the year since we'd last seen each other. She had been seeing the student therapist who had suggested that my behavior in our relationship might have been emotionally abusive. Heather latched onto this and published a third and more public zine about our relationship, badmouthing both me and Microcosm. When I told her in a letter that her actions could affect a lot more people than just me, she responded, "You know I could sink this ship by telling the truth... Microcosm will never be the same now that you are the sole tyrant."

Heather told me that it was my fault that she had to write about Microcosm. In the same message, she asked me to look some things up for her and send over some files. She told me that I was not allowed to talk about our relationship as she did not believe that I could be trusted to tell the truth and that if anyone asked I should direct them to talk to her about it.

Later that month an anxious Juliette was tabling for Microcosm at a book fair in New York City. Heather was tabling her own work at the same event. At the end of the day, Heather approached Juliette unexpectedly and shouted "Fuck you!" in close proximity to her face.

I told Heather that I wanted to make amends, but she told me that she would never forgive me.

She made a list of twenty demands. Some items on the list were places where I should not set foot lest we run into each other. Others were demands that I tell people whom she had made publishing agreements with to stop using her work. Several items dictated aspects of how Microcosm was operated. One demanded that I check myself into feminist counseling and the next asked for me to show demonstrable change in my behavior... without engaging Heather.

I immediately implemented what I could and did my best to explain the ones that were convoluted or impossible. I hoped that I could finally put this, too, behind me.

Our Bloomington office in 2007

Selling books at Mauled by Tigers Fest, Chicago, 2007

KAMCHATKA

Microcosm continued on its upward trajectory with some tremendously successful years. We had long accomplished all of my original visions and goals. Despite how much I pushed the staff to come up with new goals to work towards, people tended to be stuck thinking in the short term or feeling so successful that they couldn't think of how to ask for more.

One request was for a healthier internal workplace dynamic, but each time it came up and was discussed I got lost in the trees. I couldn't see the forest—just unrelated and isolated incidents. I believed that with enough space and time, the staff would find a functional way to manage each other and I could focus on things that I was good at. Perhaps it was because this was the elephant in the room, but everyone had a hard time talking about the big picture, or at least during strategy meetings. To rectify the geographic divide between the two offices, we started to have meetings via Skype and converted all of our internal documents onto Google Drive so all personnel could share and access an up-to-the-minute version of the same spreadsheet or document no matter where they worked or even if they were on tour.

Our short-term plans were going remarkably well also. Gradually, as the months went by, the staff came up with an answer for what their goals were: They wanted to publish more books, increase the design and editorial quality, and be proud of everything that we did. Someone in the office would find a submission they really liked or a comic book that hadn't been anthologized and hold it up and ask "Why don't we publish this book?" Everyone present would respond with "Yeah!" and they'd get in touch with the author minutes later. It was commendable but more than that it was nice to see other people taking initiative when, two years prior, I had trouble convincing our staff to even read our books.

We went from publishing 6 books in 2006 to publishing 24 books in 2007 and 29 books in 2008. This increase took its toll on our capacity and confused our fans, some of whom felt that we were compromising quality or thematics. While it used to be a major event with ceremony for Microcosm to publish a book, it was now a constant rigamarole and we were having to ask our fans to buy more. Some fans thought that it was a move to make more money, but in reality we were still scraping along and breaking even at best. Others claimed that we were trying to remove the inherent politics from our titles. But we weren't thinking about it that way—we were simply taking things as they came to us and publishing work in the author's voice without giving much direction.

We were motivated by the sheer amount of unpublished yet awesome work out there that needed a home and fit into ours.

The collective aimed higher than I ever had before, asking authors who had books with much more established publishing houses or whose books had gone out of print and needed a new home to work with us. At the same time, we doubled how many titles we were distributing through our mail order, and our overall sales doubled. It certainly helped that the collective at this time genuinely loved books and zines. Not only was the bar of quality higher but we were also actively seeking things out rather than just waiting to see what submissions came in.

Still, all was not well. No one at Microcosm had any publishing experience. While several people in Bloomington had learned bookselling at Boxcar, there is a world of difference between publishing work like developing content or back cover copy for publication and bookselling work like memorizing and reciting marketing handles to a customer. As a result, all of the books we published were awesomely unique oddball pieces. When I ran into editors from the reputable independent publisher South End Press and we were talking shop, they expressed that they needed to sell at least 3,000 copies of any book that they published. They told me that speculation about a book's sales would often cause them not to publish things that they were otherwise interested in. They were cursorily familiar with Microcosm and were surprised to hear that we had a paid staff of ten. They picked up a few of our books and I explained that we had, at that point, sold more than 3,000 of every book that we'd published, with some as high as 20,000. There did not seem to be a limit to what we could accomplish. *Making Stuff & Doing Things, Stolen Sharpie Revolution, On Subbing,* and *Hot Damn & Hell Yeah/The Dirty South* had each sold over 10,000 copies. They were in absolute disbelief and began asking me for advice. Partly it was the sales figures that were impressive, but most people were confused about how we could sell so many of the kinds of books that we developed. We broke all of the rules of covers, title, and subtitle development. Our secret was that everything we published had had a proven sales track record as a zine: We already knew that people wanted it before it went to press.

We discovered a new problem: For our first twelve years we never had book contracts. We had a simple handshake agreement based on trust and mutual respect. For most publishers the entire value of the company is in its contracts because it is the rights to certain content that create a saleable commodity. But again, we weren't thinking of ourselves as a business. Like Factory Records, the British label of the '70s that released work by Joy Division and New Order, the artists owned the work and we existed just as a middleman to bring their work to the world. This made it a greater risk each time that we paid thousands of dollars for a print run of a new book. It also set us up for bigger problems.

We had been working with an author for a few years on her third book with us when we received a phone call one day: "I was offered enough money to live on for a year to take the book to a different publisher... I still want to work together, but I want to do this."

At first I was excited. The book was scheduled to be a lead title for Soft Skull Press, a publisher that had recently been bought by an investment firm and had much greater financial means than we had. In punk-rock lore, when Green Day signed to Warner Brothers or when Nirvana signed with David Geffen, their former independent labels reaped the fruits of the resulting newfound fame in a major way. Our thinking was that if this new book became a hit, legions of new fans would discover the author's work and flock to buy her previous books—from us.

I thought that this would be our Green Day. But it didn't turn out that way. It was more like our Jawbreaker, whose major label album sold fewer copies than the previous records they had made with bedroom record labels. The new book, even with all of its marketing dollars and global distribution, sold fewer copies than any of the author's previous books. Apparently, the magic was in our development and in access to the audience that we'd built organically. The author wasn't happy with the final product either and complained that the jacket copy describing the book was inaccurate and that they had fought about the editing. Worse, they had changed the book's format from a graphic-novel memoir into an illustrated piece of prose fiction.

After the third time a similar situation played out, we caved and started using contracts as a standard practice with most of the contract protecting the rights of the artist. Just about the only thing that a contract gave us was the right to publish the book in the first place and to continue publishing it as long as we paid the royalties. I didn't like the formality of the whole matter, but it created much clearer expectations in our relationships with authors.

We also found that the longer we were around the more our authors expected from us. It was no longer an exciting success to get a book in print and into stores; they wanted certain sales goals. Authors began to feel wronged when they found out we could not sell as much as a major house. I had always felt like it was more of a personal relationship with these authors than a business one, but if they didn't feel that way they could often resent that dynamic. My inability to communicate coherently, my odd way of doings things, and my preference to engage authors as peers or friends certainly wasn't helping matters, and on several occasions this led to them feeling like I was trying to sweep their concerns under the rug.

Collective management had its quirks. Microcosm offered a health-care stipend to our staff. Our employee manual read that, in order to qualify, staffers must ask for expenses related only to healthcare. When one person spent their entire annual stipend at the grocery store at 10 PM on New Year's Eve and included a carton of cigarettes, the collective was split down the middle as to whether this was an acceptable use of organizational funds—or a violation of the health-care policy. Extensive meetings were spent redrafting the policy, as if the problem were that the language was not clear enough.

In October of 2008, our European distributor, Counter Culture UK, went bankrupt. They had a few thousand of our books in their warehouse that they hadn't paid for, worth over $10,000. Even though the books still belonged to us, they were sold at auction and the money was used to pay off the distributor's debts. Auction winners got in touch, perplexed about who the audience of the books might be and how to reach them. I explained that the books still belonged to Microcosm and they promptly stopped getting in touch. It was a huge loss for us.

A week later I opened a credit-card bill and found that we had nearly $30,000 in new charges that month. We had gotten carried away and weren't watching our expenses, and as a result we owed more money than I had ever seen. It caused me to realize that, without anyone managing the ship and paying attention to things like this before they happen, Microcosm would not last long in this world.

Disheartened, I went out and ate a whole pizza that night and felt even crummier in the morning. Somber and sobered, I spelled it out to the staff.

"We are way overspending. We need to cut back. We owe as much money to our credit card as we make in most months."

"How did that happen?" one person asked.

"Well, we published all of the books that the collective wanted to and there was no mechanism in place to put a limit on that." I explained.

I was disheartened but everyone else was energized by this problem. They proposed the most obvious solution—creating a budget—and began implementing new tasks. They discovered that we were owed almost the entire amount of our credit-card debt in overdue invoices and created the rotating task to collect on those bills each week. We made more stringent rules for what we would publish and criteria to establish whether something qualified. Realizing that their choices could undo the success of or even destroy the organization that I had built, the staff created a plan to pay me back the money that I had put in from my delivery job in the '90s: I would receive $500 a month until my entire initial investment had been repaid.

Everyone began brainstorming ways to make more money, and the first sales job was created. For the first twelve years, all of our sales that weren't the result of walking into a store and slapping a catalog on the counter had been passive. We made new books and added them to our catalog each month and waited for people to buy them. Now we switched tactics and created a phone and email list to remind stores that we existed and even asked them to buy things.

But gradually, our success increasingly became our undoing; as we did better and better each year, our fans started to feel like we didn't need their support as much as we had when we were furiously fundraising to publish our first paperbacks.

One idea that came out of these brainstorms was that we should return to our roots and go on tour with punk bands, selling our books at their shows. A few days later, I received an email from Josh, with whom I had toured in 2003, saying that he was going on tour with the popular punk band Propagandhi and asking if Microcosm wanted to come along and split a rental car.

Propagandhi's heyday had been ten years prior but they were still beloved in the punk community. We didn't have an idea of how popular they were these days but we knew that this was a great opportunity. Besides, we liked their music and their onstage politics and monologues. The tour was very different from the life of office work I'd gotten used to. Also, the audience was a lot more macho than most of my world. A drunken frat boy spilled an entire beer down the front of a shelf of books in Kansas City. I asked him to pay for the books, he threatened to fight me, and the manager kicked us both out of the club. In Kentucky a man stood at the front of the stage and unironically shouted the title of their sarcastically named second album *Less Talk, More Rock!* at them whenever the band talked between songs. "I didn't come here to see my all-time favorite band *talk*," he complained after the set. I was skeptical that he "got it," because half of the point of the band was their vocal politics.

Even so, the tour was huge for book sales, and even better for passing out catalogs and truly growing our audience, and we ended up seeking out opportunities to go on the road with more touring bands. But, while it seemed like punk tours might be the future of retail, they weren't always pleasant or easy to experience. They were often lonely endeavors. While the band members were friendly, we barely had time to say hello to each other during the rigorous schedules, so it felt like we were isolated in a room full of thousands of people. And while many fans automatically got the connection between the aesthetic & politics of punk music and our books, a lot of people were confused to see a bookstore at a punk show. During the Propaghandi tour I put together a mathematical rule: 1% of music fans at shows with over 1,000 people will buy books. Ten percent of them will ask what we are doing there or demand that we justify our presence.

At one point, Josh ran inside somewhere and asked Stefanie and I to wait in the car for him. An hour later he returned and told us that he had been meeting with Bill Ayers and Bernardine Dohrn, the two former members of The Weather Underground who had gone on to establish the most conventional success. Upset that we had been excluded from meeting people with such a fascinating past, we griped until Josh passed out some food that they had given him and admitted that he was nervous about how we would treat them.

After another week on tour it was during the show in Kentucky, at a dingy bar full of macho people we didn't relate to, that our night was redeemed when we met two young people on their own tour: Ben and Cayce were on the road with their band Mancub. It was a breath of fresh air to meet fellow DIY punks. With their pinned-on patches and animal-rights slogans, they were some of the only people that we met on that tour who seemed like peers rather than customers. There was a familiarity with them that we had been lacking, and they could clearly sense it too. They lingered at our table whenever there were lulls in the night. We talked about loving Propagandhi but not always relating to their audience.

We got back to Bloomington and celebrated the successful tour over dinner with two friends. We learned that later that night that Ben and Cayce had been killed by a truck driver who lost control and slid out on the interstate.

DIAGNOSTIC, CHECK

That fall, Microcosm was invited to Halifax for a zine fair. It was the furthest east that I'd ever been. The city was unlike anywhere else I'd ever seen, and the fair felt more like an organic community than similar events did in the U.S. I spent some time with Shawn Granton, who was also tabling there, and I told him about Bloomington. He came back with me to check it out. Shawn was unimpressed with Bloomington and that hurt me more than it should have. I have my opinions and he has his, but I was starting to lose track of what mine were.

Another Microcosm collective member had been on tour with the popular punk band Against Me! and they came through Bloomington the following week. I attended with some trepidation. Going out had always been stressful and anxiety-producing for me. Against Me! had become a divisive band. They had just signed a major label contract after a rapid ascent from their anarcho-punk roots and less than two years after writing a song that went:

We want a band that plays loud and hard every night /
That doesn't care how many people are counted at the door /
That would travel one million miles and ask for nothing more
than a plate of food and a place to rest.

They had been that band in the flesh and were great role models for other bands to be inspired by and emulate. Many of their fans were understandably confused or upset with their move to a major label. Against Me! explained that they wanted to see how far they could take their band.

I attended the show and hid behind our merch table most of the night, saying hello only to people that I knew on a relatively intimate level and fearing that people might lump Microcosm's behavior as being similar to the band's recent decisions. The move had disappointed me, but I didn't feel attached enough to want to talk about it. I definitely understood the need for evolution and pushing the envelope, but I was still more partial to their back catalog.

Midway through their set, my friend grabbed my elbow and pointed at the ceiling. There was a guy swinging from the rafters just above Microcosm's merch table. Several people were telling him that the rafters couldn't support his weight and he was about to pull down some of the light fixtures onto the dense crowd. On the back of his leg I noticed a tattoo: It was the Microcosm logo, in the same place that mine and Heather's were tattooed.

I again tried to find my place in Bloomington. I became involved with the local bike co-op and started working there in the evening, turning wrenches and helping other people fix their bikes. It was a thriving hub of social activity and I met a lot of enthusiastic and motivated people there. People were often surprised because I wasn't a student at Indiana University and that I was older than most of the staff. One night, a goth kid who couldn't have been more than twenty approached me and asked me to walk around the corner with him. I agreed, even though I was confused and a bit scared. I figured that he wanted to sell me drugs.

"I was in jail up in Michigan for a few years. I was making bad choices. I sent you a letter and asked you to send me a catalog. Instead you sent me a dozen books about being positive and empowering myself to make the life that I wanted for myself. That's why I moved here with my mom and it's why I'm here volunteering at this bike project. You turned me on to making good choices. It's why I'm clean."

"Shit, man...I mean, thanks man. I really needed to hear that right now." I said.

"Cool. Don't make a big deal about it or nothin'. I just wanted you to know."

I was floored. It was exactly the right moment to hear that. After that he started saying "hello" to me every time he saw me, and we began running into each other everywhere. It was a constant reminder that I could do good in the world. If that's what he could take from our books and it could actually turn his life around, it was exactly the dream I'd had when I was an eighteen-year-old kid cranking out zines in the small office next to my bedroom. To this day it is my greatest success.

But the more I began to create my own friendships and life in Bloomington, the more I seemed to upset Stefanie. She told me that there were aspects of my personality that she didn't like.

"Like what?" I asked.

"Well, you tend to exaggerate when you relay information." she said.

This was clear and actionable feedback on my behavior and it was easy to fix, so I immediately resolved not to exaggerate anymore. It didn't benefit me in any way that I could see, and if it was causing her to mistrust and be upset with me it had to go.

"I'm sorry. I had no idea that bothered you. I won't exaggerate anymore," I said, meaning every word.

"Well... that was easy," she said.

"Anything else I can do for you?" I asked.

"Well... you'd kind of need to change your whole personality," she said.

"I'm open to that. What specifically?"

"Ugh, just everything. I can't talk about this right now," she blurted, walking away.

Tensions flared in our relationship. I knew that I struggled to clearly communicate what I meant and still had a hard time understanding the needs of other people. I still couldn't recognize it when she desperately needed my support. This came across as disinterest or lack of caring about her or anyone but myself.

We had frequent arguments and she would quickly escalate to breaking things. It was scary, but I had experienced a similar dynamic in my childhood so it wasn't unfamiliar. Before long she would threaten to harm herself and I started routinely hiding Microcosm's entire collection of box-cutters and looking for her before she could jump off the roof of a downtown parking garage. When she got enraged, she would tear up her own art. These were the worst escalations that I had seen, and I was heartbroken and terrified. Once she threatened to harm herself and ran out the door. I was too exhausted to follow, so I made the mistake of calling 911 and reporting it as a mental-health emergency. I was just worried about her well-being and wanted to de-escalate the situation and take care of her needs. But the result was that they had to take an incident report, which felt more like damning her to a life of scrutiny and stigma than getting any kind of help.

Each time we had a fight she would eventually come home, apologize, and bring me ice cream. I told her I was sorry too and we would hug and make up, but it just kept repeating. I tried so hard to listen to what she was saying, and she was very patient in trying to explain things to me. But no matter how hard we tried we were like gunpowder and a fuse. There was only one result.

We had separate bedrooms and I had a painting that I hung in mine. It depicted an angry dad menacing a scared mom and a little boy hiding behind the stove. The boy was thinking what it would be like to turn into Batman, face his fears, and protect his mom. Of course, in my case, I imagined it with the parents' roles reversed. I would gaze at it before I fell asleep, but it wasn't the source of comfort that I imagined it would be. Instead, it reminded me of the worst and most difficult parts of my life and left them feeling unresolved. I was embarrassed for people to see it, as the meaning of this choice of decor was fairly unmistakable: I was trying to figure out how to make the pain go away.

I slowly adjusted and tried losing myself in our relationship, hoping that would make us both happy. I withdrew from socializing with my new friends and stopped spending so many nights at the bike project and playing in a band that had started to come together. I didn't know who I was, what I believed in, or how I felt about things.

My health was such that things that I had once been so good at, like remembering how to spell proper nouns, were eluding me. Because my entire skill set was based in logic, math, and statistics I was deeply embarrassed that I had failed to estimate how big Microcosm's credit-card bill would be and that I hadn't prevented the rampant spending to begin with. Microcosm was in turmoil for months.

People on my personal periphery assumed that I was somewhat wealthy after the success of Microcosm, but my personal finances were desperately struggling and I had no money in the bank. I had taken out a second mortgage in my own name on the building that was in Stefanie's name to pay for maintenance and repairs. The lifestyle that she wanted to have—going out for three meals every day and impulsively buying everything that we wanted as it was stumbled across—was more than I could afford. But after my failed relationship with Heather, I felt a duty to hang in there and do what she wanted. Keeping the relationship together was important to me, if only to prove to myself that I was not a failure in this regard. I was still deeply unhappy. But this time I was in a city where I had no close friends, and I felt trapped both geographically and socially.

Microcosm bought an old U-Haul box truck that had been converted into an RV and set up with a second fuel tank to run on waste vegetable oil. The plan was to take it on the bigger tours that we had planned. The Microcosm staff tested it out on a smaller tour in 2008. After a year off from author tours, it felt good to get back to touring as Microcosm rather than just touring with bands and piggybacking merch sales onto their draw. People were coming to see us on purpose and it reminded me that our audience was special and that we had truly built a community as well as a catalog. The people who came out to our events were much more thoughtful and engaged with the materials, and we didn't need to explain as much of the politics or motivations behind what we do. I heard a lot of inspiring talk during those ten days in the Midwest and came to believe that the Midwest was the ideal place to tour.

One night Stefanie woke me up in the middle of the night to tell me that she was unhappy with our relationship and wanted to break up. And she wanted to figure out the mechanics of how we'd divide our property and take care of the house right that minute.

I was destroyed. I *was* the problem.

While Microcosm had long been hearing murmurs complaining about our scale and capacity, we had more recently begun receiving weekly messages like these:

"As a survivor of abuse, i will not support a business led by someone who was abusive to his partner."

"Seeing as how Joe Biel is without a doubt the face of the monopolistic entity that is Microcosm (I mean, off the top of your head, could anyone name anyone else in that collective?), I find myself seething when I realize ever more how much Joe Biel capitalizes and profits from the creative output of really amazing people."

"We express our concern regarding your support of a perpetrator of abuse. The wide reach of Microcosm's distribution can be intimidating for any individual to speak out against."

I resolved to move to a desert island. I felt that, despite so much good intention and honest effort, I still did not know how to interact with other people or what information was relevant to share. Having broken up twice in a row with partners who were upset with me afterwards really made me feel like I was bringing something problematic to the dynamic.

To get some clarity and connect with my community, I took a trip by myself in the Microcosm truck to Madison Zine Fest. On the way there the right hand mirror of the truck came loose and it hung limply. Because there was no way to see out of the back of the box truck, there was no way to see what was behind me in the right lane. I was in the center lane. I knew that my choices and luck in the next few minutes could decide whether I lived or not. I was in a place in my life where I didn't particularly care what happened. It's not that I wanted to die; it's that in that frame of mind I didn't really care either way.

I thought long and hard. What did I want? Did I have more to accomplish? I could estrange myself from too much socializing and eschew dating. I did have more that I wanted to do with my life. I put on my right blinker and kept a consistent speed for a full minute, thinking that any cars in the right lane would see my stated intentions and abide by that. I gritted my teeth, closed my eyes, and started to ease into the right lane, waiting for a crash. It never came. I pulled off at the next rest stop, tightened up the mirror, and made a plan to check myself into therapy when I got home.

On the Tall Tales zine tour, Indianapolis, 2008

Getting some work done in Milwaukee on the Tall Tales Tour, 2008

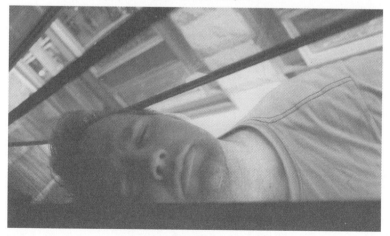

Passed out in the van on tour, 2008

SHRINKAGE

I sat in a dusty office waiting for my therapist to see me. I had picked her based on hearing a radio interview she had done and not being familiar with any other therapists in Bloomington. She seemed progressive and a little bit like a hippy but not completely without education or psychology behind her. In Heather's letter of twenty requests she said that she felt that I should see an expressly feminist counselor for therapy regarding issues of how I was treated in my childhood. Heather seemed to believe that this was the root of what continued to motivate my behavior, oddities, insistence on doing everything my way, and inability to relate to other people. Since I had no idea what the causes might be and could accept that I was different, I was open to this idea. But my initial goal in therapy was to resolve and rebuild my relationship with Stefanie.

I sat down in our first session and started blurting it all out: Two people in a row I'd dated found real problems with my personality, I was unable to relate to their emotions, and I found myself often ending up in arguments. One had gone so far as to call me emotionally abusive. I wanted to explore that and change it. The therapist looked at me.

"That's pretty intense. How about we start looking at all of the pieces of that slowly?"

"Sure," I offered.

But the more time we spent in that office together, the more I realized that she wasn't the right fit for me. I also realized how much work it would be to make the changes I needed to, and that if I was serious I would need to withdraw from my Microcosm management obligations for a while. I did extensive Internet research and began tracking down the most highly recommended books about abuse, communication, and relationships. I was intimidated but ready. I didn't even tell my closest friends about the therapy or the books I was starting to read, like Lundy Bancroft's classic *Why Does He Do That?*

After reading about case after case where someone who is publicly shamed commits suicide, I quit drinking again and I got on a train back to Portland. I needed to find a new location for our store there. Beyond that, I needed to get away from Bloomington for a while. It was time for a lot of changes.

I landed on a friend's couch in Portland and with Shawn Granton's help I found a location for the store in under two weeks. Juliette, her husband, and I built and painted shelving from the designs that I liked at Boxcar and then we priced and moved in all of the books. Elly Blue stopped by to say hello but I was distracted and aloof, as usual.

I had arrived in Portland a few weeks before the 2008 Zine Symposium. I had missed it the previous year because of my dad's funeral and was looking forward to tabling with Microcosm at the event. But Heather had re-joined the organizing body and laid it on the line: If I was allowed to attend the event, she would quit. The large group of organizers were in a difficult place because Heather had privatized a lot of institutional memory about the Zine Symposium and no one else knew the answers to certain questions or how to complete certain tasks. Numerous organizers, particularly Multnomah County Librarians, felt that they could not bar me from attending the event without an incident or some kind of neutral process beyond Heather's word and experiences. But Heather was firm and got her way in the end, though at least half a dozen other organizers quit over the issue. The remaining organizers sent me an email claiming "your presence would be a violation of our Safer Spaces Policy regarding failed mediation of abusive interpersonal relationships."

Eleanor contacted the organizers, pointing out that their behavior was directly counter to their own policy, which offered "to provide mediation at the event and not to exclude people based on interpersonal issues." I had co-written this policy and spent hours in meetings stressing the importance of having a safer space policy in the first place. But the organizers responded by simply rewriting the policy to bar me from attending.

A few weeks after we had opened the store, Heather had her attorney's courier deliver a restraining order to me there. It was intimidating but also confusing. I was no legal expert but didn't there need to be some grounds for a restraining order to be issued? Heather and I had had zero contact in almost two years. I read through the whole thing. Every piece was in place except that the order wasn't signed by a judge. Heather was trying to trick me into thinking that she had filed a restraining order against me. The organizers of the Zine Symposium referred to this fake restraining order in their follow-up message as Heather's "ongoing legal action" against me. They went on, "Individuals have contended that your presence would detrimentally infringe upon PZS endeavors to make the event one free of oppressive behavior."

When I tried to have a conversation about their stated policies and how I had violated them, they told me that they were were not mediators.

A week later I was asked to speak at the Portland Grassroots Media Camp about book distribution and I agreed. Fifteen minutes before my talk was scheduled to begin one of the event organizers found me and said that an unspecified number of people were planning on showing up to protest my presence there. I told the organizer that I wasn't comfortable with the situation. We agreed to talk about the situation later. I suspected that a big part of the problem was that during the year that I had been unable to return to Portland because of my health, many new people in the scene were hearing one-sided stories about me, a person they'd never even met. And I knew how easy it was to get caught up with gossip in the scene. I left, crying and burying my face in my pillow when I got back to where I was staying.

An old friend from New Orleans told me that he had stumbled upon a blog that Stefanie had written about me that included some pretty loaded accusations. I got in touch with Stefanie and asked her about it. She said that she had started to talk with Heather after we had broken up. "We fell into patterns of abuse," she wrote. "It was a cycle we both participated in. I wouldn't say that either of us are abusive people but that we did do abusive things to each other...

I don't want anyone to be mad at you! That wasn't my intent! It was just at a time when I needed an outlet to talk about my feelings."

Meanwhile, I asked friends in Portland who had talked openly about their therapy which counselors they would recommend. Most recommended counselors who were not seeing new clients but it became clear that Portland offered a much higher caliber of feminist therapist than Bloomington had. Eventually I found someone I felt optimistic about.

I sat down in her office and she greeted me: "So... what are you doing here exactly?"

"Oh, sorry. I thought we had an appointment... I'm Joe."

"I mean, what are you doing in Portland. Are you running from something?"

"Well, I lived here for ten years and I still intend to live here for half of the year, splitting my time between here and Bloomington."

"Okay. That makes more sense... but sounds complicated. Why go through the trouble?"

The decision had never seemed anything but logical to me.

"Well, I have close friends here. It's where I want to be but I'm not sure that I can afford to live here anymore."

Microcosm had begun doling out pay cuts as a way to balance the budget and I, along with three other staff members, had agreed to voluntary 50% pay cuts until things were stabilized. It seemed fair to me, especially since I had removed myself from management and day-to-day operations over the coming months so I could focus on getting my life in order. I would see my therapist for about four hours each week and she would take about half of my remaining paycheck in return. The rest of my time would be spent doing homework and reading.

As I continued to explain the actual roots that I had in Portland and why it felt more like home to me than where I grew up, the interviewing tone in my new therapist relaxed into conversation. We talked about my friends, how they laughed at my jokes and supported me.

When she was done feeling me out, she asked again, "So, why are you here?"

I had already thoroughly addressed this matter via email, so I wondered if this question was meant to gauge my tone and level of comfort as much as it was to see how much my voice cracked while I delivered it. I cleared my throat.

"My ex-wife accused me of... abusing her in our relationship."

"That sounds like scary stuff. Well... did you?"

"I guess I don't know. I don't know what that looks like. I don't know what that means. Not that I haven't tried to understand it. I never meant to hurt her, but she's so convinced that I did and that I meant to and that I concealed my motives that it's reached the point where I'm really not sure about much anymore." I sighed.

"Well, let's look at the things she accused you of that you do feel responsible for. Are there any parts that you feel are accurate?" she asked, trying to get me back on track.

"Well, sure. She said that I exaggerate things and withhold information. Sometimes I exaggerate things because, I guess, I worry that no one will take me seriously or understand the gravity that something holds over me if I just stick to the facts. Sometimes... well most of the time I don't know what information is relevant so I tend to babble a lot about all aspects of a situation to people and then they often have a hard time sorting out the important parts and claim later that I didn't tell them. Or sometimes I don't understand what they want to know and they just don't ask the right questions to get the information they wanted. I don't know what somebody wants when they start with questions that are really cryptic to me. I really do try but most of the time I screw it up and either say too much or too little."

As we talked through the semantics of each situation, my therapist pointed out how Heather also would withhold information at times. So, she told me, while it was good that I could admit to my mistakes and feel regret for them, the situation was complicated. She pointed out that, while Heather accused me of being manipulative, and that's generally a bad thing to do to people that we care about, it's also common practice in running a business and trying to take care of the people we love. She gave the example that, if she didn't manipulate her teenage kids every morning, they wouldn't go to school, let alone get out of bed.

I was distracted for a minute, feeling bad for her kids.

My therapist pointed out that my responses to Heather were often point-by-point semantic refutations of her statements rather than larger responses of perspective. She suggested that this was both causing me not to hear the heart of what Heather was saying while still allowing Heather to frame every situation.

I told her about how all of the newfound negativity and hate mail directed at Microcosm really ruined my day along with everyone else's. My therapist pointed out how much more negativity affects us than positive responses do: She cited a study that indicated the impact was actually ten to one, as in we need ten times as much positive feedback to balance out the negative stuff. This made sense to me. I began comparing proportions. I went home that night and received the following email:

I know this isn't what you're for, but I trust you better than anybody to send me punk-f-ckin'-rock stuff in the mail so I thought I'd give it a shot. Do you perchance know where I could find other activists in NYC? I'm fleeing a dude who likes to take me into the street and beat me, so being around some radical activists is probably going to be the best medicine for my black-and-purple heart.

To be trusted in this way by a complete stranger solely because of my knowledge of reading material was exactly what I needed in that moment and being able to help them gave me a ten-fold positive boost in my attitude.

After months of disorganized planning, I finally heard from the organizers of Portland Grassroots Media Camp, who wanted to talk about what had happened at the event. I figured that discussing the situation would be a quick path to resolution. Unfortunately, when I finally got them on the phone, they spent the time accusing me of "being manipulative" and "using people's work without permission." When I tried to respond, they called me a "liar" and shouted me down. When they were done yelling at me, they told me not to contact anyone that I believed might be responsible for spreading these rumors.

Even though they were hostile, I assumed that it was because they hadn't heard my side of the story and that if they did, it would go a long way to dispel rumors. I suggested that meeting in person for mediation might be more productive if they really wanted to talk through this stuff. I continued emailing them and trying to organize a meeting, but they were clearly not reading my emails and they continued to suggest times when I had said that I was not available.

I went home after therapy each day and did my reading and homework in secret. I tried to do no more than two hours of work on Microcosm each day before noon. I brought in Heather's letters to me, the zines she had written about me, and printouts of things she had publicly written about our relationship. My therapist examined Heather's words line by line and would ask me about anything that was a statement about me or my character. I answered as honestly as I could but felt insecure each time. I wondered how all of this reflected on me. I felt like I was on trial.

Gradually, she found patterns both in our conversations and in the things that people accused me of. She said that it was frequently mentioned that I violated people's emotional boundaries.

I asked what boundaries were.

She explained that boundaries are the rules that people live by. They dictate what someone will or won't do or allow. Boundaries allow people to set limits on how they want to be treated. My therapist thought that I might be oblivious to these communications, especially in the nonverbal and subtle ways that they are often expressed.

"That is unreal! Why wouldn't people just say when they don't want me to do something? How am I supposed to decipher this cryptic nonverbal language?!" I wondered aloud.

"For some people, it's uncomfortable to express themselves so bluntly. Some people are afraid of how others would react to that. Some people carry baggage from ways that they were treated in the past and have fears as a result of it."

I was completely perplexed. Who had created this elaborate and nonsensical system? Why hadn't anyone ever told me about it? What was the point? How did everyone else know about it but me?

On my way out the door one day, I asked what an abusive person does to get better. My therapist handed me a phone number for a batterers' group but told me hold off on calling for a while. That night, I found a seemingly relevant passage from Lundy Bancroft:

Abusive men come in every personality type, arise from good childhoods and bad ones, are macho men or gentle, "liberated" men. No psychological test can distinguish an abusive man from a respectful one. Abusiveness is not a product of a man's emotional injuries or of deficits in his skills. In reality, abuse springs from a man's early cultural training, his key male role models, and his peer influences. In other words, abuse is a problem of values, not of psychology.

This was helpful, but it didn't address my fundamental questions. How could I know whether my values were abusive? How could I know whether my early cultural training was? Bancroft seemed to hold little hope for changing these values; his focus was on getting others away from people who have them.

The next time I sat down on the familiar couch that by now I knew every detail of, my counselor took a goading tone.

"Don't you think that Heather deserved to be treated this way, for the way that she treated you?" she said in a much louder voice than usual.

Feeling a little dominated, I replied "No, I don't think so. Plenty of what happened between us was my fault."

"But she probably did get what she deserved, at least a little bit, right?"

"I'm not sure what that would accomplish." I mumbled.

"It would show her what happens when she disrespects you!" She was yelling now.

I stared at the floor. "I don't think these things have a cause-and-effect relationship."

My therapist lowered her tone. "I don't think you have an abusive personality. If you did, your tendency would be to blame Heather for what happened and refuse to take fault yourself. Someone with an abusive personality can explain within an inch of their life how the abused person provoked and deserved everything that they did and thus how it was not their fault. An abusive person has a very hard time avoiding these tendencies, but I don't see them in you. I haven't even seen subtle indications of them."

My therapist went on to explain that there was an important distinction between abusive behaviors, that most people are responsible for at some point in their life, and an abusive personality. We discussed a news story about the various kinds of abuse.[11] Abusive behaviors can be seen on any school playground, where one kid calls another fat or stupid in order to make them feel bad. An abusive person, on the other hand, is a narcissist, a socially agile and intentional manipulator of other people's emotions. They can, through systematic intention, extract everything useful from people before discarding them. They're the kind of person who knows your insecurities and your goals and knows how to trick you into doing what they want. I, on the other hand, couldn't tell you much about anyone else's emotions or insecurities. Nobody would describe me as "socially agile" at this point in my life.

I asked how it could be possible for Heather to believe so strongly that I was an emotionally abusive person.

Sometimes, my therapist replied, a person has an abusive relationship in his or her past, something triggers the fear of that in the present relationship, and the image of "abuser" is projected onto the partner. Without some major insight, it leads to a breakup. Especially if the first experience was with a parent, the person who suffered the abuse has to do a lot of work in order to stop recreating those dynamics in other relationships.

"From the sounds of how you describe it, your communication could be so fractured that you are both taking very different things from the same conversation."

I asked my therapist if she could write me a note saying that she found me not to have an abusive personality. She thought about it for a minute and then asked rhetorically, "Do you really think that would make anyone feel better?"

11 Eleanor Beardsley, "France Moves To Outlaw Mental Abuse In Marriages," *All Things Considered, January 8, 2010, http://n.pr/1Gjbyqg*

Still, as I left my appointment that day, I felt like there was hope for me. I was ecstatic and began calling my closest friends and delivering the news.

"I just got out of therapy and my therapist says that I'm not abusive!" I exclaimed into the phone.

"That's awesome! I changed my own tire on my car when I got a flat today!" my friend said with equal enthusiasm.

"Ummm, that's not really the same thing. Congrats on your achievement, but the life implications are a bit greater with my news," I muttered and hung up.

The next friend I called at least said, "Congrats, man! I'm not sure that I totally understand but that sounds like great news!"

That's about where I was, too. The implications were much greater than I could yet realize.

Two days later I returned to the familiar couch and asked, "Well, if I'm not some kind of crazy narcissist, then what is it? What do we do next?"

She reminded me that, in virtually every complaint about my personality, the underlying factor was that I had not noticed or appropriately responded to a boundary, a limit that promotes integrity, that someone had tried to set. We spent weeks going over and over these incidents.

Then things got personal: My therapist asked me if I could afford to pay her more per hour. I was already paying her half of my income so I responded immediately that I could not. She asked me to think about it and I explained that more thought wouldn't be helpful, as I had already done the math in my head.

A few weeks later, the incident that she wanted to discuss was our own. She said that it had felt like I was dismissive of her needs and concerns. She pointed out that I had rejected her request immediately and without an apology. Perplexed, I again explained my financial situation. She said that this wasn't the point. She was trying to set a boundary and I had dismissed it without even apologizing. I took her point, apologized, and asked a lot of questions. I had a few actionable lessons here.

As I was leaving that day, I mentioned in passing that Heather had once gotten upset with me when I told her that I didn't see any emotional communication in people's facial expressions. My therapist seemed to have an "aha!" moment at this. She suggested that it might be an indicator of Asperger's Syndrome.

I knew it was true even before I was tested properly. When I did take a test, I landed in the 90th percentile. It just felt unbelievably right. While I had joked that I had Asperger's for years, I had waited far too long, until every disaster had left a finger pointing at me and I just couldn't put it off anymore.

I've heard dozens of Aspies express a similar feeling of comfort in this diagnosis. It was the greatest revelation of my life to date. Slowly every pain, hardship, and depression in my life that others didn't seem to experience could be explained by and traced back to a single word. For most of my life, I had "friends" all over the world but without any kind of emotional proximity; they respected the projects that I had built and engaged with me because of what I did rather than because of actual closeness.

I discovered Simon Baron-Cohen, one of the world's foremost experts on Asperger's and director of the Autism Research Centre at the University of Cambridge. He lists four defining traits of AS:

- Persistent and intense preoccupations;
- Unusual or bizarre behaviors;
- Impaired social reasoning abilities and the inability to apply social rules properly; and
- Clinical-strength egocentricity.

I felt like the poster child for each of these items. I was quite content to go on and on about any subject that I deemed interesting to anyone within earshot. Even if I could stop talking about my obsessions, I couldn't stop *thinking* about them. As for unusual behaviors, anyone who has watched me sort my 27 pills per day into caps for each meal until my next trip can attest that it's best not to test my focus by interrupting this process. Perhaps the third trait should have been clear after Stefanie had to explain to me that it was not an appropriate time to do gym stretches spread eagle on the living room floor while her ex-boyfriend came over to socialize. The last trait really ties it all together. When Heather told me she was moving out, my immediate response was "But the bed is yours! What will I sleep on?" And three years prior, when she said that she was going on a 30-day Amtrak trip around the South, my response was "But I'll get really lonely!"

These weren't choices or learned behavior. Each was caused by neurological differences that made it impossible to relate to others in certain ways. I processed every experience that I had only in relation to myself. Other people's emotions were completely confusing unless I could relate them to my own experiences or emotions. If someone was willing to spend enough time explaining how and why they felt a certain way, which they usually were not, I could slowly eke out their intended meaning or how my initial response had been inappropriate. Most of my life I did not feel comfortable or even natural looking people in the eye while they talked to me, even after it was repeatedly demanded of me. My needs always came first, if only because they were the only ones that I was aware of. I've been told my whole life that these things are a result of not caring or trying. In fact, I tried *so hard* every day but still couldn't seem to figure out the secret code that everyone else seemed to communicate in.

I read an article by Baron-Cohen[12] that made the issues make a lot more sense to me. It said that the socializing problems with Asperger's essentially come down to a lack of empathy. Empathy is a high-stakes commodity: the ability to interpret how someone else is feeling. Without empathy, one just cannot undestand what someone else is experiencing. Empathy calls us to help others and tells us how not to hurt them. Sympathy is the result of empathy after understanding what kind of response is needed. I came to realize that I had always related best to other people who had trouble with empathy.

I learned about emotional reciprocity: The instinct to smile when someone smiles at you, something else that Aspies often lack that and is often

12 "The Empathy Quotient: An Investigation of Adults with Asperger Syndrome or High Functioning Autism, and Normal Sex Differences" by Simon Baron-Cohen and Sally Wheelwright, *Journal of Autism and Developmental Disorders,* Vol. 34, No. 2, April 2004.

misinterpreted. Then I learned about mirror neurons, the part of the brain that allows animals to understand the emotions of others from birth. It's the part of the brain that allows us to recognize that a smile means that someone is happy. These neurons inform our emotions and create the building blocks for empathy. People with Asperger's still have mirror neurons, but these neurons are much less sensitive than those in neurotypicals, people not on the autism spectrum.

It's not that I don't have empathy. I just don't have very much of it, medically speaking. The things I had empathy for were typically not human, such as my blanket scrap as a child. When, as an adult, I found a discarded Winnie The Pooh doll missing an eye on the side of the road, I picked it up, brought it home, and washed it off because I felt bad for it and thought it was lonely. The intellectual part of me knows that a stuffed animal does not have feelings, but that was a rare moment where my empathic impulses made a decision for me. When I took an online empathy test, I scored a 7 out of a possible 80 points, which is consistent for someone with Asperger's. When I took an online test about how to evaluate the emotions of dogs from looking at pictures of them, I scored a 95%. I've often felt closer to the dogs in my life than the people.

When I see a person who has crashed a bicycle, I can relate that to my own experience so I will stop and ask whether I can help. But the more that I learn about empathy, the more I realize it's complicated. Most experiences result in multiple emotional responses. For example, when April, who was kindly letting me sleep on her couch at this time, broke up with her long-term partner, my thoughts were, "Okay. I guess I won't be seeing him around the apartment in the mornings." A neurotypical would likely have an empathic response of feeling April's pain mixed with relief in letting the difficult relationship go.

I had been emailing the mediators for four months and suggesting meeting times without anything materializing. They did not respond to most of the emails but finally responded to say that they did not consider our conversation to be "mediation." The only thing that we'd agreed to do was "talk about the issues," but we seemed to have different goals and I didn't know what their goals were. I asked about meeting face-to-face with mediation, thinking that things might go better in person than they had on the phone. Despite how uncomfortable they had made me feel, I still thought that we shared the goal of making everyone feel better. I believed strongly in community-based restorative justice efforts.

Two months later the mediators still had not agreed to any of the times I had offered to meet. A month later their email address began bouncing. A few weeks later, I was asked to leave an anarchist café and was told that it was because I had "failed the accountability process." I tried to explain that there hadn't been an accountability process. The Zine Symposium organizers began to use the same language. No one had used the word "accountability" to describe the communications as they were happening. In her letters, Heather referred to them as "the mediators." I had a bad feeling that this would all come back to haunt me again.

THE SPECTRUM

Even though it was a huge revelation for me, I was embarrassed and ashamed upon the realization sinking in that I had Asperger's. Navigating these challenges had already caused so much pain in my life, and explaining it to neurotypicals for the rest of my life sounded as exhausting as socializing with them had been for 32 years. Sure, I could mask my symptoms in the short term when I *really* needed to, like on a first date or when applying for a loan or hanging out with new people, but masking the symptoms just made it *more exhausting*.

One thing I'd always struggled with was not giving people advice when they just wanted me to listen to their experiences and commiserate. For me, everything is action-oriented and fixing shit up—so when someone came to me with a problem, it was logical to assume that it was because they wanted help with it. This is an Aspie trait but also traditionally male. I really thought that I had the best answers for everybody. Worse, this brand of giving unsolicited advice was often encouraged in my communities. At least it was easy to change once my therapist explained it to me.

I had been obsessed with things for as long as I could remember. When I was four years old I somehow learned about breakdancing, decided that it would become my career as an adult, and talked about nothing but breakdancing until I fell face first onto a vent in our kitchen and cut a wide gash open out of my chin. I was rushed to the emergency room. By the next day I had become obsessed with growing up to become a professional Lego builder. I'll have that long scar on my chin for the rest of my life.

I learned that most Aspies are diagnosed as children, usually after they have trouble in school. But the Asperger's diagnosis was not formally recognized until 1992, and I was too old at that time to be tested or for it to be noticed. Parents are often diagnosed when their children show signs of Asperger's, which is genetic, but I didn't have kids. Thus I had managed to escape diagnosis for most of my life. Instead, I had to awkwardly bumble through life not knowing why everything seemed so much more difficult for me than it was for everyone else around me.

But as I read more over the next days and weeks, I also came to see Asperger's as an advantage, a superpower. The more I thought about it, the more I realized that all of my successes in life were a result of Asperger's. If I didn't have "clinical-strength egocentricity," I never would have had the gall to start a publishing company based on my vision as a seventeen-year old, funded by my under-the-table delivery job at the Italian restaurant. I certainly wouldn't have stuck with it for twenty years and counting. If I hadn't had "persistent and intense preoccupations" I certainly would not be spending every minute of the day using mathematical formulas to determine which books to publish, how to distinguish them from existing books in those categories, how many to print, and deducing what questions to ask to save thousands of dollars at the printer. I certainly wouldn't have spent years of my life poring over spreadsheets, convinced that I could solve all my problems simply by creating the proper equations within them. As James Elder Robison says about adult Aspies in *Be Different: Adventures of a Free-Range Aspergian*, once people sought me out for my competence, they were usually willing to look past my eccentricity and strange behaviors, which allowed me to respected instead of bullied.

Of course, everyone still thought I was odd, but I could live with that: I was successful *because* I was odd. Or maybe all of these neurotypicals were odd. Who can really say?

For the three days until I saw my therapist again, I reveled in each realization as it came to me, often while riding my bike and heavily distracted in traffic.

I had so many questions by my next appointment. Lundy Bancroft's *Why Does He Do That?* had left me with a fairly hopeless view of what happens after someone is deemed to have an abusive personality. A major theme of the book is that all effort should be exerted towards caring for the abused person rather than attempting to work with the abuser, mostly because the statistics on people who show sincere changes are so grim.

I looked into cases of Aspies' being referred to as abusive by their partner. It seems that the combination of egocentricity and lack of empathy can be interpreted as malicious instead of oblivious. In case studies I read about in psychology journals, I found many situations where the neurological differences and literal understanding of phrasing led to an Aspie's actions' seeming insensitive or even underhanded to their neurotypical partner. The lack of empathy could feel not only cold but sadistic. In one example, the neurotypical wife tells her husband, "Don't let that man set foot on our property." In response, when the man visits, the husband lays out boards for the visiting man to walk on. To him, he's following orders and respecting his wife, but to most reasonable people it looks like he's manipulating the situation to do what he wants in spite of her request.

The examples from my own life were very much to the point: When I continued to be friends with someone after he had sexually harassed Heather, she believed that I was condoning his actions. To her it was a disrespectful betrayal. But I felt that one incident was not defining of his character and that staying friends gave me the ability to discuss these things with him. He did change over time and we are still close fifteen years later. But in Heather's mind, it was another careless choice.

At work, similar moments of confusion were happening. I shared ordering duties with two other people for stocking our store. We used a system similar to the one at Boxcar, where we put our own requests next to customer requests and then submitted a monthly order. At one point, I ordered one copy of a title that all three staff members were featured in, as well as many of our authors. It had been a contentious book because it had numerous factual errors, especially about the history of Riot Grrrl, but I figured that our customers and staff would like to at least flip through it and draw our own impressions. The day that it arrived, I put it on display, mostly because it was so oversized that it wouldn't fit on any shelf.

"Oh. We got *that*. I had avoiding ordering that on purpose," my co-worker chimed in.

"Sure. It might be weird but did you know that you're in it?" I beamed.

"Yeah, that's cool I guess," he responded and let it drop.

Based on that conversation, I concluded that we were on the same page. I hadn't broken a policy but, looking back, I think he felt elbowed around. He was doing his best to give me nonverbal communication that he wasn't okay with it and thought I was ignoring his requests. Over the course of a year of events like this, he became so frustrated with me that he quit. Since we had never once had an argument or a disagreement, I was shocked and confused. When I asked our colleague Juliette about it, she seemed equally confused that I did not know how he felt, as they had apparently talked about it often.

One of the most frustrating aspects of being accused of abuse was that there wasn't anything specific and concrete. I had been horrified by the accusations and wanted to change, but without a clear set of directives I couldn't figure out what to work on after the boundaries conversations with my therapist. Worse, my requests for specific feedback were seen as trying to undermine the accusations. Once again, I was missing the forest for the trees.

It began to make sense why there were never clear, specific accusations about how I was abusive. I had never hit anyone and rarely got outwardly angry as an adult. When I hurt people's feelings it was typically through unknowing insensitivity rather than by being cruel or cunning. I knew only how to understand what was literally being said to me. If the resulting blunders hadn't been so hurtful, they would have been funny.

My therapist explained that in some cases two people's communication can be so fractured and they can miss each other so intensely that both experience it as an abusive relationship. Heather felt judged and undermined when my choices didn't align with hers. I began to understand, through examining the incredible volume of Heather's letters and emails with my therapist, that Heather felt judged by me for every choice she made, from taking the bus to dressing a certain way to painting the bathroom to getting a new couch to spending money frivolously to letting the water warm up before she washed her face. Feeling my scrutiny and knowing I would do all these things differently had, over time, eroded her confidence in the choices that she knew were right for her.

Over time, my seemingly irrational and peculiar behavior left her to feel like I was up to something or that my actions were meant to harm her. The tension between us worsened when I did things she hadn't expected, even little things. Once, when I said that I was leaving work, I ran into a friend outside and talked for an hour. When I went back inside to get something I'd forgotten, Heather said she believed I was "up to something." The awkwardness caused me to communicate less, causing more confusion and assumptions.

It is entirely common for people who actively feel abused to respond in kind. It's defensive. It's what they know. It messes with their head. It creates a bullying cycle. And Heather did many things right out of the abuse textbook in an apparent attempt to regain power in our relationship. She would call me names and ridicule me in front of customers and other staff. She would tell me how I felt or why I did things or what I had meant by a statement. Such situations were made more difficult when she was hurt by what she had interpreted as my meaning and refused to hear my intentions. She would often tell me that what I had experienced in a situation was not valid because it was not *her* experience.

I remember bringing up to our marriage counselor in 2003 that I felt like Heather was engaged in a power struggle with me, but Heather disagreed. I was perplexed and wanted the power struggle to stop. I didn't understand why she behaved this way. The ways she had treated me eroded my confidence in turn, locking both of us into a downward spiral for years.

I always got along remarkably well with people who are strongly logical and other Aspies, but I almost always missed it when someone was expressing a boundary to me. This led people with clear boundaries to create distance from me, people with unclear boundaries to continue to engage with me and expect different results, and people on the spectrum to clarify their position until we were understanding each other and communicating well.

It was important to me not to see Asperger's as an excuse for my behavior so much as a roadmap for preventing it from continuing to happen. I was still responsible for my behavior. Asperger's explained why it had happened, but it didn't justify it.

With this much new information to interface my life around, I reduced my therapy to two hours per week and agreed to work on a new feature-documentary project with my longtime collaborator, Reverend Phil. I needed to develop my confidence again as well as taking on a project to keep myself busy. Phil and I had been collaborating since our 2002 documentary *Do You Copy?* and he had patiently taught me most of what I knew about documentary filmmaking. But six years later, the tables had turned and I was the one teaching Phil new tricks. After a few months of tossing ideas around, we settled on *Aftermass: Bicycling in a Post-Critical Mass Portland,* a history of bicycle activism in Portland since 1971.

We hit the ground running and began scheduling and shooting interviews. Quickly we found our way down the block from the Microcosm store to the BikePortland news office. I found Elly Blue sitting there, apparently now a reporter. We scheduled an interview with her for the next day but when we came back she wasn't there, so we interviewed her boss instead.

Because their office was just a few doors down from the Microcosm store I bumped into her again the following week.

"Oh, sorry. Something came up," she said. We re-scheduled for the following day.

I conducted the interview while Phil ran the equipment and everything went well. The next day Elly came into Microcosm and started asking me questions about myself. I had an appointment for my fourth eye surgery later that week and explained that there was a two-week recovery period when I would be confined to dark rooms. She suggested that she could bring me food during this period and asked for my phone number.

The first time she came by she dropped off some food and left. A friend later admitted to coaching Elly on my diet, as what I was able to digest was quite complicated by that point in time. That weekend, Juliette came by to read my emails to me and to type responses as I dictated through the darkness. Before she left, I asked her to text the ten most recent people in my phone and invite them over to visit. By chance it happened to be Valentine's Day. Elly must have been among those invited because even though she didn't know any of my friends she happily showed up, staying after everyone else had left. I asked her to put in my eye drops for me before she went home. I was falling asleep.

After another week of recovery I was developing cabin fever and growing a wicked beard so I put on my dark sunglasses and took a blind walk to the Microcosm store, where I had forgotten my razor. It was a Sunday, but I noticed that the door to Elly's office was open so I stuck my head in and said "hello." She was surprised to see me and even more surprised that I had walked the twenty blocks without being able to see. She was reviewing a cargo bicycle and offered to give me a ride back to where I was staying. The only problem was that she hadn't mastered balancing an extra 200 pounds in the back, so she dumped me onto the sidewalk three times before giving up and offering to walk back with me.

I accepted, and we began a routine of spending time together every few days, going on walks and talking for hours. By the time I could see again, we had a nice day of sitting close in the park and then going on a walk on the trail by the river. As the sun was going down, we sat on a bench watching the river and talking about what we each wanted out of a relationship. It was something that neither of us had done consciously before. Perhaps it was reaching our 30s and creating intentional paths, but it made me feel close to her, and like there was already investment and value in the relationship. A serious talk like this, before there was much risk, made proximity and empathy less intimidating and made it feel like we could invest deeply.

I felt like I understood her motives and which parts of her past were exciting and which parts were painful. It gave me greater perspective to explain my own life goals out loud and to learn that she shared many of them. She hadn't grown up with the benefits (or unclear boundaries and downsides) that punk rock offers, so she had different perspectives and opinions. Elly had the curiosity and inquisitive nature from her years as a reporter. She had a particular curiosity and analytical view of accountability. She also found other aspects of my life interesting, such as how I mended every hole in my pants with a patch. She wanted to hear the stories from my life and was curious about what I'd learned from punk. Most people I knew didn't want to discuss punk lore, such as how Bob Stinson's presence had intimidated Paul Westerberg into writing great Replacements songs. These stories, true or not, were taken so deeply for granted that they were passing references and footnotes. Several times I witnessed people turn their backs and walk away if someone told the story in conversation. But Elly not only wanted to hear these stories but also had a unique perspective on them. She would connect them to her own experiences and observations about other topics and scenes. It was refreshing to have common interests—at least in analyzing the dynamics of a situation—without feeling like I had to be or do anything.

A week later, Elly pointed out how I created symmetry when decorating my bowls of yogurt before I ate them. She noticed how I made sound effects to illustrate or comment on what was going on around me. But instead of teasing me, she found it charming. Elly knew how to talk to me and knew what questions to ask to get the information that she wanted. She had attended a nerdy liberal arts college ten years after dropping out of high school, and said that learning to interact with her fellow students there had taught her to get along with and appreciate people on the spectrum. She took some of the same tests I did, and while her score on the empathy quotient test was three times what mine was, it was still low enough to allow her to relate well with my mostly logical brand of communication. She communicated intellectually rather than emotionally, which is probably why she came across so gruffly in our first two encounters while I tried to flirt with her.

Of course, I had also changed. My first year in therapy had taught me skills that I began employing immediately. I watched for subtle expressions of boundaries when I talked to people. I acted more slowly and asked more questions to make sure that I wasn't overstepping or reacting inappropriately to something. I knew more about what to look for in people's facial expressions. I learned that a slow response or none at all indicated some kind of hesitation.

As a result of this dynamic, Elly and I both communicated well to each other and we both put up boundaries as needed. I found that setting firm boundaries of my own from the beginning left me feeling respected and valued in the relationship. She knew that when I asked for some time to myself that it wasn't a statement about her, and she gave me my space. When I was initially hesitant about moving in together or having a house at all, she knew to take a step back instead of pressing the issue. Setting those boundaries and seeing her respect them set me at ease, and soon we were living together. Well, I was staying at her house more nights than on April's couch, where I was technically "living." We spent many hours discussing logic, finances, and mathematical solutions to problems. Before long, with the help of Kickstarter and a solid group of friends, Elly had started her own publishing business despite not having any money to her name.

Gradually I realized that I would have to tell other people about my Asperger's.

I remembered a time when I had paused mid-conversation with Stefanie to write a note that said, "Support other people; show empathy. Don't give advice." She was incredibly annoyed with me and I didn't understand why. "But I'm learning how to be a better friend." I said.

She rolled her eyes. "Do you see why that's annoying?" I didn't.

I thought that the vast multitude of moments that we'd experienced together like this one would allow her to see my Asperger's realization as a framework to understand all of my oddities. I called her.

"What is it?" she asked cheerfully.

"I had a breakthrough in therapy." A strong lead, I thought.

"Yeah?"

"My counselor believes that I have Asperger's and that's why... well, I have such a hard time understanding people, reading nonverbal communication, and with empathic understanding."

"... <sigh>"

"I know that I used to joke about it but this is different. She thinks this is why I can't recognize the expression in people's faces."

"Joe, you don't have Asperger's. I know a high-school student who does... he can't tell when other people are joking."

"I can't tell when other people are joking! How many times have you seen that happen with me?"

"I guess so," she said. "It just sounds like an excuse."

"It's not an excuse. It doesn't make me any less responsible for who I am and what I do. It's the first roadmap that I've had that makes sense to me."

"Whatever. I gotta go." She hung up.

That experience sucked. For the first time in my life I felt at home in my body and mind. I realized that I couldn't be friends with people who were going to deny my experience. Fortunately, the next person I told said, "Well... that's not exactly surprising." The next few people were not surprised at all either. A few said that they had long suspected it.

"Are you sure?" one close friend asked. "It doesn't seem right. You function so well."

I pointed out the litany of things I was responsible for in the being-insensitive-to-other-people's-feelings department.

"But I've seen you be emotional."

I explained that Asperger's didn't turn me into Spock; it created a complicated relationship with my own emotions and an inability to empathize with others.

The people who argued with me about it didn't really understand what Asperger's was, what it looked like socially, and what it meant. I'm not brain damaged or intellectually inferior. My brain is just different. I still have emotions—in most cases I have more intense emotions than other people. My principle disability caused by Asperger's is the inability to communicate effectively with other people, thus, ironically, making it difficult to explain that I have Asperger's to people that I've known for a long time.

In order to better understand my own socialization, I read about the kinds of people who have relationships with people on the spectrum. Obviously, Aspies date other Aspies and get along splendidly because they speak the same language. And while Aspies encounter neurotypicals every day in all aspects of their lives, it is often the people with unclear boundaries who allow Aspies into their lives against their better judgment and are constantly frustrated with their behaviors. People with poorly developed emotional boundaries often don't self-advocate. They sometimes misunderstand the social dynamics or just expect problems to change over time without addressing them directly.

Thinking about it, I saw both sides in my own life: I would easily become highly emotional, argumentative, or defensive. My unclear boundaries often caused me to give advice, blame others, or accept blame at inappropriate times. I would often feel guilty because of someone else's negative feelings or problems. When I realized that it was my unclear boundaries that had caused me to go with Heather to see her student therapist despite seeing how no good could come of it, I resolved to change immediately. It was liberating to realize that I didn't have to do something just because someone asked.

The more I thought about other people in my life, the more I saw the impact of unclear boundaries. They did things that they did not want to do when someone asked them and then complained about it later. When I asked Juliette if she could warehouse Microcosm's books in her basement when we moved out of Liberty Hall until we opened a new store, she immediately agreed even though later she said that she didn't want to. When I would email Heather to ask things like "What was the name of that Ice Cube movie that we were in the background crowd shot of while we were in the Vancouver train station?" she would always reply willingly, creating a hazy line in my mind of whether or not we were still friends. When Stefanie wanted to hire an exterminator for the Microcosm offices and I said that we didn't have the money at the time, she said that she would pay for it. I said that was fine if she really wanted to. But later, she said that she hadn't meant it; she was only "being nice" and had expected me to respond by understanding how important this was to her and offering to pay after all. But I couldn't hear communications like that.

Now I understand that someone might be sending conflicting nonverbal communications simultaneous to their verbal communication. As a result, if it's someone I have had problems communicating with in the past or don't know very well, I am careful to ask what I think is the same question two or three different ways to make sure that I am understanding their response.

It was a revelation to find out that the behaviors of most of the people around me were influenced by the feelings of the people around them. It didn't mean that they were bad people, but it did mean that I had to be especially careful in dealing with them. It explained how people who were so annoyed with me would continue to stick around until their cup overflowethed with frustration. They speak a language that I am incapable of ever learning in the same way. It wasn't that I *didn't* understand other people's emotions, it was that I *couldn't*—at least not in the innate way most people could. There are ways that I can use my intellectual skills to mimic emotional conversation, such as knowing what expressions to watch for and learning what questions are appropriate when. But as I practiced these techniques, my strategy would have to be cautious and intentional as I learned a foreign language that most people were born speaking.

I made a resolution to actively seek relationships with people who had healthy boundaries so I wouldn't run so much risk of having to predict and manage their emotions as well as my own. Realizing that I could proactively make the decisions that were right for me really changed everything in my thinking.

Our store in Portland, 2010

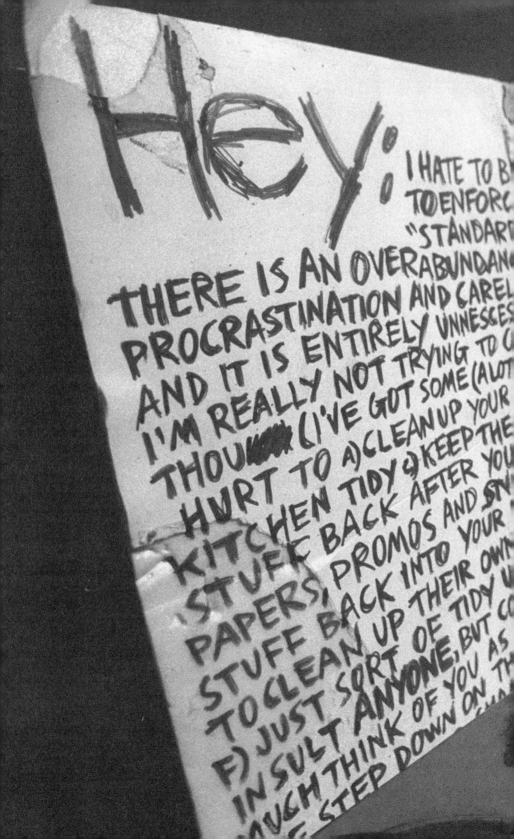

Section

IV

From Orange
To Pink

SUBMISSION & BOUNDARIES

In mid-2009, Elly and I moved into a 98-square-foot camping trailer parked in a friend's yard in the middle of the city. When the remainder of my possessions arrived from Bloomington, I noticed that the painting of childhood Batman standing up to his tormentor wasn't among them. But after my time in therapy, I found that I didn't want to reflect on my past in that way anymore. Even better, I felt that I had a firm enough handle on my therapy and myself to re-enter the public sphere.

In June, on Heather's demand, I posted a public statement apologizing that my actions had hurt people, how I had learned from this experience, and what exactly had taken place. I hoped that a public statement would help to defuse the situation and allow people to move on. Each person in the collective seemed to think I was crazy for posting it, though they each had their own reasons. Despite their objections, I believed it would be the right thing to do. I was wrong. Instead, strangers begun to publicly mock my statement and claim that I was blaming the problem on a corn allergy. People made Internet memes that said "Together we can end Joe Biel." Things began appearing online proclaiming such bold statements as "It is no big secret that Joe Biel, the co-founder [sic] of Microcosm Publishing, has been called out for abuse in his former marriage, as well as dishonest business dealings." The anonymous users of the Internet had turned me into an object; a cultural reference point about the importance of standing up against abuse.

A few weeks later, Microcosm received an email that read,

So I've been ordering from and distroing catalogs from Microcosm for years but I only just found out about the shit around Joe being really emotionally abusive. Basically, my question is, is the collective doing anything about that? Making any response to it? I'd really like to continue to buy things from Microcosm but I don't feel alright doing so with no action taken.

And then another email:

We were disappointed to hear of allegations against Joe Biel, the face of the Microcosm Collective. These allegations include suggestion of poor labor practices, as well as allegations of emotional abuse by past partner(s), friends, and employees... Is Microcosm really run as a collective? Is Joe taking steps towards dealing with his own issues regarding the allegations of emotional abuse made against him?

After eighteen months of not being part of management, I took a trip back to Bloomington and started engaging in administrative meetings again. The collective was divided about how to deal with the issue. Some people wanted to ignore it. Some people wanted to publicly respond to rumors, especially since most claims had no basis in truth. Some people referred to it as "bullshit." Mostly people wanted to add it to meeting agendas. We talked about it over and over without coming up with a clear resolution.

Upon getting to Bloomington and looking at the submission pile, I discovered that the Microcosm collective had declined to publish numerous titles from people we had a long history of working with that I felt fit our vision, that had a lot of merit, and that I knew would sell. I revisited them with the collective, asking why they had been rejected. Some managers cited similar items that hadn't sold well. Others simply didn't like the submissions in question. Some expressed that they still were not confident in making the decisions about what we put money behind. After two meetings where I unsuccessfully tried to make the case for rejected projects, two people suggested that I start a new company to publish these titles. Everyone else agreed and it was decided that Microcosm would distribute items I published on a case-by-case basis. It felt like a good solution to a complicated dynamic and I began saving money to start the new publishing company.

In July of 2009, Microcosm had its first breakout hit, a book called *Make Your Place* that had hand-written and -illustrated instructions for sustainable housekeeping. It was the first time that we propelled a book beyond the insular bubble of our DIY punk subculture, though that wasn't what we were trying to do. We just thought it was a cool book. But it turned out that it could appeal to three different generations of the same family, which none of our other books were likely to do. The book was featured on a popular mom blog and spread to other popular websites, and we sold over 5,000 copies in one week alone. Our small, scrappy distributor had failed to get the book listed on Amazon, so the only place to order it was from our website. The resulting cash infusion was a huge relief. It allowed Microcosm to stop bleeding money and get our long-term credit-card bills under control.

With this book's intergenerational success in mind, I started to develop titles and publish work under the name Cantankerous Titles. One of the things that had begun to frustrate me about Microcosm was that it seemed that every year I got older but the audience stayed the same age, inherently limiting what we could publish. When I would bring this up to the collective, who were all younger than I was, they expressed that they liked the age range that we published for. There was pushback against making any changes. So while Cantankerous also published books for people who wanted different perspectives on popular topics and probably had some access to punk growing up, these readers were likely ten or twenty years older than Microcosm's primary audience. I was excited to be able to relate to and stay engaged with the work I was publishing and the people that I was trying to reach.

After I had put out a few releases and planned a dozen more, cartoonist Tom Neely contacted me via our mutual friend Dylan Williams.

"Hey, uhhh, I was wondering if you wanted to publish this book that I made with some friends. It always sells out at conventions but I haven't done much with it. It imagines what it would be like if Henry Rollins and Glenn Danzig were in a relationship, like Tom of Finland, but not sexual," he said.

"Ummm, that sounds *really* specific. I'm not sure that I could sell a whole print run in my lifetime. I don't think management at Microcosm would go for it either. I'm not sure that it's a good fit. Does anyone even know who those guys are anymore?" I wondered out loud.

"If you can't sell enough, I'll buy all of the ones that you can't sell," Tom said.

As predicted, after a close vote, the Microcosm collective passed the project up. But with Tom's offer on the table and the fact that this was exactly the kind of book that I loved, I agreed that Cantankerous Titles would publish it. After another very close vote, Microcosm agreed to distribute it. The book that Tom delivered, *Henry & Glenn Forever,* was tongue-in-cheek punk sociology that was heavy on making fun of idol worship and demonstrated how homoerotic punk is. It was perfect.

I contacted 1984 Printing, a small print shop run by two old friends, and sent them the book. I was on a Microcosm tour in early 2010 when the book came back from the printer. The book was listed on Microcosm's website, without any publicity effort or a single email sent. But somehow during its first month the book was reviewed by Carrie Brownstein on NPR and featured in *Entertainment Weekly* and *LA Weekly.*

The book didn't have a publication date or a trade distributor, so it wasn't available on Amazon or in stores. As a result, Microcosm sent out orders for the entire first printing of 2,500 copies in the first two weeks while we waited for 1984 to reprint it. In the coming months, the book appeared in major music magazines, on MTV's website, on Twitter several times per day, and in almost every other kind of media that I know of. All without a single publicity pitch sent out. Later, when a campaign was launched, the response was generally, "Well, everyone has already covered this, so why would we?"

The success of *Henry & Glenn Forever* firmed up my self-confidence at a time when I really needed it and showed me that I could do things outside of Microcosm.

The rumors about myself and Microcosm were spiraling out of control as they traveled through the grapevine. The accusations against me were not specific and it seemed that because of that, people just inserted their worst imagination. On one message board, strangers accused me of "domestic violence" and "sexual assault." The scene that I had built on the construction of didactic invective was applying this same logic against me.

Increasingly through 2009 and 2010, people started getting in touch with management to insist that the Microcosm collective hadn't taken enough of a stand against abuse. They demanded a public response. Gretchen, one of Microcosm's authors, got in touch in June of 2010, and said "In order to feel comfortable continuing to be published by Microcosm, I need to know from each collective member that they don't think Heather was crazy or that the attempts to deal with the situation are a witch hunt. I would need to know from each member that the collective recognizes that Joe still has issues with control and manipulation." She closed the email by mentioning that she had once felt uncomfortable talking on the phone with me after she had sold books that she bought from Microcosm to a store that we normally deal with, in violation of her contract.

Another example of my problematic behavior that she mentioned was that I once forwarded each collective member's individual design feedback (with the names removed) and did not understand why she found this unhelpful and hurtful. She said, "the communication/manipulation models Joe uses are patriarchal." She also said that, in order to continue working with her, I must submit myself to an accountability process.

Confusingly, perhaps as a token of good faith, she also signed a contract for a second book. At the bottom of the contract, she hand-wrote an additional clause: "[I] promise not to undermine Microcosm's awesome work and dedication and completely respect the awesome deal Microcosm gives the author and promise not to take advantage or go ballistic."

Gretchen's first book had sold relatively well, but the staff was running into lots of problems working with her. When the first book went into a new edition, the reprint was delayed for months because Gretchen and the staff couldn't agree on a cover. When the collective wanted to make any changes at all, even editing for grammar and punctuation, it became so tense that no one wanted to engage with her. Abe, a new staff person in Bloomington, agreed to bear the burden, saying, "She already hates me, so there is no reason for her to hate anyone else." When the collective decided to stick with Abe's design, Gretchen was so upset that she proposed a policy that Microcosm would not redesign book covers that were submitted. Abe explained how artists and designers work together and the collective held their backbone and declined Gretchen's suggested policy.

The collective discussed Gretchen's other demands and concluded that making private statements would be a good way to move beyond the issue. Even though her work wasn't anywhere near our most popular, Gretchen was trusted in our social community and she was a bellwether of opinion. Two staff people again sent me emails that said, "This is bullshit," but overall it seemed like people believed that the issue was important even if they didn't like the way that it was being handled. The staff were all genuinely afraid that alienating our most loyal and insular base over this issue could bankrupt Microcosm. Everyone agreed that capitulating would make the harassment stop. Everyone made their statements, though they were not all well received; Gretchen told Juliette's husband that he was "disgusting and disappointing" because he referred to the situation as "Joe and Heather's issues." But after everyone in the collective had made a statement that they took abuse seriously there was silence.

Privately, I got in touch with Gretchen. I told her about the skills that I was learning in intensive therapy and explained that I had long ago complied with Heather's demands. I told her about the media-camp organizers who had offered to talk about the issues then a year later referred to it as "accountability," and how so much of the situation was a result of distance and communication breakdown. Gretchen offered to put together an accountability group and, not knowing what else to do, I agreed. After a lifetime of misunderstanding social mores, I was accustomed to deferring to other people telling me what was socially appropriate. I had come to accept that I had no way of navigating these issues on my own and thus no way to conceive of boundaries around them.

Trusting people on this issue had always served me well and I felt that, despite all of our conflicts, Gretchen was a member of my community who I could trust.

A week later, the collective received, from an email address that nobody recognized, a series of strange questions:.

1. *Does Microcosm have a policy for who represents Microcosm at conferences?*
2. *Does Microcosm have a policy to make sure reprints and things it prints have permission?*
3. *Does Microcosm have a policy on zine writers' rights to sell their zines/ books that you've printed?*

The questions were misleading and confusing. While we had clear and functional policies on all of these things, the staff felt uncomfortable and ignored the questions. Employees at Microcosm were overworked and had received so many emails in the previous year claiming that the organization "supported" or "denied" abuse that they had stopped engaging or responding. Whoever sent the questions complained that the Microcosm staff was neither cooperative nor taking the abuse accusations seriously. The mysterious email address got in touch again and clarified that the questions were coming from an anonymous group of people for the purpose of accountability. The collective responded this time.

Gretchen was still contacting the collective. She accused Stefanie of being my pawn and accused the collective of "preferring to become paranoid" and demanded that in order to continue working together, every Microcosm staff person must write and agree upon a group statement saying that I was abusive and the steps that they were taking in response.

Stefanie was the messenger this time. "Dear god I am so over this shit," she wrote to me. "I think [Gretchen's] boycotting us will sink us at this point. Regardless of whether we all agree with her concerns, it seems like we should at least acknowledge them." Feeling like this was a path to resolution, the collective again complied.

Someone posted Microcosm's statement on a news website and one confused comment posited, "This Joe guy isn't a rapist or a snitch (at least from what I was able to discern from the article) at which point putting someone's name next to "abusive behavior" all over the Internet can have some serious repercussions, especially for a group's dynamic. I would *never* post something like this about my group if I even remotely intended to mend the issue." But the typical response was more along the lines of: "Zinesters and punks: Boycott Microcosm. There are plenty of other zine distros that sell zines about support & consent whose collectives don't violate those principles."

The collective's fear of losing its fan base was causing the organization to quickly destroy itself from within. Gretchen requested a fourth statement, this time on Microcosm's website, saying that the previous statement felt "unofficial" and "insufficient." The staff again complied.

Alone in Portland, I was answering long strings of questions in emails from the same anonymous accountability group. A longtime friend of mine, Amy, who had experience and a nuanced view on accountability, helped me by reviewing my responses to questions and making sure that they were appropriate. If not, we discussed why not.

The accountability group said that their goal was "helping people identify and change behavior." This sounded good, but they did not say why they were qualified to do this and got upset when I asked. They did not share a timeline or outline of events and rarely signed names or offered introductions. They asked questions like a trained psychologist would:

1. *What behaviors have you identified as problematic in past (or present) relationships?*
2. *What did you hope to accomplish through the action and/or what was the fear?*
3. *Then write what specific thing you could have done differently?*
4. *What you could do differently in the future if similar things come up?*

These questions seemed reasonable and helpful, and I answered to the best of my ability. But further communications did not go smoothly. One of the members of the group shared a story of a painful experience in their own life and became upset when I responded with my own experiences and a related news story. They said they did not believe that my counselor was a feminist and did not agree with her "views about abuse." They said that my feelings of frustration about the last attempt to mediate weren't fair, since people were volunteering their time to a difficult task.

Rumors began to fly about me: that I was dating a nineteen-year-old, that a sexual assault had been involved, that I earned a $300,000 salary, that I had a trust fund, that I was stalking Heather, that I had curtailed an accountability process. The group demanded that I admit that I had been trying to violate Heather's boundaries when I'd sent her the note three years before telling her that I'd forgiven my mother. The group insisted that I was asking too many questions about the process.

Elly offered them a testimonial about my character, but they were not interested. For several months we went back and forth. They sent me dozens of probing questions each week and responded angrily to the answers I'd spent hours writing. Finally, Amy raised objections about how the process was being run and its lack of transparency. She explained that giving me busywork was not healing or illuminating. She asked for a phone call to better clarify the terms of the relationship and offer feedback. In response, the accountability group told Amy that Gretchen had promised them they wouldn't have to talk to anyone on the phone and that the process would resolve quickly. Upon questioning, they revealed that they did not in fact have professional training and that, despite her bias, Gretchen had been taking an active part in the anonymous group all along.

So instead, Amy talked to Gretchen on the phone and outlined her areas of concern. In response, Gretchen yelled at her, "How dare you question the process?" Disheartened, we both lost tremendous respect for someone who we had once felt was a person that we had looked up to.

As time went on, the stress was beginning to wear on me. Five months into the accountability process, I passed out after getting out of a public pool and cut my head open on the concrete. I spent the next three weeks in bed and still have a scar behind my eyebrow to remind me of the incident. It was a sobering event. Everywhere I looked in the world, I saw hard, unforgiving concrete. As I recovered from the concussion and later some broken ribs from a separate incident, I spent the next nine months walking around, looking at the ground, thinking about how uncompromising everything is, and how our society is not constructed to catch you if you fall.

After six months of emailing back and forth with us, the group said they didn't have more time and that the agreements they had made with Gretchen were not being met. They issued a statement saying that, while I had met all of Heather's logistical demands, they could not confirm that I had changed my behavior. They admitted that they had not committed the time or energy necessary for a process to occur and that they recommended that people with professional training in my active community should meet with me face to face. They concluded with "We do believe Joe is working to understand and change his behaviors. We do not believe this gives him a clean slate."

It felt unfair for them to have agreed to commit to this, not disclose agreements, and then quit, citing that it should have been done face to face instead of through email and that they did not have professional training. It made me question the ideals of restorative justice and the fabric of the community that I had spent my whole adult life investing in. I walked away feeling hurt and sad.

The following month, Gretchen got in touch to say, "I really don't care what you do next. I have no faith in you." This was particularly disheartening. She mentioned in passing to Stefanie that my communication style reminded her of an ex she once dated. I couldn't understand why she was taking so much offense at such seemingly minor slights. I wondered if the situation represented something greater to Gretchen.

Meanwhile, Heather posted yet another update about the situation on her blog, stating that if you were a feminist, you should boycott Microcosm.

At Microcosm, we had long discussions about what to do next. This issue had slowly become the most time-consuming in Microcosm's history. Disheartened after the previous year and struggling to rebuild morale, the collective decided that other people should take over aspects of company ownership from me. I was fine with this. I had long ago given up control and I didn't expect Microcosm to last much longer. Management made online documents that made all information available to all staff at all times, changed job duties and did cross-trainings so that people could transition between duties more easily, and equalized the hourly wage across the staff of eleven so everyone felt more like an equal. However, despite these management efforts, all of the staff was feeling increasing negativity, burnout, exhaustion, and stress. Two more people quit and Microcosm did not have money to replace them. The staff wanted to publish books, not deal with my Asperger's or spend time explaining how they *do* take abuse seriously. Operations began to run painfully behind and orders were shipping a month after they were placed. The financial problems that Microcosm had always faced were once again coming to a head as morale collapsed. In internal management conversations, workers wondered aloud if the company was ending.

Some of the staff had children who depended on their income from Microcosm. So even though it had been over a year since I'd received a paycheck from Microcosm, I began lending Microcosm large sums of money from *Henry & Glenn* sales so that they could pay for operating expenses and payroll. While I wasn't overly optimistic, I wasn't ready for the dream to be over yet.

Despite the year of back-and-forth communication, transparency, and concrete change, Gretchen decided to discontinue working with Microcosm. She was under contract to publish her next book with us and we had been working on the manuscript. Suddenly we started to see publicity that indicated that she was self-publishing it. The collective voted to not enforce the contract. They shared the feeling that Gretchen would find a way to make it look like their fault that she had betrayed her agreements. After publicly acknowledging that Microcosm had offered her the best deal as an author that she could find and that there had not been problems in the first five years of working together, Gretchen proceeded to break every clause she'd added to her contract when she had promised not to "undermine Microcosm's awesome work and dedication," "take advantage," or "go ballistic." In a public statement on her blog, she accused me of lying and charged Microcosm with being complicit.

It was another huge blow to the morale of the organization. The collective decided not to respond and not to continue engaging with her. I proposed to the collective what I would have done: point out the way she claimed to be more of an expert on our internal dynamics than the people actually involved, the way she denied the perspectives and experiences of people closer to the situation, and the way she overlooked facts that did not support her case. But the staff was exhausted and agreeing on the statements that they had made had already taken a huge toll. No one was in a position to go back to the drawing board and create another public response to Gretchen.

I could understand that. But on a personal level it was devastating. I knew that it would condemn me in the eyes of many strangers who would assume that the chain of events that led to this moment were much more severe than what had happened.

I wanted to understand why I only ever heard of accountability processes failing. In fifteen years of involvement with DIY punk rock, I realized that I had never heard of a single success. I remembered back to the process that I had been involved in in 2003 and how frustrating it had been before ultimately being unsuccessful.

Two other people got in touch over the next several months, each offering to operate an accountability process. But the offers were both rescinded after both of them were called out for their own abusive behavior and summoned to submit to an accountability process of their own.

Gretchen was the bellwether of the only family that I'd ever felt close to: The DIY punk community. The fact that she was electing to push me out of my family was upsetting. Worse was the revelation that this construct that I had long believed in as a better method for creating change in the world and putting it on a pedestal was lacking in basic methods or even structure. It wasn't actually a better way of solving our problems. No one showed up to the accountability table with any empathy, only a hammer looking for nails. When they didn't see any nails right away, the people running the process would demand to know where the accused was hiding the nails. There were no professional skills or even room to take things like my Asperger's into account. The process was doomed to fail from the start. And worst of all, so many people in our punk-rock family seemed to be either afraid to point out the problems or utterly lacking the analytical skills to understand why it didn't work. Many people had a hard time looking at what had gone on or figuring out what was and was not being said, who was pushing them to say it, and what agendas and biases those people had. When other concerned people did raise questions like this, they were again shouted down and told that they were supporting abuse. If we were going to change the world, I thought glumly, we at least needed to learn how to have a restorative justice movement that worked.

I dug deeper in my own case and found out that a vocal blogger had pushed Heather to "go public" against me in 2007, challenging her to share her experiences and name names. The blogger, it seemed, had a long history of demanding for accused people to be ostracized from communities in situations that she wasn't involved in. She referred to the recent spate of rumors about me as "actual evidence," but there was no evidence anywhere to be found—just raw emotions, feelings, and conflicting perspectives. The same blogger, I learned, is the one who had shamed Gretchen for continuing to work with Microcosm. Gretchen had eventually bent under this public pressure and took a public stand against me. It was the kind of bullying that was doing nothing but continuing cycles of abuse.

Despite referring to the situation as "my least favorite subject," Heather made six different zines about our relationship across ten years. She began to publicly mock and shame Stefanie for having entering into a relationship with me despite having been "warned." Stefanie had requested that her experience in our relationship not be shared as part of public discourse in the "campaign" against me, but people had a hard time respecting those boundaries. Quotes from her appeared on multiple websites along with the editor's requests for people to boycott Microcosm and me.

Elly pointed out to me that people were being asked to take sides without being allowed to argue or even ask questions. Strangers insisted that I had not learned from my mistakes and hadn't changed. When anyone hesitated or asked questions, they were accused of "supporting abuse." When anyone publicly expressed even mild skepticism or concern, a campaign would be mounted against them. There could be no end and no resolution, just an open wound hanging in the air. The cycle of bullying and abuse continued. It brought back every terrible experience from high school. It reminded me of the bullying I had faced before my Asperger's-fueled obsessions had carved a respectable niche for me. And it only caused more hurt to whatever it touched.

I came across an article that Gretchen wrote shortly after my accountability process ended.

If [an abuser wants their] name cleared, no amount of accountability process is going to clear it. It is something that comes with the passing of time and a sincere, noticeable change of self. It seemed like such a powerful thing, to sit down and tell the person who had assaulted you all the ways they had been fucked up, and to tell them what you expected them to do, and for someone to be there—especially that part—for someone to have your back. That in itself sounded incredible but the follow-up sounded like a nightmare.

I was confused. Rather than being about resolution and healing, as I had been led to believe, it sounded like a recipe for feeling better for a few hours—winning the battle to lose the war. At least I agreed with one part of the essay: "In most cases attempting to do an accountability in a thrown together group is going to be a disaster... Jumping to accountability is so similar to jumping to retaliation. It's not generally what's going to make things better. Especially when it's used in place of a deeper form of support and exploration and feeling and rebuilding of strength and solidarity and connection." But then why had she gone to such great lengths to create such a haphazard process?

I had made mistakes and hurt people. It took a long time to understand that my low empathic ability, difficulty noticing people's boundaries, and inability to navigate a lot of social norms were the reasons that I continually ended up in these situations. But now that these things were under control the most striking thing to me was that there was no way to communicate this, rebuild the scene, and move on.

Ann, a former editor of a feminist magazine, had volunteered to help Microcosm make these transitions and create a healthier organizational dynamic. Ann reached out to Heather in an attempt to mediate, but Heather declined, saying something was 'off' in her message that she couldn't put her finger on.

How would progressive, thoughtful people deal with abuse in our society? It seems like that conversation was being lost in individuals' eagerness to prove that they could take a stand. I kept looking for touchstone resources, but I never found any. Author Kristian Williams told me about a similar accountability process that he had witnessed and pointed me to an article he'd written about the mounting problems he'd seen with issues around accountability on the left. He expressed that feelings often got so heated that people felt unsafe sharing their feelings or experiences. "Several people— mostly women, interestingly—told me they were afraid to say anything about the controversy, lest they go 'off-script' and find themselves denounced as bad feminists."[13]

It had been a huge revelation to learn about boundaries and start to apply them in my day-to-day life. But now I realized how much more I had to learn. It was my own faulty boundaries that had led me into two consecutive relationships where I was very uncomfortable and also into the unreasonable demands of an author and an accountability process run by anonymous strangers. My lack of boundaries had led me to not manage the organization I'd founded and held dear while everything I had delicately and intentionally built was lying in shambles.

Finding this learning experience about boundaries, emotional intelligence, accountability, and restorative justice so full of potential, I put it on my to-do list to publish work about building healthy relationships and focusing on resources that demonstrate ways that the community can support each other.

13 Kristlan Williams on failure of accountability processes, http://bit.ly/1ROgR2t

Setup at San Francisco Zine Fest

A WHOLE NEW WORLD

The landlord who owned the property that Elly and I lived on asked us to vacate for a month while he cleaned up. So Elly and I came up with what became the Dinner & Bikes tour and headed out on the road together in late 2010. It was another important step to realizing that I could have successes and professional growth outside Microcosm. For so many years, Microcosm had felt like my safety net—yet one that had so many restrictions and confines and that wouldn't grow with me as I changed and developed.

Dinner & Bikes was something completely new. Elly and I were not speaking as representatives of a larger organization; we were just two people with opinions, some expertise, and a range of new perspectives on the bicycle-transportation movement in the U.S. We put together a presentation, showed some of my short films, and sold lots of books and bicycle T-shirts that I had designed. We stuck with noncommercial and nontraditional venues, partly because that's what I knew how to reach. Over time we found that being in church basements instead of lecture halls created a more authentic dynamic at the events and opened things up to more audience engagement.

Within a week we found ourselves hurriedly changing into our dress clothes in the bathroom of the library in Cheyenne, Wyoming. The presentation that night was for city employees to learn from us about bicycle-oriented development, and I watched as women old enough to be my mother rushed to write notes about what I was saying. Because I held no college or professional training, I felt like a fraud. Elly reassured me that our perspective was in fact valuable to professionals who are largely fed talking points and don't often hear the kinds of things we present. We talked about the value of grassroots action and the relationship between advocacy, leadership, and activism. It felt like I was once again building a new touring circuit. It was the breath of fresh air that I needed: To bring my existing areas of interest to a new audience and not just be stuck in arguments within an echo chamber. Even if it required dressing up, it was certainly more punk rock than many things I'd done in my life.

After several years tucked away while finding myself, it was also a way for me to re-enter the public sphere and add to my persona. This tour showed me that I didn't need to drop all my former interests and activities and become "normal." I could chase my values in a new way, speak to a new audience, and fully realize my ideal self.

Because I'd never been close to my own family, I thought that the DIY punk scene would grow and change and accept me throughout my life, as I imagined a biological family would. The didactic politics, acceptance of rumors, and the lack of value placed on analytical skills made me wonder whether the

DIY punk scene was the right place for me. The problem wasn't just the level of public scrutiny and bullying being directed against me. It was heartbreaking to realize that this kind of behavior had been directed at other plenty of other people throughout my involvement in the scene. It was a hard lesson to learn so late, that, even if the majority of people who made up my former subculture still wanted to associate with me (and the more vocal ones had become increasingly clear that they didn't), I didn't want to spend my life enmeshed in that scene anymore. It's a didactic snake pit where right and wrong are written in black and white. My life was full of grays and nuances. I realized that I could set a boundary and decide to build something new. And I could invite the people with similar frustrations or who still valued my work to join me.

I started to think longer term and realized I needed some serious investment in self-care. I used the money that I'd made from *Henry & Glenn* to put a down payment on a house in Portland. The gears started grinding on what else I could accomplish if I started to take a more active role in my life after so many years of being passive.

We moved into the house in the last few days of 2010, and by the first few days of 2011 I found myself too weak to get out of bed. After a week of this, Elly found a doctor willing to do house calls. She concluded that I was somehow not absorbing the nutrients from my food. Eventually when my gut was tested, they discovered that the number of colon infections I had was off the chart and had pushed out my digestive flora.

A nurse friend came over and told me that the only real solution was to cut out all sugar from my diet. No doctor would tell me to do that, she explained, because the compliance rate was nonexistent for getting patients to quit eating any sugar. "It's harder than quitting heroin," she said.

The Biel Stubbornness Gene kicked in. I quit immediately.

The first three weeks were miserable but after that the cravings went away and I adjusted my diet. My digestion slowly came back and then my energy did too.

In May of 2011 the entire staff of Microcosm traveled to Bloomington for the annual all-staff meeting. The collective had requested that we put all work on hold so we could sit down and talk through our problems. At the meeting, many coworkers met each other for the first time. We had a massive agenda and four days to work through it. The stakes were high. Microcosm had become unable to pay year-end bonuses over the past four years, had exhausted its lifetime savings of $50,000, and was only able to pay people for up to 32 hours per week while the company needed many more hours of work to be done. Even so, there were months when healthcare and even basic operating costs could not be paid.

In the months leading up to the meeting, Juliette told me she was unhappy and felt disrespected by her coworkers' communications. She asked me to mention to the collective that the meeting notes almost never explained the decisions or conversations from the meeting but simply repeated the agenda. The collective had created a system of peer reviews for everyone to fill out about every other staff person. We both agreed that this was potentially divisive at a time when we all needed to stick together and support each other. Each person would receive six or more peer reviews. This process would consume at least 40 paid hours of staff time. There was no clarification about protocol or what the consequences of poor reviews would be, if any. Juliette and I put our feet down that we would not participate until the system was more refined.

Most of our internal communications in the previous three years had been over email which, on top of the financial situation and overworked conditions, often led to confusion, the misreading of other people, and emotions flaring. Sometimes when someone needed a question answered to do their job, they would have to wait days or weeks and ask repeatedly. Sometimes people would take unannounced time off and hold up workflows. But the collective didn't have a protocol to manage people and no one had the heart to fire anyone. Trust had slowly eroded and people were taking sides, even though in reality few viewpoints were actually in opposition to each other.

Ann had traveled from Minneapolis to facilitate the meeting because she believed in the Microcosm project and both its process and product. The mood in the meeting was tense but optimistic. I felt largely removed from the organization and disinvested but Ann urged me to realize that people looked up to me and that I influenced the dynamic more than I realized. At various points numerous people were threatening to quit and other people were threatening to fire them. I suggested that splitting into two separate organizations based on geography might solve the communication problem but this idea was immediately shot down. At several points I went out into the hallway to support Stefanie and help her calm down. It wasn't a comfortable dynamic for me but it felt right and I was more confident in it than I expected. But, at the end of the week, I was crying when Stefanie and Juliette were at odds, and Stefanie offered to quit. Stefanie said that she felt supported by me but not by others. Just as it felt like wounds were starting to heal, everyone ran out of time and most people headed out of town. I promised I'd come back soon but it was already clear that this would not be good enough.

When I got home, I spelled out my own boundary: All staff and collective members need to agree to communicate about their ideas, grievances, and problems; cease gossip and rumors within the organization; pack and ship weekday orders within 24 hours of receipt; cease to be rude and disrespectful to other staff; assume that all other staffers were operating with good intentions; enforce all policies; terminate four-time violators; and begin to operate on a defined budget within our income. If these terms were not met by the end of the year, I would quit. The situation was making me too crazy for it to be worth staying on otherwise.

I was being dramatic but everyone was frustrated, exhausted, and being dramatic. No one could keep track of everyone else's needs and as a result, I reluctantly accepted promises from most of the remaining staff that these matters would change. Other people were similarly frustrated that their needs were not being met. I discussed the matter with Ann, who said that in every private conversation that she had with other staff members they had each expressed liking me as a person but having trouble managing the company with me. Two more people quit soon thereafter.

As the company's owner, I was legally responsible for our debts and what we couldn't pay ended up on my personal credit cards, so I still had quite a bit at stake. If it weren't for that, I would have quit as I walked out of the meeting that day in Bloomington after having witnessed the disarray and blame being thrown around in every direction. Nonetheless, I trusted the collective. They had all been varying degrees of close to me at various times. Abe said that he would feel comfortable continuing his involvement in the collective only if I took more leave from management and others began taking on ownership roles. My personality was too dominating and people listened to me disproportionately because I had so much more experience, he said. I agreed as long as my conditions were also met. Besides, I wanted to finish work on *Aftermass*.

We finally agreed on a bold step forward. On August 16, 2011, Juliette purchased 50% of the company for the sum of $2,000. After being closely involved for our six most tumultuous years, she said she was proud and excited to have her name on the bank account. I continued to own the other 50%.

In the first week after I formally withdrew from management and again stopped attending administrative meetings, the collective fired Stefanie, closed the organization in Bloomington, moved the warehouse and mail order operations to Kansas where Juliette now lived, and approved signing a trade-distribution agreement with Independent Publisher's Group.

A week later, Juliette called me with this news.

"How are you going to pay for the move?" I asked. "There is no money."

I received no answer. It hadn't been discussed.

"Why did you fire her? I don't think that's fair at all. She doesn't deserve that."

Stefanie was furious and began to badmouth the organization publicly. She asked me to talk to the collective and see if they would reconsider. I tried, but Juliette stood behind her decisions. I was getting the impression that my needs would not be met, so I began my exit strategy.

After three and a half years of intensive therapy, my counselor told me that we had accomplished everything I had set out to in my initial goals. Unless there was something else, we were finished together. I didn't feel ready yet. I stammered to come up with some more goals. She explained how we had thoroughly covered each one that I could think of. I asked how a person "heals" from Asperger's.

"The process is called cognitive behavioral therapy (CBT) but that's not something that I can help you with. You'd need a specialized psychologist. They would teach you how to mimic the behavior of a neurotypical person in social settings so that you can 'pass' most of the time. I can write down some references."

I made some appointments with specialists. In the meantime, I began to focus my study on CBT issues at home. While I had always cried at movies, I felt like this made me a bit of a nerdy softie. I didn't understand this behavior in the context of my dull mirror neurons or my lower empathy response. But when I discovered the TV show *The Office*, I realized that I could learn empathic responses of all kinds from it. Just like laugh tracks on old comedies or sad parts in movies, the situational storylines of *The Office* were laden with emotional responses. The writing of the show made it clear when to feel sorry for a character and when to feel awkwardness, remorse, joy, or sadness. Because so much of the humor of the show is about inappropriate workplace behavior, it helped me to understand not only why the behavior was inappropriate but also how it might be responded to appropriately. I watched every episode of the show but would have to pause it often because I felt the emotions so intensely.

This experience and my continued study also led me to realize what good hands-on management could do for Microcosm. So much inner turmoil had been caused by my inability to resolve conflict, however small. The culture of the organization was one of forgiveness and looking the other way when staff people were actively damaging Microcosm. Collective members had to advocate for their own individual needs, and the collective noise from members expressing their needs was making it impossible to hear each other. I read a dozens of books about collective structure and business management. I came to understand that management is just as important a job duty as filling mail orders or doing data entry. It required intentional time dedicated to it in the same way.

I came to understand the importance of recognizing the hierarchies, privileges, and responsibilities needed to give each staff person an opportunity to discuss concerns, problems, or grievances and to give management the wherewithal to make decisions based on these issues. By trying to pretend like we were all equals at Microcosm, we were doing a disservice to not only our individual skills and backgrounds but also to ways that each person was more or less equipped with various social privileges.

I was on the fence about keeping up with CBT. I went to several appointments with two different specialists, but neither was quite right and I was running out of money. But in 2011 at BookExpo America, the largest publishing trade show in the U.S., I had an illuminating encounter. While hurriedly walking to a meeting I literally bumped into Temple Grandin, who is famous for her books about turning her autism into a superpower. She was standing in the middle of a crowded walkway waiting for her book signing to begin. When we collided, she did not respond in any way. I apologized. She just looked at me. I recognized who I was talking to and exclaimed how much of a fan I was of her work. She still just looked at me. She was clearly overwhelmed but in a way her lack of any coherent reaction also hurt my experience of having an interaction with someone that I am a huge fan of. On one hand, she's the poster child of autism so of course her social skills are going to be limited. But I couldn't help but wonder how many times I had had a run-in like that with one of my fans that left them disappointed.

One of my favorite things about being an Aspie is that, unlike neurotypicals, our intelligence and brain development never stop growing. We pay attention and refine our model until it's bulletproof. Even though I was weird, I could continue to learn how to fill in a lot of the missing pieces of cognitive retraining to appear as a neurotypical and stop hurting people's feelings. This encounter with Temple Grandin made me realize that I should hire an expert to help me flesh out my cognitive development.

During my first appointment with my new doctor, we talked about the basics of CBT.

"Most people make eye contact when they are having a conversation, while you tend to look at the floor or avert your eyes."

I fixed my eyes on the psychologist.

"It's easier to focus and think about the answer to the question when I'm not distracted by someone's face," I responded.

"Do you find it difficult to understand when or how to join a conversation? Has 'free' time at school or work been a source of anxiety for you?"

I nodded feverishly.

"Most people don't speak in monotone. It makes it harder for other people to understand the meaning behind what you're saying and what your emotions are."

I made an immediate mental note to always talk with inflection and began using it to cartoonish effect in conversation.

"To most people, it comes across as rude or uninteresting to talk for more than three sentences unless you are telling a story or asked about your areas of expertise. Do you find that you have a problem with this?"

"Ummm... definitely." I made another immediate note to limit myself to three sentences each time I spoke in a conversation.

He reviewed my history and again pointed out that my key issue seemed to be my inability to notice when someone was stating a boundary.

"When someone tells you that you hurt their feelings, you shouldn't just explain yourself; you should apologize first."

I made another mental note and nodded in response, contemplating how many times I had broken that rule before I knew about it.

"When you make a request of someone, there are many different ways that they can express apprehension or state a boundary. Sometimes it's not necessarily a boundary that they are stating, but they will want to talk through what they are agreeing to in order to set their expectations correctly. Look for these moments and ask more questions if you aren't sure that they are consenting."

I nodded. I got what he was saying but the particulars always felt so difficult in the moment. This was where my difficulties often were.

The information sheet that my CBT doctor gave me included strengths of Asperger's, too. I am more inclined to be honest with friends and family. I am skilled at tasks like double-checking spreadsheets and data entry when others would become bored or fatigued. With clear strategies, I could improve in my social skills. I had already developed the last skill on the list, a sense of humor, especially puns and wordplay.

Meanwhile, Cantankerous Titles was growing quite a formidable catalog but nothing was selling nearly as well as the original *Henry & Glenn* book. I ordered supplies for my home office and built a website database.

It was working, but I felt lonely, missing the social and teamwork aspects of Microcosm. Reflecting on that and knowing that the money from Cantankerous Titles wouldn't last forever, I got a job teaching documentary filmmaking for adults at a private school. After working closely with a middle-aged woman who was making a documentary about her deceased father who had lived his whole life in the closet, I was in love with the job. It was heartwarming and powerful work that had many of the same attractions that I had loved about Microcosm. But soon the school was contacted by someone named "Paulie" who told the administrators that I had a "long history of partner abuse" and had "refused to be accountable."

The school shared the email with me and asked me about the situation. I explained what had happened. It was clear that the administration did not want to deal with this. After my quarter was over, I was not asked to come back.

I got a new job teaching nonfiction writing development, which I was also excited about, but again the school was contacted and asked not to work with me. Student enrollment was low, and the entire nonfiction track was canceled before I began teaching.

I was asked not to attend or table at numerous events that year, including the Chicago Zine Fest. They explained that their justification was that the Portland Zine Symposium had done the same thing. When I pressed them for answers, they told me that a "concerned member of the community" had gotten in touch with the event organizers when they saw that I was confirmed to be there and had warned them about my "past behavior" and "ongoing issues." The same thing happened when I booked film screenings. I tried to reason with people but over and over, each set of event organizers simply said that they didn't have time to look into or deal with the situation so it was easiest to ask me not to attend.

Dinner & Bikes Tour, Lafayette, IN

THE OTHER SIDE

By January of 2012 I came to the realization that, even if I was bullied wherever I tried to go professionally, at least I was going to do exactly what I wanted to, which was publish books that could have a positive impact on the world. I had built up Cantankerous Titles to become my job and planned to leave Microcosm completely. Juliette was going to buy my 50% ownership of Microcosm. By cutting deep into the budget, in June of 2012 Microcosm paid me back the last of the money that I was owed for *Henry & Glenn*. Next, Juliette and I created an agreement and a timeline to buy my ownership. I let Juliette know that I wanted to begin printing and selling design work and publications that I owned instead of licensing them through Microcosm.

Meanwhile, low morale, fatigue, and financial strain were continuing to collapse Microcosm. Communications and finances were in such bad shape that each purchase of badly needed office supplies became a tense negotiation resulting in hurt feelings. The only other full-time person besides Juliette quit in frustration a month after the 2012 all-staff meeting, leaving Juliette as the sole manager of the company. As collective members quit, she hired her roommates and family members to work part time. It was slowly becoming a family business, which was neat to see. But Microcosm had debts in the neighborhood of $50,000 and I was still liable for them. I was getting a bit nervous that the company might not ever be able to pay for them. But I trusted Juliette. We had overcome many, many obstacles together, and I believed that we had a strong relationship.

Stefanie continued to contact me and pleaded for me to come back to Bloomington and take care of her while she was weak after surgery. I cared about her but something seemed curious about her request. Wasn't there someone closer to home that she didn't have complicated emotional history with? It had confused and hurt me that this person who knew me so well denied that I had Asperger's after I was diagnosed. When she continued to call and plead for me to come, I reviewed the ways that I had allowed her to treat me over the last five years and changed my phone number.

I visited Juliette at the Kansas Microcosm offices for a week before our Dinner & Bikes tour. We had a plan that I would share everything I knew about Microcosm's finances with her. All week she put off the conversation while my tourmates bristled impatiently. They wanted to know why we were in Kansas for a week. Eventually, Juliette and I sat down and talked for a few hours but we never got to discussing finances. Instead she told me that she had a cousin with Asperger's and that I didn't seem disabled similarly to him. I explained that Asperger's affects people differently and that I had developed a lot of workarounds in my social skills and confidence over the last 30 years. She seemed unconvinced. While she said that our in-person communication was always pleasant, the company's downward spiral over the previous few years had scarred her pretty badly. Former staffers began insisting that my half of Microcosm had no cash value; Juliette got nervous about the financial risks, and our agreement fell apart.

When I got home in June, Juliette brought me a counterproposal: We would split the company in half rather than having her buy my half outright. I would continue to publish new books and she would take over the massive distribution arm of the business. The good news was that we'd each receive over $100,000 in inventory, rights, database software, and equipment. We'd each work with the staff at our separate locations and, most importantly, we'd each be able to manage our own company. So many of the problems that we'd had over the years were a result of not having clear management roles. It was a good solution and a good time for each of us to get our houses in order. Moreso, it was a good opportunity for me to apply everything that I'd learned about CBT and business management. I was optimistic. More good news was that we would have a new book coming out in July from our best-selling author whose previous book's sales had bailed us out of debt three years prior, also in July. But the staff wasn't working as a team this time, and everyone seemed focused elsewhere, myself included. This time, though, the sales were not enough to bail out several years of accumulated debt, which meant that we'd each be responsible for half of the remaining $36,000 in back debt.

By August 2012, when I returned from two years of managerial leave to accept the offer, the events with Heather were eight years behind me. During the past six years I had closed the gap between my self-image and the public's perception of me. I refused to feel ashamed any longer because my self-image was much sharper and clearer. I knew who I was and I knew how I felt about things. I had finished my therapy, cooperated with accountability, complied with the twenty things that Heather had asked of me, and completed my massive soul searching mission. I felt ready to take on the challenge of running the company again while also having a healthy personal life without continually being asked about my past relationships.

Having three to eleven bosses who did not agree with me, let alone each other, had taken a major toll not only on my day-to-day feelings and morale but on the expectations of our fans and authors. It was also an opportunity for me to change course and steer Microcosm to evolve and become what it needed to be, thematically and financially, to sustain itself for another sixteen years. I really hadn't expected things to shake out this way and I had long abandoned the hope of a decision that could leave everyone happy. The more that I thought about it, the more this felt like a great solution.

I met with the staffers who would remain in Portland and we discussed the change. One person said he wanted to move on during the transition because he was doing more freelance art than he could manage, but everyone else was excited. They said they saw what I saw: Microcosm could be run with more structure and under one roof for the first time since 2006. We could have clear and simple communication. We were all enthusiastic and had a party.

But before we could continue to celebrate, there was still a long way to go to pay off that debt. After splitting the company, our average income each day was reduced by 70%. I had offered Juliette preferential placement for receiving online orders as a kindness, but it was hurting us badly. We needed to make about $1,800 per day to pay our bills but were struggling to earn $300. I contacted Juliette about monthly payments towards the debts. She said that they didn't have any money either.

I had intended to spend that summer finishing the final sequencing on *Aftermass* and had an editor coming from the Bay Area to work on it with me. But before long it was clear that I needed to go back to doing freelance work as well. I did design work for hire, made some Kickstarter videos, shot an all-day cargo-bike race demonstrating disaster preparedness, and even shot a wedding video. I was working seven day a week and doing twelve-to-eighteen- hour days. I consolidated Cantankerous and Microcosm into one company. I tabled at events on the weekends, knowing we needed to raise every dollar that we could to pay those debts. My stress was at eleven (out of ten), and I knew that my body couldn't maintain that kind of pace for very long.

Worse, the other half of Microcosm went from saying that they didn't have enough money to pay the debts to saying that they were not willing. It started as "Sorry, I can't afford it this month" but within eighteen months it turned into "I'm not going to pay."

I had been longtime friends with Juliette and her then-husband and I wanted them to succeed, so I tried to be patient and supportive. She had been my favorite staff person to work with across seven years and had believed in Microcosm even after I had given up and moved on. At their request, I had created a working budget and balance sheet for their business. I had been spending hundreds of hours scanning and paginating over 600,000 pages for their company without asking to get paid for the work. But, at the same time, it rattled me that, despite our agreement, I had somehow become responsible for everyone's share of the debt. I asked them to pay even $100/month as a sign of good will.

That was when Juliette told me that she had made amends with Heather and that she and previous staff had convinced her that I was intentionally taking advantage of her, even though the whole arrangement had been her suggestion. Anonymous trolls on the Internet had been saying that the only way "the community" would support Juliette's company was if they took a strong stand against me. At long last, they did. The cycle of bullying was a powerful one.

Later that week I received a letter from a longtime friend. She said that she kept hearing that I was "a manipulative and intimidating person." She went on to say, "This confuses me because I've seen nothing but kindness and sincerity from you... I just don't feel comfortable being friends with you anymore."

A few weeks later, the owner of a seemingly similar publishing company asked if we could have a private conversation. We walked outside into the brisk morning air and he said that while our interactions had always felt pleasant and he'd enjoyed talking to me, his staff was so concerned about the rumors about me that they were refusing to ship packages to Microcosm. The conversation felt respectful and while it was disappointing, I felt good about it until I bumped into this on his blog a few months later when he was publicly criticized for hosting an art show for one of our authors.

"A while back, upon finding out about the trouble from Joe Biel to a handful of real-life personal friends, I decided to stop selling to or buying from Microcosm...I don't feel important or informed enough to pass loud judgment or take up space in this discussion, but he has clearly harmed people I care about, so I decided to personally limit ties. Microcosm has published books from my best friend in college and artists I've been friends and collaborators with for 15+ years ... I am insecure about everything forever and welcome conversation, criticism, suggestions, perspective or whatever about this (and really anything else I'm doing ever), getting called out makes us better people. I'm posting this not to be self-righteous or defensive but in an attempt to clearly state whats going on and what my current thinking is."

Confused that this was the opposite of what he had communicated to me in person, I attempted to get in touch a few times and received no response.

I was hurt and upset. But I was also no longer willing to try to appease everyone and look the other way. Elly and I sat down and Googled "How do I deal with being bullied?" The most telling and appropriate response was the first one, "Talk to an adult."

Once Microcosm got our ship righted we began pursuing legal grounds to collect the money and our property that Juliette still had not sent to us. It was one way to set the boundary that I was no longer allowing myself to be walked all over. Unfortunately, we ran out of money before she did and had to settle the case without getting paid a penny. She responded by spreading rumors that I prosecute others with regularity when the only other lawsuit I've ever been involved in was her countersuit. And craziest of all, it seems likely that Juliette's legal bills amounted to more than the $18,000 that she owed us in the first place.

This was another difficult lesson: Boundaries cannot protect you from everything.

A packed house watching Aftermass in Columbus, IN in 2013

THE UNDERGROUND IS BIGGER THAN THE MAINSTREAM

Under the collective-management system, Microcosm had never fully taken advantage of the resources provided by the big trade distributor we'd signed on with, Independent Publishers Group (IPG). IPG offered a way to get our books stocked in independent bookstores and wholesalers across the U.S. and Canada. They also would routinely have sit-down meetings with major retail chains, businesses that would not ordinarily accept a meeting with a publisher as small as Microcosm.

Working with IPG was a major departure from the values of direct distribution that had driven us well for the first fifteen years. I had pushed to essentially launch our own distribution company, but the collective had chosen to sign on with IPG instead, and I inherited this decision. I chose to accept it as an ideal opportunity: We didn't need to give up our direct distribution in order to add quite a bit in sales through IPG.

While the notion of placing our books into chain stores was foreign both to our ethos and to our history, it felt like the right way to spread our politics to reach a different kind of person who wasn't already familiar and on board. In 2001, when we had labored over the decision of whether or not to sell thousands of books to Tower Records, we were eventually happy with the decision to do it and we received many letters from people who were thankful to have discovered us there. That decision had introduced many new minds to the politics and aesthetics that we were peddling. In the wake of a bad few years that had divided our once-reliable base, reaching a new audience had now become a matter of survival.

In the ideal relationship, the publisher sits down with the trade distributor to develop a title before the book is even written. The author's skills and the publisher's budget and resources are considered along with the distributor's expertise in how to ideally tailor each book for the market. The publisher bears the risk and so has the final decision, but the distributor will often provide quite a bit of feedback. I am told that a great publisher knows which 50% of distributor feedback to take to heart.

I began to see this distribution relationship as a way to evolve Microcosm. It wasn't necessarily bigger or better. As we worked with IPG I was gratified to reaffirmed my suspicions that in many ways the underground was still much bigger than the mainstream, especially in terms of book sales. This distribution relationship was different. And after sixteen years as a book publisher I needed a way to evolve my understanding, engage my interest, and learn new things. Besides, Microcosm would remain independent and it was a great way to place our ideas in places where people wouldn't be expecting them.

Our relationship with IPG allowed us not only to think differently and aim higher but also to publish a broader range of work that we couldn't have sold into our usual range of specialty underground newsstands, record stores, and textile shops. In June of 2013 IPG placed my old friend Eleanor Whitney's book *Grow: How To Take Your DIY Project And Passion To The Next Level & Quit Your Job* into major Canadian bookstore chains and Urban Outfitters and as a gift for graduates in the entire Canadian university system. We sold 5,000 copies before publication, which we had never done before.

As we neared the end of 2013, after borrowing huge sums of money, numerous desperate and pleading phone calls to our credit-card company asking for a few extra days to pay, and many long months from a dedicated all-volunteer crew, a new day was dawning for Microcosm. The old debts were finally under control, and the staff, including me, began to get paid again. We began carving out our financial future. I was crossing off items from my lists at a new record rate.

My new management skills were bearing fruit, too. Upon request from our senior staff, I started giving anniversary presents and spelling out how much I appreciated everyone individually. I felt honored that each of these people had stuck with us through such a difficult transition time. I had learned how to spell things out and offer proper expectations so people had a good idea of how things would go. More than anything it was their loyalty and relationships that meant so much to me. Microcosm's mission and our message were deeply meaningful to them, so much so that they had worked for free for fourteen months alongside me.

In August of 2013, I left the office early one day because I was grumpy. As I rode my bike home I wondered whether I had overstepped my bounds or stomped out in a way that had hurt other people's feelings. I sent an email to everyone to apologize. Unanimously each person said that I did not seem grumpy or inappropriate. My CBT training was working! I learned when to be watchful that I might offend others and learned to check in afterwards. It was even better to find out that I hadn't done any harm.

Microcosm's home in Portland since 2010 had been a wide, open warehouse with tall ceilings. We had used it as a store until splitting the company, when we built giant lofts in the front room so the office staff could sit ten feet up to avoid constant questions from retail customers. We shared the huge building with four different print shops. There was a giant skateboarding bowl in the back that was used enthusiastically one day by four Japanese tourists. We were grandfathered onto a lease from the '90s, paying virtually nothing each month.

In September, one of Microcosm's volunteers asked the owner of one of these print shops where they wanted their mail placed each day. Accounts vary about what happened next, but when I walked in the door fifteen minutes later, the owner was shouting, "Quit fucking with me! You're an asshole. Get away from my printing press! I pay rent here! Let's go out in the parking lot and settle this." It really did seem like he wanted to fight our volunteer instead of telling him where to put the mail. I stepped between them, cooled the situation, and convinced everyone that no one had meant to escalate to this degree.

All of our staff had watched this neighbor's mental state deteriorate over the previous year, but now there was no way to deny that we had to move. He smoked industrial amounts of marijuana every day, worked 14-26 hour days, and when we greeted him on his way in the door each morning he merely grunted incoherently in response. One night two of our staff members found him passed out on the concrete floor. I was afraid that he was going to die in the building.

It was hard to think about giving up our '90s rent but I quickly realized the advantages that a dedicated building might be able to offer us, aside from not having to give a police report. I began looking around for a new office. Three months later I found a building on North Williams that had formerly held a financial consultancy and a medical lab. It became apparent that our rent would quadruple no matter where we moved. But in exchange, we could choose a more prominent location and we would not need to negotiate any building changes with four other tenants. The building on Williams offered a deck, a separate warehouse, a great retail location, and my first office where someone couldn't walk in from the street and interrupt my work. While the real-estate situation hadn't much improved since 2006, this particular building was zoned primarily for office use, which caused it to sit vacant for eighteen months. As a result, we were able to negotiate a 20% reduction in the price.

More importantly, Microcosm was in a much more stable financial situation each month. I had time for organizing predictive bookkeeping and now that I managed the company I could allocate money into budgets as was necessary to arrange for the organization's best interest. We signed an agreement in November of 2013 and moved in across the end of the year.

Along with the move, Microcosm settled on a new focus. We embarked on publishing a series of books that presented a new and challenging perspective on a familiar subject that allowed readers to look at the world around them in a new way. The books were ambitious and much more difficult to work on, giving me renewed interest in being an editor and publisher. I realized that I could now truly create the kind of books that I wanted to see in the world, something I hadn't been able to do fully since Microcosm had grown to its current size in 2008. In December, 2013 we published *Bikenomics*, Elly's book making the economic case for bicycle transportation. It impressed me both in its brilliance and in her ability to really take the narrative to the next level. I honed our catalog to four lists: The classic DIY series, vegan cookbooks, the aforementioned Real World list, and Comics Journalism. I hadn't fully realized how exciting the opportunity to manage the company could be. I had been complacent for so long that I had forgotten these were actual choices that I was allowed to make and that nothing was set on autopilot.

Between August 1, 2012 and August 1, 2014, our sales through IPG increased by 150%, going from 10% of our bottom line to 25%. As a result, by November of 2014 we were finally able to pay off all of the debt that had been incurred before I was managing the company.

Once the debt was under control, I spent much of my time ruminating on what had previously gone wrong in setting the culture and priorities of the organization. In the past, many people had become burnt out because they invested *too* much energy and belief in Microcosm. There had been too many expectations, too much hope, not enough time, not enough money, and too much faith. Worse, there had been an idea that if everyone just worked every minute of every day this balance would shift. It didn't, because no one was reviewing a grand plan and direction for the company. The collective members had been too busy doing their individual tasks and resolving interpersonal disputes to sit down with financials projections and goals, and were unable to change strategies to reach them.

Part of the problem was that I had set the expectations and demands too high. People saw my level of unmatchable commitment and felt pressure to meet the immediate apparent needs of the organization instead of taking the time to change the culture and reset the timing, schedules, and demands of what we were capable of. From 2003 until 2012, we were working harder instead of smarter. For years our entire staff would work seven days per week, even if it was just a few hours here and there on the weekends. They weren't asked to do this, but they saw other people doing it so they matched the culture that was in place. This was burning people out, one after another.

The increasingly low wages were another huge problem. Overwork and low pay created stress, health problems, and frustration for everyone involved that never relented. Perhaps most importantly, Microcosm needed a way to prioritize the individual needs of its staff, even if they were different from person to person. Because of my Asperger's I had special needs that had rarely been met at Microcosm, often with other staff people not wanting to acknowledge it or discuss how it impacted all of us. I didn't want anyone else to have this experience.

Starting in 2012, I set out to meet people where they were at in a way that created better results for both the staff person and for the organization. I sat down with each person every other week and talked about their observations, needs, and frustrations. I carved out time for managing the company instead of just doing my own piece of the work. In May of 2014, I created a new budget and figured out that, based on the consistent income we were already earning, we could cut six published titles per year and afford to give everyone a 40% raise within twelve months. I created a new organizational culture where people could bring their problems to me to solve and we'd talk through them. I created new priorities, such as hiring special-needs people who had no other place to land and creating an environment where they could not only be happy but could thrive. I was beginning to feel quite accomplished in all that we'd overcome.

On December 19, 2014, I had breakfast with Elly before biking to the office. She was unusually glum and solemn. After I left for work each day, she worked on her own publishing company alone from her home office. She told me that she missed the daily camaraderie of working with others and needed a change. I lingered longer than I normally would have and we went over her options. After an hour she casually suggested that it might make sense to combine our companies.

I did the math in my head. It made a lot of sense for both of us. Within 48 hours, we had counted up her inventory, reviewed her lifetime accounting history, and signed a contract. We merged our companies and she received an ownership share of Microcosm in return. She took over half of my work as Microcosm's first ever "Marketing Director."

For years I had desperately wanted someone in my life that I trusted implicitly and could go to for advice who was my intellectual equal. By talking about our boundaries and aspirations and working on them together, Elly and I have been together for seven years and now work across a desk from each other too. It's not to say that we have never had disagreements or miscommunications. Early in our relationship, Elly brought up that I would constantly make reference to her coffee habit, even in front of strangers. She said that she felt teased about it. I apologized, realizing that I had turned something that was cartoonishly entertaining to me into a sensitive issue for the person that I cared about the most in the world. Nobody likes to feel made into a cartoon and with clear instructions like these, I could stop immediately. Elly trusted me and we moved on.

In 2015, her best friend pointed out how Elly's emotional intelligence had improved dramatically over the last seven years and said she felt that I was 97% responsible. So we've been able to help each other. It's not only the most mutually supportive relationship I've ever had, it's also the first time that I've ever felt truly understood. When something that I do bothers her, we can talk about it, find our way to the root of the problem, and resolve the underlying issue. I trust her, I know how to communicate with her, and I find that each time I begin to explain myself to her, she already knows what I'm going to say and assures me that it's going to be okay. But still, we can talk about it if I want to.[14] When I can come home and be comfortable in my skin in our home every day, I recognize the value of applying 38 years of hard-won lessons.

---

14 We even wrote a book on communication together, *Manspressions: Decoding Men's Behavior*, Microcosm: Portland, 2015.

The new staff navigated rumors about me and the company with much better boundaries than the old staff did. While it upset some people, it wasn't a major source of stress or losing sleep. People would be bummed to run into gossip in the course of doing their job but not heartbroken or ready to quit over it. If anything, encountering gossip reinforced staff loyalty and points of view. After four years of therapy, I understand the emotional needs of others much more and can talk people through conflicts and low morale. I continue to read books about management and apply new leadership skills as necessary. These days, when hardships or transitions come up, we create a strategy as a team and talk through them. Now I brief people as they join the team about my behavior, oddities, and personality so their expectations are properly set.

No longer encumbered by the collective system, the staff now has clear direction about how to do their jobs. We no longer need to stop the works when we run into a new problem and figure out how everyone is comfortable proceeding. Instead of shaping a proposal until it is no longer disagreeable to anyone, we act based on what needs to be done for best interest of the organization. And at the end of the day everyone goes home from work and rests.

In November, 2014, Microcosm achieved its goal for raises six months early. The following May everyone received another 25% raise based on our increased sales. I adjusted the budgets and income on my spreadsheet to calculate that we could afford a further raise for everyone in November of 2015 and we also achieved that. The total amount that we pay our staff has increased by 227% since 2011. I am now able to give the entire staff living wages in an increasingly expensive city.

Microcosm's sales peaked in 2009 and were in steady decline for the next four years. So it was incredibly exciting when, at the end of 2014, we discovered that not only had we ended that slump but it was also actually our best sales year of all time! In 2015, we began a new distribution arrangement with Legato Publishers Group, the first sales team to truly understand the audience for our books. They increased our sales to bookstores for new books by 900% that year—partly because the bar was so low but also because they knew how to frame our work and put in the necessary time to understand and describe each book. I revisited our budgets and concluded that sixteen books per year was our ideal number. This, along with a steadfast and committed staff set a new sales record yet again, making 2015 an even better sales year than 2014!

It felt good not only that the staff stuck it out to get to the end of the rainbow but also that I was able to reward them with something more than positive words and a healthy working dynamic for doing so.

RECONCILIATION

Brian Heater, a blogger for Boing Boing, sat me down in his Queens apartment in 2015 and we talked for over three hours. It was one of the most in-depth interviews ever about Microcosm and its trajectory. The tone was casual and conversational but we kept bumping into unknowns. How was I, a punk rock publisher who had brought the SST Records model to books, evolving after twenty years and a wildly changing industry? I asked Brian what my personal elevator speech should sound like and he brushed me off, saying "You shouldn't worry about selling yourself." I tried to explain that I was ending up in situations more and more where people didn't understand my history and didn't know where I had come from. He said "You don't want to get stuck having to do that. Let people appreciate you for who you are. Show, don't tell."

While I am proud that Microcosm's mission remains to help people without making them feel bad, I wonder what my life might be like if I hadn't been degraded daily during my childhood and had finished college or had more opportunities. I don't regret my choices but I also don't see myself or my experience reflected in film or literature. It's rare to see a protagonist I can see myself in, which is why seeing the documentary *Billy The Kid* was so exciting. I'm still ashamed to tell people that I have Asperger's. For many people in my life, reading this book will be the first time that they learn about it. I guess that I'm still afraid of their judgment and of again watching the narrative of my life slipping out of my hands. So to see young Billy, a young teenager in small-town Maine, wear his heart on his sleeve, socialize with other kids, and even profess his love for a girl—that's powerful stuff. That is a role model. Many of the people who were once influential in my life aren't relatable anymore. People I grew up with in punk rock often went deeper underground after some moments of achievement; they talk about success as if it goes hand in hand with compromise or selling out. But I've found that I can carve my own path independently without compromising my values. And I can shine a light behind me so people that relate to my experience can follow.

On the Amtrak trip home from New York City, I was recognized by a fan who began declaring my achievements to the train car. She was old enough to understand the longevity of my work and, although I was a bit embarrassed, I felt proud. It felt nice to be recognized and seen as notable still. It had started to feel like my prime had passed.

My creative peak had happened way back when I was nineteen years old and just channeling all of my nervous energy into something constructive instead of destructive. But I had been deeply unhappy then. I didn't know who I was or how I felt about things. I was so focused on creating that I had never paused long enough to figure out how to be comfortable in my own skin. Twenty years later, I was happy, I was still constantly creating things, and I knew what I wanted and why. I took the time to unravel what had created me.

There were plenty of times over the years when I just wanted to come across as "normal," whatever that meant. I wanted to blend into a crowd and disappear and not trip over my own two feet on the sidewalk. Part of me worried that CBT would take away not only the quirks that made me difficult to get along with but also everything that made me interesting, capable, and creative. That is, until I caught my entire leg on fire while burning some dangling threads on a pair of cut-offs one summer. There was really no way of explaining *that* incident away as something that neurotypical people do, not even punk rockers. I had never experienced pain like that before. In the past I would have seen this experience as a suitable punishment for doing something stupid. But my weeks of soaking the burns in the bathtub offered plenty of opportunity to learn from my mistake. My emotional maturation had come full circle.

No amount of cognitive re-training can make me neurotypical. I still make mistakes and do or say things that come across as callous, but now I can avoid having a meltdown 95% of the time when someone questions my habits. I found a balance that doesn't totally cripple my confidence or functionality. I can harness my intellectual understanding of mirror neurons to communicate what I want to in conversation. This has allowed me to improve immensely as a public speaker, at making jokes, and just in communicating what I want to in private conversation. At work now, there is a clear method for resolving a conflict, as well as solving a problem. If I am not communicating well with an author or staff person, there are other people for them to talk to. But the internal communication problems at Microcosm have ground to a halt now that everyone is under one roof, we trust each other, and I have learned how to read empathic responses from others and listen to nonverbal communications. Trust goes both ways and it's easier to have empathy.

I don't know whether it's just because of the passage of time or also because of my personal transformation, but nowadays when I read something that I wrote years ago it feels like it was written by someone else, a stranger. When I'm going through boxes of old things, I often uncover incredibly involved and meticulous to do-lists that reveal my former ways of thinking. Six out of seven items will be crossed off and I now can have the gratification of crossing off the last thing on each list. I don't relate to that person anymore; I'm just curious about him. What motivated the list, what I was thinking, and why do I have no recollection of former eras and obsessions in my life? Sometimes the events of my past are so far removed from my current thinking that even after struggling for an hour over a list I can't decipher what I might have meant by something like "remove lines."

It took time, but I figured out how to harness my superpowers. I suggested to Elly that we use the 2015 Dinner & Bikes tour as a vehicle to talk about classism, gender, and racism through the lens of bicycling. She loved the idea. We developed it together. It never would have seemed possible in the past to use the skills that punk rock taught me about societal power structures to push a mostly white room to talk about privilege. We created a new touring network that connected these dots and brought these ideas to a new audience. We framed the conversations so that underprivileged people did the talking—in the films, in the discussion, and in the summations. I had successfully steered the same priority of channeling the most silenced voices of society back into the conversation—just as I had accomplished with zines. The difference was that this time we set a boundary so that we were paid a living wage to do it.

After our event in Brownsville, Texas, a kid emerged from the crowd while I was going through my rituals of packing up the projector. He was carrying a gear catalog from an electronic-bicycle company and was also wearing the hat, shirt, and branded coat advertising the same company. I assumed he was a marketing person or a sales rep. Instead he launched into an extensive monologue about how he rides his e-bike through all of the drive-thrus in his town and works hard to normalize that behavior. He detailed his vision for public solar-charging stations for the bikes that people could utilize while they are watching a movie or at the mall. He was particularly excited about one specific brand—it costs $10,000 but he was ready to fundraise for everyone in his town to have one. He had a vision, and he couldn't stop talking about it.

After a few minutes of blathering, he told me that he had Asperger's. I tried to slip away but he followed me. I felt a little bad—not only because I'd behaved like this for the majority of my life but also because I knew how painful it was and how you couldn't turn it off even when you watched your own behavior drive people away from you. I remembered something that my psychologist had told me during CBT social-skills class: "Neurotypicals socialize for reasons other than sharing information." At the time it had totally blown my mind. I wondered what would be the best way to support another Aspie passing me in the night like this.

Despite the other people that wanted to talk to me, I chose to focus on him instead. It's the way that I would have wanted to be treated at that point in my life. To the other people trying to talk to me, he probably seemed selfish and inobservant, or even rude, but it's likely that he was just stuck in his own head. So, instead of brushing him off, I stuck around and let him keep talking, offering a few points of conversation and trying to connect him to the other people milling around, some of whom also seem interested in e-bikes.

Moments like this help me recognize how far I've come and how my role has completely reversed. Without a punk scene to nurture me and accept me for who I was, I'm fairly confident that I wouldn't have made it out alive to make it to CBT training. And I do worry about the people who don't have punk to accept them or who are pushed out of punk communities for being different. It took a ton of work to get here, but it was worth it. I will always be disabled, but I also have superpowers and a community that has stuck with me.

I've returned the favor to that community by always making myself available to offer free advice to anyone who comes to me, whether they want to know about publishing or just a personal issue that I've written about. With twenty years of publishing experience that I had to scrap together through trial and error, I figure that the least I can do is create an easier way to learn and connect the dots for others. My only rule is that I help only people whose work is "punching up," challenging taboo subjects and power structures by pushing against people that have greater power in society than they do.

I've learned to listen more and talk less. This way, I'm more likely to understand others a bit more. I remember the tone of my last conversation with each person I meet and try to resume it when I see them again. I let people have different opinions from mine, even if they think it's somehow okay to sit down while playing guitar. I think about when it's worth disagreeing with someone else and when to let things go. And I believe that showing empathy for others, especially blathering e-Bike Aspie, is the only way to put a pressure valve on the pain of living in a world full of other people's truths that are different from our own.

As I drove our van away from the venue that night, Joshua drunkenly made a comment that I drive like I've still got a bit of a suicidal instinct in me, like I still haven't shaken all of my habits. I take risks. But it's not because I am deeply or secretly unhappy. It's because risks result in payoffs as much as they result in pain and heartbreak. And at this point in my life, I want all of the adventure and payoffs that are possible.

I spent my twenties sculpting elaborate sandcastles that interested people in my innovative thinking—and then watching as the tides ripped them apart. When I rebuilt them out of concrete in my thirties, people didn't seem to think it was as interesting the second time around. It's a lot harder to set a vision into concrete, and it takes a lot more time to catch notice in the shorter attention spans of the Twitter era. Making changes isn't as easy either. I've chiseled my manifesto into stone where it's harder for other people to remove or change the island that I've built. But it's the one I can stand behind, the one I can be proud of.

On the last day of the 2015 tour, I looked back into the empty venue, noting where 70 people were sitting not too long ago, and I thought about how proud my teenage self would be.

The National Republican Congressional Committee's

2007

Congressional
Order of Merit

presented to

Joe Biel

In recognition of commitment, loyalty and dedication of service
to the Republican Party and the United States of America.

After the AP newswire story about me in 2007 there were some creative attempts to get money out of me and I've jokingly been registered as a Republican since 2000 so I can vote in their primaries.

*Left:
Licensed
reproductions of our
logo on medallions.*

*Right:
Fan art submitted by
an intern applicant*

*Left:
a bootleg of my work
that I found in Medellin,
Colombia*

*Right:
Unlicensed t-shirt in
Chicago. Whose logo does
that remind you of?*

*It's one of
the most
flattering
things to
have met
dozens of
people who
have my
artwork
tattooed on
them all over
the world.*

About The Author

Joe Biel is a writer, activist, filmmaker, teacher, founder of Microcosm Publishing, and co-founder of the Portland Zine Symposium. He has directed over 100 short films and four feature documentaries: *$100 & A T-Shirt: A Documentary About Zines in Portland* (2004), *Aftermass: Bicycling in a Post-Critical Mass Portland* (2014), *If It Ain't Cheap, It Ain't Punk* (2010), *Of Dice & Men* (2006). He is the author of *Manspressions: Decoding Men's Behavior* (2015), *Make a Zine!: When Words and Graphics Collide* (2008), *Perfect Mix Tape Segue, Bipedal, By Pedal, CIA Makes Science Fiction Unexciting: Dark Deeds & Derring Do* (2013), *Bamboozled: An Incarcerated Boxer Goes Undercover for John McCain's Boxing Bill* (2013), and *Beyond The Music: How Punks are Saving the World with DIY Ethics, Skills, & Values* (2012).He tours with his films with the DinnerandBikes.com program and has been featured in *Time Magazine, Publisher's Weekly, Utne Reader, Portland Mercury, Oregonian, Broken Pencil, Readymade, Punk Planet, Spectator* (Japan), *G33K* (Korea), and *Maximum Rocknroll.*

SUBSCRIBE TO EVERYTHING WE PUBLISH!

Do you love what Microcosm publishes?

Do you want us to publish more great stuff?

Would you like to receive each new title as it's published?

Subscribe as a BFF to our new titles and we'll mail them all to you as they are released!

$10-30/mo, pay what you can afford. Include your t-shirt size and month/date of birthday for a possible surprise! Subscription begins the month after it is purchased.

microcosmpublishing.com/bff